The Spatial Organization of New Land Settlement in Latin America

Dellplain Latin American Studies

The Spatial Organization of New Land Settlement in Latin America

Jacob O. Maos

Land settlement in Latin America has become a subject of growing concern as governments renew efforts to develop agrarian potential and to relieve the pressure on overpopulated rural and urban areas. In this book, land settlement is viewed as the development of resources, both human and natural. The spatial organization of land settlement is examined in light of social and spatial patterns that may complement economic activities, lead to viable communities, and facilitate the provision of social and cultural amenities. The farm family is seen as the basic socioeconomic unit, and the family farmstead as the basic spatial nucleus.

Dr. Maos is associate professor in the Department of Geography, University of Haifa. He has served as a consultant to various United Nations agencies and is on the board of directors of the International Rural Housing Association.

DELLPLAIN LATIN AMERICAN STUDIES

PUBLISHED IN COOPERATION
WITH THE DEPARTMENT OF GEOGRAPHY
SYRACUSE UNIVERSITY

The Spatial Organization of New Land Settlement in Latin America

Jacob O. Maos

Dellplain Latin American Studies, No. 15

Routledge
Taylor & Francis Group
LONDON AND NEW YORK

First published 1984 by Westview Press

Published 2019 by Routledge
52 Vanderbilt Avenue, New York, NY 10017
2 Park Square, Milton Park, Abingdon, Oxon OX14 4RN

Routledge is an imprint of the Taylor & Francis Group, an informa business

Library of Congress Catalog Card Number 83-51156

ISBN 13: 978-0-367-29623-0 (hbk)

ISBN 13: 978-0-367-31169-8 (pbk)

Contents

Tables

Figures

Preface and Acknowledgments

The problems surrounding rural development have been amply described in professional literature; however, most of these studies have remained on a descriptive level. While several normative models, which purport predicting the outcome of alternative courses of action, have been developed in economic theory, many physical planning aspects, especially in rural areas, still have not been treated. The arbitrary separation between the spatial organization of settlements and their subsequent economic behavior has diverted the attention of planners from the potential inherent in spatial and social patterns of rural settlements. Even in new land settlement, the spatial rationale sometimes remains unquestioned while almost every other aspect is critically examined.

Some examples aptly demonstrate this point. In a treatise by an interdisciplinary group of experts from the M.I.T. Center for International Studies, the main ingredients for successful agricultural development were identified.[1] A detailed list was formulated which included physical, economic, organizational, cultural and motivational, and knowledge factors. Surprisingly, the interrelationships among these factors and their arrangement in space and time were left unmentioned. The fact that new land settlement accounts for only a small part of the total agricultural production could explain the absence of spatial aspects from those factors considered to affect agricultural development; however, the opening of new lands occupies an increasingly prominent place in the policies and allocation of resources in many developing countries.

Current planning theories regard the marketplace as the crucial element in lending viability to rural settlements. The notion of market, however, is understood primarily in terms of the local peasant market. Mosher, in line with this concept, proposes the construction of a grid of farm-to-market feeder roads which, in combination with other inputs (i.e., fertilizers, credits, agricultural extension services, etc.), is expected to modernize agriculture.[2] Although the incentive of the market need not be underrated, especially in traditional rural structures,[3] it is difficult to perceive of the peasant in the triple role of tiller, hauler, and peddler as a dynamic factor affecting agricultural development. In new land settlement the provincial marketplace may even become an obstacle which would best be by-passed.[4]

Johnson also regards the market system as a primary motivating force, but within a broader context of centralized locations which could serve as bases for development of the region's human resources.[5] Nelson, who addresses himself specifically to new land settlement, cites the factors crucial to the success of settlement as selection of site; selection of settlers; preparation of infrastructure; provision of capital by settlers and authorities; organization of central services and project administration; land allotment and farm size per family; and tenure conditions.[6] He admittedly concentrates on economic feasibility, but the physical planning related to these inputs is barely mentioned. As an inevitable conclusion of short-term economic objectives, Nelson advocates spontaneous settlement--a solution which is contradicted by the principles and criteria expounded in this thesis.

The student of rural spatial organization will be hard pressed to find updated normative material on land settlement. Among the few studies and writings on the subject are the publications by the Settlement Study Center in Rehovot, Israel, which are applicable to some situations in developing countries, and others that direct themselves to specific areas, such as the comparative study of land settlement in Ceylon.[7] The writings by Weitz on the transition from subsistence to specialized farming include important insights into the spatial aspects.[8] Various studies by Yalan and co-workers define useful criteria and principles of rural physical planning.[9] The structuring of rural services has received scant attention although it stands out as a key factor of rural development, second only to the economic basis of settlement. Contributions in this area include, among others, studies by Prion and Maos. The U.N. Economic and Social Commission for Asia and the Pacific has published guidelines for the planning of rural centers with a view to developing pertinent methodologies based on the experience of recent land settlement.[10]

A combination of descriptive matter and conceptual analysis, which is indispensable in formulating planning strategies, is offered by Dorner, Dozier, L. Smith, Thiesenhusen, and Warriner.[11] Many other authors delve especially into the intricacies of subsistence farming. The bulk of studies on Latin America, however, concentrate on urban problems. Several studies concerned with specific variables of land settlement emanate from diverse countries engaged in rural development (e.g., the Polders scheme in Holland, or rural development of the Mezzogiorno).

A good deal of information can be found in nonconventional publications most often available in the countries themselves. Most of this material, however, is mimeographed and tends to become extinct after several years. Some international cooperative programs operating in the area of agricultural development and land settlement have sparked the elaboration of a conceptual and technical framework for land settlement which is widely disseminated in Latin America and several Caribbean countries. Regional and international entities, such as the Organization of American States and United Nations' specialized agencies, are also collaborating in the field of land settlement and have published on the progress of their activities.

This book is an attempt to clarify the significant spatial aspects of land settlement, with the hope of formulating planning criteria which are compatible with the generic characteristics of development areas in Latin America. The argument put forward is that the failure of planned settlement can often be traced to its spatial organization--a repeatedly overlooked factor. How important is the component of spatial organization in new land development? The adequate organization of rural settlement enables the provision of health and education, as well as production along modern lines which may improve the economic status of the involved population. A crucial condition, however, is the need to preserve flexibility since physical plans, once incorporated into the landscape, are difficult to modify. The reviewed case studies and models suggest that social and spatial patterns that complement economic activities are conducive to the formation of viable communities. Viability is, in the long run, the most important criterion of successful settlement.

The data used in this dissertation stem from studies and planning work by the author in Israel during 1958-1965; consulting work in rural housing and physical planning for the Pan American Health Organization, Regional Office of the World Health Organization in Latin America, during 1964-1975; information compiled during brief study tours to the Netherlands, Italy, and Spain; project reports and plans collected from governmental, regional, and international institutions; and general literature on the subject. In this work I have drawn heavily upon the conceptual framework developed by Professor Raanan Weitz in his numerous writings. In the spatial and physical sphere, I owe much to the late Professor Emmanuel Yalan, who was my tutor and long-time co-worker.

During my stay at the Johns Hopkins University, I profited immensely from discussions with fellow students and professors in the Department of Geography and Environmental Engineering and cherished many a conversation with Dr. Abel Wolman who let me share some of his insight and experience. This work would not have been finished without the constant encouragement of my friends and colleagues, Lipa Kam, Donald Davidson, and Luis Dorich T. I would also like to express my sincere thanks to David Harvey and M. G. Wolman, whose challenge and guidance greatly assisted me in developing this manuscript.

Finally, to my wife and companion of always and to my children, who bore the full brunt of my struggle with this book with patience and understanding, I extend my thanks and love.

NOTES

1. Max F. Millikan and David Hapgood, No Easy Harvest; The Dilemma of Agriculture in Underdeveloped Countries (Boston, 1967).

2. Arthur Theodore Mosher, Creating a Progressive Rural Structure to Serve a Modern Agriculture (New York, 1969).

3. Sidney W. Mintz, "Peasant Market Places and Economic Development in Latin America," The Graduate Center for Latin American Studies, No. 4, Vanderbilt University, Nashville, Tenn., 1964.

4. Gunder A. Frank, Capitalism and Underdevelopment in Latin America, Historical Studies of Chile and Brazil (London, 1971).

5. E. A. J. Johnson, The Organization of Space in Developing Countries (Cambridge, 1970).

6. Michael Nelson, The Development of Tropical Lands: Policy Issues in Latin America (Baltimore, 1973).

7. UDA Walawe Project, A Comparative Study of Two Regional Planning Alternatives, Settlement Study Centre, Rehovot, Israel, 1971.

8. Raanan Weitz, From Peasant to Farmer: A Revolutionary Strategy for Development (New York, 1971); also, Integrated Rural Development: The Rehovot Approach, Publications on Problems of Regional Development, No. 28, Settlement Study Centre, Rehovot, Israel, 1979; and R. Weitz (ed.), Rural Development in a Changing World (Cambridge, 1971).

9. Emmanuel Yalan, The Design of Agricultural Settlements: Technological Aspects of Rural Community Development (Jerusalem, 1975); Emmanuel Yalan, J. Maos, and L. Kam, Land Planning of the Agricultural Co-operative Village, The Rural Building Research Centre, Haifa, Israel, 1963; Emmanuel Yalan, J. Maos, and L. Kam, The Influence of Farming Rationalization on the Planning of Scattered and Gathered Settlements, The Rural Building Research Centre, Haifa, Israel, 1964; Emmanuel Yalan, H. Finkel, L. Guttman, and Ch. Jacobsen, The Modernization of the Traditional Agricultural Village, Publications on Problems of Regional Development, No. 11, Settlement Study Centre, Rehovot, Israel, 1972.

10. I. Prion, Development Trends of Spatial Rural Cooperation in Israel, Publications on Problems of Regional Development, No. 3, Settlement Study Centre, Rehovot, Israel, 1968; and Líneas Generales de la Planificación Integrada Rural Regional en las Zonas de la Reforma Agraria, Ministry of Agriculture, Israel, 1973 (mimeo). See also, J. Maos, "The Spatial Organization of New Land Settlement: Experiences and Trends," GeoJournal, Vol. 1.4 (1977), pp. 29-35; and "The Efficiency of Rural Services in Dispersed and Concentrated Land Settlement: A Comparison," Geographical Research Forum, No. 2, Occasional

Papers, 1980, pp. 33-43; and United Nations Economic and Social Commission for Asia and the Pacific, Guidelines for rural centre planning (New York, 1979).

11. Peter Dorner (ed.), Land Reform in Latin America: Issues and Cases, Land Economics Monograph Series, No. 3, University of Wisconsin, Madison, 1971; Craig L. Dozier, Land Development in Latin America: Case Studies of Peru, Bolivia and Mexico (New York, 1969); T. Lynn Smith, Studies of Latin American Societies (New York, 1970); William C. Thiesenhusen, "Technological Change and Income Distribution in Latin American Agriculture," Paper presented to the VI Interamerican Conference on Agriculture, OAS, Lima, Peru, May 27-June 2, 1971; Doreen Warriner, Land Reform in Principle and Practice (Oxford, 1969).

1 Introduction

> Success in settlement schemes is, after all, nothing but the process of reducing or minimizing the number of failures.
>
> A. J. Schwelm
> Some Thoughts on Colonization

Many Latin American countries are increasingly shifting their efforts toward developing rural areas. The general aim is to relieve the situation in depressed regions, to offset migratory pressures on urban centers, and to accelerate the transition from subsistence farming to modern agriculture. The productivity of the land and the capacity to sustain a given population density in existing rural areas are hampered by the shortage of cultivable land and lack of infrastructure such as irrigation, access roads, and other production factors. These problems are exacerbated by poor land management, absentee ownership, excessively large holdings, or the fragmentation of land ownership and overcrowding. In addition, the dispersion and small size of rural communities frequently restricts their ability to absorb and support modern amenities.

The growing realization that the industrial and service sectors will be unable to generate sufficient employment in the foreseeable future, combined with the need to reform obsolete agrarian structures, has led governments to look at opening new lands for rural and urban settlement. However, despite the substantial amounts that are being invested in numerous enterprises, planned land settlement has not lived up to expectations. All too often projects have lapsed into stagnation, while attempts to stimulate regional development by implementing policies of settlement dispersal have served merely to accentuate the dichotomy between urban and rural areas.

In spite of the outstanding and promising advances in agricultural technology, the majority of traditional rural communities in Latin America are still very far from achieving anything near their production potential. The most available resource, that of labor, is largely underutilized due to inadequate and inequitable allocation of other resources or suppressive institutional systems which fail to induce increased production efforts. Agrarian reform has wrought substantial changes, primarily in land tenure, but has not yet produced a wide-scale transformation of rural structures. The upgrading of traditional rural settlement is unable to keep pace with population growth in rural areas. The deterioration of economic conditions and consequent migration to urban centers is often faster than the modernization of agriculture. Rehabilitation of already settled agricultural areas is tedious due to distorted physical patterns and fragmentation or pulverization of holdings, and because any selective process with regard to the farm population is not possible.[1] Cultural restraints, technological weaknesses, and the primacy of village and kinship loyalties constitute barriers to large-scale enterprises.[2]

The importance of modernizing rural areas and integrating the rural population into the mainstream of economic and social development has been repeatedly emphasized by the U.N. Economic Commission for Latin America, by the Charter of Punta del Este,[3] and in high level meetings such as those of the Ministers of Health of the Americas.[4] The general view is that development in most Latin American countries must take into account the prospects of an overwhelmingly large rural population, with agriculture being potentially the principal source of employment. It has been pointed out that by strengthening the rural sector migration can be retarded and diverted to stimulate the growth of smaller urban centers, thereby alleviating pressure on the larger cities. Programs have been outlined in the areas of construction, water supply, nutrition, housing, and physical planning. Effective action, however, is notably lagging.

The mounting problems related to urban and rural development have caused renewed interest in the subject of interregional disparities in economic growth. Two areas, in particular, are of special concern: the alarming proportion of unemployed in developing countries; and the need for a more equitable distribution of benefits.[5] Recent studies indicate that development programs in the last decade have actually widened the gap between the poor and the middle class in the less developed countries by underscoring economic growth and industrialization. National and international development strategies of the 1960s placed an excessive and unbalanced emphasis on the growth of the domestic product and did not give enough consideration to production and consumption patterns and the effective use of labor. Leading economists concur on the importance of agriculture in economic development. In contrast to underdeveloped countries, economically advanced countries had both a higher productivity rate and more land under cultivation before industrialization occurred.[6] The vital role of agriculture has been summed up as "expanded food, expanded markets and an expanded supply of funds to the modern sector."[7] The rate of improvement in agriculture is among the principal indicators listed by economists in appraising economic growth.

The concern over unemployment has also brought agricultural improvement to the fore as an important tool to combat rural poverty. A study in Colombia concluded that the country's nonagricultural sectors could not be expected to generate enough employment in the medium term to approximate full employment, implying that faster growth in agriculture was necessary and that the hitherto prevailing trends of migration and urban growth would have to be altered.[8] However, maximization of employment, or equitable distribution of benefits, are still regarded as unconventional goals which have only recently been recognized as basic problems.

Agricultural development is usually viewed as a short-term transitional phase of economic growth rather than a way of life. Nonquantitative properties such as social stability, quality of life, well being, or even health are generally ignored. Some disciplines hover on one aspect or another but, to borrow a phrase from Kindleberger, they have not yet produced a single theory of growth. Regional planning disciplines which focus directly on the spatial distribution of human activities, perceive rural planning strategies foremostly in economic secular terms. Attempts to apply regional theories to rural development planning have frequently failed, particularly since they are based on the principle of economic polarization or domination.[9] Diverse strategies based on balanced versus unbalanced growth, agglomeration versus deglomeration, and other approaches have been advocated and applied at various times. The shifting of some of the growth potential to smaller urban centers, for example, was identified with rank-size, as well as with the growth-poles theory of Perroux which was widely disseminated among planners in Latin America. One of the advantages of the latter scheme seemed to be the integration of economic and spatial planning by both decentralizing and deliberately creating growth-stimulating imbalances.[10] Nevertheless, attempts to induce development through growth poles only accentuated the dichotomy between urban and rural areas, with the familiar migratory effects now generated by the chosen centers. Basically it remained an industrial-urban oriented strategy and, even where the region profited by such development, the polarization had debilitating effects on most of the region's rural population. Planning criteria were primarily based on economic efficiency measured by traditional benefit-cost parameters, and the application of such criteria to comprehensive development schemes remains questionable. Few of the evolved theories fully appreciate the human factor as the critical element and final purpose of the developmental process.

The very center-periphery relationship between town and countryside may be a key factor in rural retardation in Latin America. Rooted in behavior patterns established by centuries of exploitation and colonial subordination, this relationship continues to thrive on the cultural gaps within the local population.[11] The same relationship is duplicated in the periphery of the small rural town. The latter, instead of generating growth by offering basic facilities for distribution and supply, lives mainly by extracting the dismal wealth produced by a servile rural population. The effective development of a rural region may require a systematic substitution of the traditional hierarchy of central places by an adequately balanced structure based on reciprocal economic and civic interests.[12] Past experience has shown that the rural population has to be organized in viable communities in order to become amenable to economic and cultural integration. Communities must likewise be spatially organized in an optimal way, making it possible to provide amenities and to direct their production for the purpose of achieving economic status. At the same time, maximum flexibility must be preserved to fit varying developmental stages since physical plans, once carried into effect, are extremely difficult to modify.

Land reform programs now under way in Latin America pose challenges which are markedly different from developmental problems encountered in the past.[13] Yet, few valid techniques have been elaborated to suit modern rural settlement. While the opening up of new land has become a significant element in regional development, many plans envisage first and foremost the maximization of farm output. Invested capital often assumes the physical form of roads, dams, irrigation, and drainage schemes, while human problems receive only scant attention. The expectation of risk in such ventures has risen with the accumulation of failure and this attitude has caused a negative reaction to increased efforts in land settlement which can only gradually be overcome. The hope remains that progressive settlement on new lands, in its various forms, may become a catalyst for interaction between rural-agricultural and rural-nonfarming communities. New employment opportunities in services and processing and the linkages generated by a dynamic farming region may lead to reduced rural migration, may relieve the pressure on urban centers, and may enable a deepening and spreading of development on a regional scale.

NOTES

1. Craig L. Dozier, Land Development in Latin America: Case Studies of Peru, Bolivia and Mexico (New York, 1969).

2. John M. Brewster, "Traditional Social Structure as Barriers to Change," in Soutworth and Johnston (eds.), Agricultural Development and Economic Growth (New York, 1967), pp. 67-98.

3. "Charter of Punta del Este," Boletin de la Oficina Sanitaria Panamericana, Vol. 51 (1961), pp. 477-493.

4. "Special Meeting of the Ministers of Health of the Americas," Buenos Aires, Argentina, October 1968, PAHO Official Document, Vol. 90, (1969).

5. Robert S. McNamara, "Address to the Board of Governors," International Bank for Reconstruction and Development, Nairobi, Kenya, 1973.

6. S. Kuznets, "The Present Underdeveloped Countries and Past Growth Patterns," in Morgan and Betz (eds.), Economic Development (Belmont, Calif., 1970).

7. W. W. Rostow, The Stages of Economic Growth (Cambridge, 1971).

8. United Nations, International Labor Organization, Toward Full Employment: A Programme for Colombia (Geneva, 1970); United Nations, "Report of the Committee for Development Planning," Document E/5126, United Nations, New York, 1972.

9. J. G. M. Hilhorst, Regional Planning: A System's Approach (Rotterdam, 1971).

10. D. F. Darwent, "Growth Poles and Growth Centers in Regional Planning--a Review," Environment and Planning, Vol. 1 (1969), pp. 5-32.

11. Gunder A. Frank, Capitalism and Underdevelopment in Latin America: Historical Studies of Chile and Brazil (London, 1971).

12. See for instance, John Friedmann and Mike Douglass, "Agropolitan Development: towards a new strategy for regional planning in Asia," in F. C. Lo and K. Salih (eds.), Growth Pole Strategy and Regional Development Policy (Oxford, 1978), pp. 163-192.

13. T. Lynn Smith, Agrarian Reform in Latin America (New York, 1964).

2
The Conceptual Framework

LAND SETTLEMENT

Ambiguities are difficult to avoid in a topic as diffuse as land settlement. Throughout the literature such terms as reform, settlement or resettlement, and colonization, with prefixes such as rural, agrarian, land, etc., are used indiscriminately. Related terms such as "spatial organization" and rural, physical, or regional planning, usually refer to the same field. Some definitions perceive land settlement as the planned and controlled transfer of population from one area to another for the purpose of raising living standards;[1] as projects involving planned social change that entail population selection, population resettlement and, subsequently, population control; or as the permanent settlement of nomadic or pastoral population and the centralization of cultivators.[2] The descriptions testify to the breadth of the subject.

In a limited sense land settlement can be regarded as an organized attempt to establish people on the land in a relatively permanent manner; but, broader implications lie in the changes brought about by the introduction of new physical features into an area, and the activation of a formerly passive rural population. Although involving only certain segments of population, land settlement is part of and complementary to rural development because of its diverse effects on the traditional rural structure, both at the individual and institutional levels. Settlement on new lands provides the opportunity to:

1. choose the type of farming and socioeconomic, as well as administrative, climate in which the settlement can operate;
2. incorporate functional devices for production services and amenities;
3. avoid certain adaptation problems that usually result from a change in status and which often generate social rifts and frictions;
4. create administrative and planning capacity without

getting entangled in the additional complexities of traditional settlement;
5. increase production through added acreage (since the increase in productivity on existing acreage is invariably slow);
6. open new land for settlement to landless peasants and future population that cannot expect employment in other sectors;
7. relieve pressure on overpopulated depressed rural areas, and attract migration away from the large urban centers;
8. tap new resources of land, minerals, crops, etc., and develop infrastructures that will generate linkages to other sectors;
9. achieve a more balanced population distribution by creating and reinforcing rural growth poles.

Many Latin American countries possess extensive reserves of national land, especially on the eastern slopes of the Andean ridges and the tropical lowlands. Some vacant forest and savannah regions are already being used for resettlement from highlands and other overpopulated areas. Roads are being built into the llanos of Colombia, Venezuela, Brazil, and other countries where farming and ranching have expanded and created new settlement nuclei. Much of the virgin land is considered to be of marginal quality and the raging controversy as to the feasibility of settlement and its long-term ecological impact will probably have to be resolved by experience and studies of existing settlement. The need to focus attention on less favorable ecological zones was emphasized by the U.N. Food and Agriculture Organization. This group noted that intensive agriculture is limited at present to irrigated and high rainfall areas of mild temperatures, probably occupying no more than 30 percent of the world's potential arable land. Opening up new land may be necessary "both to meet longer-term food needs and to alleviate social inequalities."[3]

The considerable expanses of land available for settlement in Latin America are not entirely vacant and some areas already contain spontaneous settlement. Such pioneer colonization can eventually provide advance information on a region, but may also result in economic and social waste and interfere with the orderly planning of land use. This is well exemplified by the problems encountered when introducing new settlement patterns into an amorphous landscape of archaic rural towns, private estates with their adjacent hamlets of laborers, and dispersed squatters isolated in the brush or clinging to roads and rivers. In such a diffuse spatial situation, new land settlement may either exert a stimulating influence or succumb to the typical apathetic pace of the rural fringe.

Considerable resources are currently being directed toward the development of new lands through construction of penetration roads and other infrastructure. Several countries have created regional development authorities; some have policies designed to attract private investments into virgin areas.[4] But the general emphasis is increasingly tending toward state-initiated and planned settlement, often in conjunction with agrarian reform programs. This approach is dictated both by economic efficiency and welfare criteria, since substantial public investments must be accompanied by the proper motivation of settlers, by agricultural extension services, and by adequate supervision.

The experience in land settlement, though widely scattered, has created a professional movement with a common vocabulary and similar basic concepts. However, land settlement schemes have seldom been evaluated in a systematic fashion. Exchange of experience and knowledge among countries is equally rare.[5] The spatial aspects of rural settlement planning, in particular, have remained relatively unexplored in contrast to the more sophisticated tools developed in urban planning. Land settlement schemes along modern lines are undoubtedly an abrupt departure from conventional conceptions which may require adjustment by planners as well as by settlers. The spatial abuse of new lands by uncontrolled agglomeration or excessive dispersion, may lead to a repetition of marginal conditions in repressed rural areas. Implicit in land settlement, as a discipline, is the spatial interrelationship between human, natural, and technical resources. It includes therefore, not merely the planning of facilities and efficient production, but also the spatial organization of the family farmstead, the village, and the intervillage group, in a way that will conduce ascending levels of cooperation, regional organization, and subsequent economic growth.

GENERIC DEVELOPMENT AREAS

A genuine need exists for the development of spatial criteria which can be adapted, with necessary adjustments, to a wide range of situations and localities. The question then arises: is it possible to speak of land settlement in Latin America in a generic way? Rural communities everywhere contain distinct features and idiosyncrasies. Factors such as topography, climate, political structure, or dwelling patterns are so divergent that any noncategorized treatment runs the risk of being highly unscientific.

Nevertheless, in regard to new land settlement in most parts of Latin America, a generic treatment is deemed legitimate for several reasons. First, although marked differences exist between countries and regions within the same country, these are often variations on similar themes. Common heritage and historical experience have resulted in typical behavior patterns associated with most Latin American people, acting as common denominators throughout the entire cultural sphere. Several authors have commented on this common denominator of Lusitanian-Iberian culture, classifying most of the rural population as "peasants" in terms of their position in the national structure.[6] Throughout most of the South American, Central American, Mexican and Caribbean areas, these peasants react to the basic problems of land, employment, amenities, market forces, religion, and other values in a similar fashion. The common cultural background is especially noticeable among communities in which the peasants farm mainly for subsistence and control the land they cultivate. These communities can be considered representative of a large sector of the Latin American rural population from which the human material for land settlement originates.

Furthermore, in spite of the differences in physical environments, the fundamental needs of human settlement have remained basically unchanged for analogous transitional periods in which the peasant moves from subsistence to more advanced forms of cultivation. In most settlements agricultural land use and organizational patterns have followed the same basic rules whether the settlement is situated in the arid north of Argentina, the tropical Amazon basin, or the temperate slopes of the Andes. Life styles and production, when organized in planned patterns, cut across many differences in background.

The impact of the European Conquest and subsequent colonization movements drastically changed native traditional structures. Even the oldest vernacular preserves only faint traces of ancient forms of social and spatial organization. Planned new land settlement, though containing new elements, does not constitute a radical departure from prevailing notions regarding the development of agricultural villages.

The change from traditional to planned-modern settlement is, in itself, a traumatic experience due to new physical and social environments to which the settler must adapt, as well as the mastering of new farming techniques. Although "acclimatization" problems will occur, difficulties are usually less accentuated in a new environment than they would be in the peasant's traditional setting. Social processes may also be influenced to some extent through the spatial arrangements of the site plan.[7]

Except for a few resettlement projects, the participation in new land settlement schemes is mostly voluntary. Participation and selection procedures depend upon the traditional land-hunger and population pressure in rural areas. These and other incentives (e.g. amenities), compensate for difficulties in adaptation. On the other hand, certain impositions on the settler are dictated by both economic and welfare criteria. The settler must accept relocation to a village neighborhood, systematic allocation of production inputs, and at least temporary abdication of his right of decisions over management and marketing practices.

The concept of generic development areas is formulated in this study primarily with respect to human and social dimensions; the settlement area is perceived, in a deterministic way, as a result of human intervention. The guiding principle is that, while the scheme must be technically feasible and adequately endowed, the crucial factor for success lies in the human element. In the general context of Latin America, the population that vies for settlement is considered to be a group with common traits and goals.

OBJECTIVES AND APPROACHES

Regional planning theories are invariably based on economic activities and the development of natural resources. Human resources, especially in rural areas, are sometimes overlooked while planners concentrate on economic aspects.[8] The importance of the human factor as a chief moving force can be proven by the many regions which have enjoyed economic growth in spite of a lack of natural resources or particular comparative advantages.[9] Agriculture as a major economic sector is similarly underrated. The function of agriculture is regarded by many as a prelude to growth, not growth itself.[10]

Regional development is conceived in this study as being for the benefit of people who live or settle in the region. Land settlement--as a component of such development--is approached accordingly in terms of the human potential inherent in rural areas, while agriculture is regarded to be the main resource and tool for socioeconomic transformation. Hence, the ultimate purpose of land settlement is not merely to grow more food, but to "plant" more people. While objectives assume different connotations according to prevailing ideologies and political concepts, the common goals of family farm land settlement can be described as, (1) maximization of the number of families settled in farming and ancillary services; (2) maximization of employment in the area of settlement; (3) achieving optimum levels of services and amenities; and (4) creating a propitious social milieu. These objectives must be obtained without impairing farming efficiency, with future options left open for the rationalization and diversification of production, and with enabling expansion into nonagricultural activities.

Two goals are usually associated with agricultural development projects: those designed to develop agriculture as a stable and viable industry, and those aiming to improve both the economic and social structure of an area by integrating all sections of population into a system of productive relationships based on rising skills and equal opportunities.[11] Spatial organization as perceived herein focuses on the second goal, and is aimed at the simultaneous development of human and natural resources. The socioeconomic advancement of the rural population is seen as a precondition for the absorption of amenities in health and education and the general enhancement of well being.[12] The major emphasis is on new land settlement--an area of increased efforts by national and international organizations. However, a spill-over effect onto various facets of traditional rural settlement can be expected through the dissemination of new technologies and modern concepts of organization.

The conceptual framework for modern land settlement involving family farms embraces three interdependent factors:

1. Subject--the human element as planning object (rather than the economic sector or activity) including three distinct levels: first, the family, the basic spatial and socioeconomic unit; second, the community of small landholders, a framework for social interaction and the basic level for planning and implementation; and last, the region of associated rural settlements, the framework for cooperation and achievement of economies of scale.
2. Process--the transition from subsistence to modern agriculture including the evolutionary phases of subsistence farming, mixed or diversified farming, and specialized farming.
3. Means--the infrastructure involved in the development and transformation process, consisting of physical, human, and institutional infrastructures.

The role of each of these elements and the ways in which they interact should be of special interest.

The Family Farm

As a socioeconomic unit, the family farm is considered to be the basic spatial element in the settlement model and the allotment of land resources is based on the projected income and working capacity of the rural household. The characteristics of the family farm render it suitable for increasing agricultural production, maximizing employment, and providing equity in income distribution--objectives which have been in the foreground of development policies. The use of the family farm as a basic planning unit is justified by the traditional desire of the farmer for individual ownership. At the same time, this form is deemed economically efficient in relation to other types of farm management. Its special importance, however, lies in the special circumstances of rural areas in most Latin American countries. Family farming enables the activation of an untapped labor reserve to increase productivity per acreage with methods that are labor rather than capital intensive, and also to generate continuity on the farm, thereby stemming the flow of population from rural areas. Furthermore, family farming remains the basic form for which agrarian reforms are structured, despite recurring experiments with collective farming.[13] It should be pointed out, however, that the family farm may serve as a transitional link to more advanced associative settlement patterns.

The initial phase of the family farm during its growth from subsistence to full-fledged mixed farming entails, in spatial terms: adequately sized holdings offering acceptable income opportunities; farmstead space and siting that fulfill the requirements of dwelling and farmyard development; and distances to work and services adjusted to the abilities of the household members.

The Community

The integration of land settlement in an orderly process of socioeconomic development could hardly be effected at a reasonable pace and cost when concentrated on the individual family. Likewise, the provision of basic services such as health or education is highly inefficient with families dispersed in the traditional manner of isolation. Hence, the community has been adopted as the basic level of action in the process of development, consisting of a group of family farms bound to a cultivable tract of land with houses situated within the same area and receiving its basic services from the same community center. The concept of a modern rural community reflects a socioeconomic framework in which the peasant farmer is master of his own decisions, either as an individual holder or as partner of a larger production enterprise. Such a community is governed by a democratically elected leadership which engages in a continuous process of community development and which can be identified as a bargaining group, especially in purchasing, marketing, and processing its produce.[14]

Spatial criteria must respond to the interrelated functions of habitat, work, and successive growth. The most salient of these are: (1) physical layout enabling the progressive utilization of economies of scale in selected production services, e.g. heavy farm machinery, aerial spraying, etc.; (2) flexible arrangements of farm holdings to preserve future options for land use and agrotechnical innovations; and (3) amenities similar to those enjoyed by urban communities, especially in health, education, recreation, and municipal services.

The Region

The concept of a regional framework in which the structure of land settlements, both new and traditional, is incorporated is rather versatile and may be adapted to the needs of the planning process. The region is often conceived of as a subsystem,[15] or as an operational region whose boundaries may be determined by political, administrative, geographical, or institutional criteria. The region thus defined allows for adequate scales of service levels, concentration of technical and financial resources, and diversification of economic activities besides the agricultural sector which will provide employment for excess labor in the region and increase the communities' participation in the national economy. The regional framework will assume additional dimensions and significance through the institutional infrastructure which will eventually grow from the initiative of the rural settlements themselves.

The spatial requisites of such a regional structure can only be spelled out in general terms, namely: the adequate integration of community infrastructure with the national communication network to facilitate transportation and active exchange of goods and services. Also significant are dynamic employment and living opportunities available within the bounds of the region for the sons of farmers. The process by which the region is affected by institutional infrastructure is discussed in Chapter 7.

The Process

The concept of transitional phases from subsistence to modern farming is adopted from Weitz[16] who outlines the characteristics of each of the evolutionary stages in family farming, delineating subsistence farming as the stage in which:

> output and consumption are almost identical, and the staple crop--usually wheat, barley, sorghum, rice, or corn--is the chief source of caloric intake. Output and productivity are low and tools are simple. Capital investment is negligible, while land and labor are the key production factors. Labor is underutilized; workers are fully occupied only at seasonal peaks and largely idle during the rest of the year. Requirements at peak seasons determine the upper limit of the size of individual farms. The peasant cultivates only as much land as his family is able to work without recourse to hired labor.[17]

As the underutilized resources of the subsistence farm are gradually brought into fuller use, the transformation to diversified or mixed farming begins. Staple crops no longer predominate, and other products such as fruit, vegetables, and livestock produce marketable surpluses that can provide cash income. This transformation is regarded as a breakthrough enabling the family farm to make better use of idle land and family labor by introducing new crops in slack seasons; by adding livestock; by making better use of seeds, fertilizer, and water; and by the use of manure, the rotation of crops, etc. The full-fledged mixed farm eliminates the disguised unemployment so characteristic of the subsistence farm and ensures increased income security through diversification.

While the transition to mixed farming is usually an evolutionary process, it can be accelerated by the systematic dissemination of techniques, improvement of infrastructures, marketing incentives, etc. New land settlement offers a special opportunity to generate this transformation pragmatically, within feasible limits of time and resources. However, the improvement of the peasant's social and economic conditions must be accompanied by the removal of factors inhibiting increased production and the improvement of skills in agriculture. Among other things, full utilization of the settlers' potential requires the removal of the crippling effects of disease and health hazards and the provision of training and educational facilities.

Specialized farming, the most advanced phase in agricultural development, is described by Weitz as:

> . . . a direct outcome of a rise in the standard of living, biological and agrotechnical progress, and the expansion of national markets and international trade . . . . Production is for the market. The emphasis in resource utilization is no longer on land, water, and labor; capital, technology, and research play a prominent part. Specialized farms vary widely both in size and function. They range from hothouses for the intensive culture of fruit, vegetables, and flowers, to vast wheat farms, where intensive and ingenious use of mechanization enables one family to cultivate a thousand or more acres. The common feature of all specialized farms is the emphasis on the cultivation of one particular crop.[18]

Weitz points out that the economies of scale derived from capital-intensive specialized farming do not require the merging of small holdings into large-scale units that employ hired labor, but can be achieved by family-operated farms through better management, adequate investments, and a comprehensive support system for those services whose efficiency is determined by scale. The main characteristics of each of the evolutionary phases of farming--subsistence, mixed, and specialized--are summarized in Table 2.1.

Infrastructures

Physical infrastructure is usually conceived of as a tool for development and has clear spatial denotations. The human infrastructure, in turn, has both quantitative and qualitative aspects and includes the capacity of man

TABLE 2.1
Distinguishing characteristics of the three phases of farm evolution

	Phase		
Characteristics	Subsistence	Mixed	Specialized
Composition of output	one dominant staple crop and auxiliary crops	diversified	one dominant cash-crop and auxiliary crops
Purpose of production	domestic supply	domestic and market supply	market only
Work schedule	seasonal	balanced	seasonal
Capital investment	low	medium	high
Income security	low	high	low
Ratio of income to value of output	high	approximately half	low
Farmer's professional know-how	low and specialized	medium and diverse	high and specialized
Dependence on a supporting system	none	partial	full

Source: R. Weitz, From Peasant to Farmer: A Revolutionary Strategy for Development (New York, 1971).

to contribute to the improvement of his own social and economic conditions. The institutional infrastructure includes organizational frameworks, regulations, and statutes delineating, for example, the range of economic programs. Of particular importance are the political and administrative structures, and organization of financial and credit systems, and the cooperative framework.[19]

While investments in physical infrastructure usually enjoy undisputed priority, few concrete policies exist regarding the human or institutional infrastructure. The discrepancy in the allocation of resources is partly due to a certain reluctance in delegating a more active role to the rural population in view of its traditional backwardness. The development of human resources is conceived of as a two-phased process in which the participating population is expected to assume a major role in the institutional development only after having reached a certain, yet undefined, level of capability.

The institutional bodies that partake in rural development can be broadly described as (1) government; (2) non-government public agencies; and (3) local or regional organizations which spring from the rural population of the region. Governmental entities contribute mainly to the development of the physical infrastructure. Frequently their most effective function is in macroplanning and control, relating regional developmental activities to other government programs. Their organizational structure usually is not oriented toward the promotion of institutional infrastructures. The task of detailed planning and the establishment of local institutions is generally performed by semigovernmental or public agencies, such as settlement or agrarian reform entities. These agencies are better suited to concentrate on human resources and institutional development. The managerial capacity of a country or region finds its expression in the professional teams or "promotor" groups which act as catalysts in the organization of local socioeconomic enterprises. One of their functions is to phase themselves out by progressively delegating management responsibilities to local elements so that the agency can transfer its efforts to new regions.

The role of government, public, and local institutions, as well as that of private enterprise, and the scope of the relationships involved in rural development have been reviewed extensively. However, the consequential process of development from the beginnings of the family farm to rural regional cooperation has not yet been sufficiently explored. The leading argument of this book states that the appropriate sequence, from the family unit to the intervillage structure, is an indispensable prerequisite for the evolution of described technical and social processes.

METHODOLOGY

Unlike urban planning, the critical area in rural settlement is the individual farmstead, where dwelling and production functions remain closely intertwined. It is the aggregate spatial organization of farm families and their relationship to work and services that determine the successful merging of individual farmers into constructive associations that can make rural life more rewarding. Other input factors, physical, economic, organizational, and cultural, are necessary too in order to generate agricultural development. However, the spatial aspect stands out alone among the man-made physical factors as the rigid planning element in the settlement scheme, the most difficult to modify once implemented.

In light of the conceptual framework outlined in the preceding chapter, and given the development areas existing in Latin America, what would be the model for planned land settlement? The planner, concerned with the immediate problem of making spatial decisions for permanent land settlement, has several possibilities open to him: (1) to plan the settlement along indigenous or traditional patterns; (2) to emulate patterns from countries or regions that are at a more advanced stage of development; (3) to synthesize past experience, in both spontaneous and planned settlement; or (4) to adopt new or nonconventional approaches to fit the specific conditions at hand. Any one of these possibilities involves some inference and transfer of knowledge acquired from previous situations. In the absence of a normative model the pragmatic planner will attempt, therefore, to: (1) analyze pertinent real-life situations; (2) define the vital criteria for "successful" land settlement; (3) formulate guidelines for the spatial organization of new land settlement; and (4) design layout models that can clarify the salient physical aspects. In conformity with this approach the following study includes an analysis of recent land settlement case studies of selected projects, and a comparative analysis of graphical layout models. The resulting conclusions and their implications in regard to higher levels of rural organization will be dealt with in later chapters.

In terms of spatial units and corresponding levels of activity, the main areas to be examined comprise: (1) the farmstead as a spatial entity, with the farm family as a basic socioeconomic unit; (2) the village, its spatial dimensions, and the rural community; (3) the group village or intervillage space, and the structure of services; and (4) the planning-region or functional region, related aspects of regional cooperation, and urban-rural integration.

NOTES

1. G. R. Belshaw, "An Outline of Resettlement Policy in Uganda, 1945-63," Paper presented to the Conference of the East African Institute of Social Research, June, 1963.

2. Raymond Apthorpe, "A Survey of Land Settlement Schemes and Rural Development in East Africa," East African Institute of Social Research Conference Papers, No. 352, January, 1966.

3. Addeke H. Boerma, "Global Approach to Agriculture Problems," Survey of International Development, Vol. 10, No. 5 (1973).

4. Michael Nelson, The Development of Tropical Lands: Policy Issues in Latin America (Baltimore, 1973).

5. Albert O. Hirschman, Development Projects Observed (Washington, D.C., 1967).

6. Charles Wagley, The Latin American Tradition: Essays on the Unity and the Diversity of Latin American Culture (New York, 1968); and, Doreen Warriner, Land Reform in Principle and Practice (Oxford, 1969).

7. D. Iatridis, "Social Scientists in Physical Development Planning: a Practitioner's Viewpoint," International Social Science Journal, Vol. 18 (1966); Gary Yoshioka and Robert Athanasiou, "The Effect of Site Plan and Social Status Variables on Distance to Friends' Homes," Proceedings of the 79th Annual Convention, American Psychological Association, 1971.

8. Resources for the Future, Design for a Worldwide Study of Regional Development (Baltimore, 1966).

9. Raanan Weitz, Spatial Organization of Rural Development, Publications on Problems of Regional Development, No. 3, Settlement Study Centre, Rehovot, Israel, 1968.

10. Charles P. Kindleberger, Economic Development (New York, 1965).

11. Tarlok Singh, "Planning and Productivity in Agriculture," in Economic Development: Issues and Policies (Bombay, 1966), pp. 117-150.

12. Abraham Horwitz, On Health and Wealth, Pan American Sanitary Bureau, Regional Office of the WHO, Washington, D.C., 1967.

13. "Relaciones entre la Reforma Agraria, la Planificación Nacional y la Planificación Regional," Seminario de Planificación Agrícola Regional, Bogota, Colombia, 5-10 June 1972.

14. Yitzhak Abt, "The Institutional Approach to Agrarian Reform and Related Tax Problems," unpublished lecture, Lincoln Foundation, Hartford University, 1966.

15. J. G. M. Hilhorst, Regional Planning: A System's Approach (Rotterdam, 1971); see also J. Friedmann and C. Weaver, Territory and Function (London, 1979).

16. Raanan Weitz, From Peasant to Farmer: A Revolutionary Strategy for Development (New York, 1971).

17. Ibid., p. 16.

18. Ibid., p. 18.

19. I. Prion, Líneas Generales de la Planificación Integrada Rural Regional en las Zonas de la Reforma Agraria, Ministry of Agriculture, Israel, 1973 (mimeo).

3
Spatial and Social Patterns of Rural Settlement

DISPERSED AND CONCENTRATED SETTLEMENT

Agricultural settlements in all parts of the world reveal a vast array of forms and patterns. The rationale of their creation and evolution has continuously interested geographers and planners concerned with rural development and has been subject to numerous studies. As in several other sciences, the classification by types was an initial step toward analyzing the principal characteristics of rural settlements and assessing their relative merits. Settlements are generally identified by their morphological features, the way in which the farmsteads are grouped, or the field system as traced in the landscape. Descriptions of villages usually convey an idea of their geographical setting (e.g. hilltop settlements) or other conspicuous landmarks, such as linear villages along roads or waterways. Most settlements, however, are perceived according to their degree of dispersion or concentration.

The diversity of approaches and criteria proposed for identifying rural settlement patterns testifies to the multiplicity of involved factors. Meitzen used ethnic criteria in classifying rural settlements in Central Europe, attributing the concentrated villages to German, dispersed settlements to Celtic, and round villages to Slavic origin.[1] Demangeon initially based his classification on morphological features, according to agglomerated or dispersed patterns.[2] The agglomerated group included: (1) long or linear villages (eastern and northern France), many of them oriented to roads, rivers, or relief; (2) massed villages; and (3) star villages, in which commercial functions brought about expansion along main roads. Dispersed settlements were divided into: (1) linear; (2) nebular; (3) hamlet; and (4) completely scattered types. Since many important characteristics were lacking in this classification, Demangeon later developed a functional scale which defined the various types of settlement according to their field system: (1) villages with open field systems; (2) villages with contiguous fields, chiefly in marsh and forest settlements (the low countries and Central Europe); and (3) villages with dissociated fields (mostly in the Mediterranean area).[3] While this classification applies primarily to the agglomerated settlements, the dispersed settlement patterns were based on a genetic scale: (1) primary dispersion of ancient origin; (2) intercalated dispersion, with scattered farmsteads of medieval foundation intercalated between villages; (3) secondary dispersion, by which an originally agglomerated village became dispersed; and (4) recent primary dispersion, as in the settlement of the United States in the nineteenth century.

Variations of these criteria were used by Christaller and others. Classifications based on the quantitative method of density measurements have not produced satisfactory taxonomies with respect to rural settlement, since combinations of gathered and dispersed farmsteads frequently occur within a single region.[4] The differentiation between concentrated and dispersed patterns has also been examined from a social and economic standpoint.[5] The division between regular and irregular, or tight and loose settlement, remains nevertheless arbitrary. Academic interest in the structure of rural settlement has further sagged with the surge in urban sciences which tend to regard rural settlement as an intermediary stage toward urbanization. The continuous reorganization of agriculture in both centrally planned and market economies and recent land reform in developing countries, however, has revived the interest in the cause and effect of the diverse spatial patterns. One particular area of controversy involves the social efficiency of concentrated settlement patterns as opposed to the impressive productivity records achieved on the dispersed farm in countries such as the U.S.A., Holland, and Denmark.

The study of spatial patterns of rural settlement involves two basic approaches: the empirical, designed to discover and generalize the principles governing the development of rural structures; and the analytical, directed more toward the formulation of normative models and based on lessons gleaned from real-world experiences. The differentiation between concentrated and dispersed patterns is a significant step in either method. Analysis of existing farming patterns may be based on the assumption that form follows social and economic interactive functions in a given environment, and that the evolved pattern bespeaks its quality. Frequently, however, the current form reveals only the last embodiment of a series of changes. It will usually be easier to discern a certain pattern in regulated, rather than in spontaneous settlement, but even then it is difficult to hypothesize on the changes which the settlement underwent.

Broader classifications including such factors as agglomeration, field association, or underlying social organization have been attempted, but become quite complex and cannot be coerced into systems of facile generalizations.[6] A more promising approach to the geography of rural settlement may lie in appraising patterns in terms of forces which tend toward concentration or dispersion. Such forces may be internal, involving agrarian and social organization, or external, chiefly those of economic and environmental character.[7] The use of criteria based on the dynamics of a settlement was similarly suggested by Vidal.[8] This conception of settlement dynamics depends not so much on particular morphological characteristics, but rather on the trends and potential generated by the combination of a settlement's spatial and social organization.

FARMING STAGES AND THEIR SPATIAL REQUIREMENTS

The issue of agglomerated versus dispersed patterns can be examined in light of activities on the family farm. These revolve around three spatial components: (1) the farmstead, consisting of the farmhouse and farmyard installations; (2) the agricultural plot, consisting of one tract of land or dispersed lots; and (3) the service center, where all economic, social, and municipal facilities are located. These three components can be grouped in different ways, but generally they form two basic patterns: the dispersed, in which individual farms are isolated from each other; and the agglomerated, in which farms are grouped in definite physical entities or villages.[9]

In the dispersed pattern the farmsteads are located within their cultivated areas. This pattern is convenient for the working activities of the farm. Distances to the fields are minimal, thereby reducing the commuting time to work and lowering transportation costs. The disadvantages of dispersal, on the other hand, include high costs of infrastructure and utilities, services that are less accessible and consequently less efficient, and difficulties in institutional development and cooperation among farmers. The emphasis in the dispersed pattern is on the relationship between the farmstead and the cultivated area rather than on the interaction of the farmer and service facilities. The agglomerated pattern on the other hand, is based on the village, a well-defined entity of farmsteads and services surrounded by cultivated plots.

The patterns that conform to each developmental stage of the family farm reflect different priorities which must be reconciled in the settlement plan. The subsistence farm, from which the settler originates, usually cultivates only limited acreage. The farmstead and its relationship to the cultivated area and external facilities remains simple. There is little need for economic services since most of the produce is destined for home consumption. Where the land has a low carrying capacity and, consequently, the area required to support one family remains relatively large, peasants generally live in a dispersed pattern. In areas of intensive cultivation the agglomerated pattern predominates. However, agglomerated patterns can also be the result of security or environmental conditions, irrespective of land-use intensity. Intensive cultivation may also be combined with primary dispersion when land settlement started in a spontaneous, or pioneer-fashioned way. The seasonal character of subsistence farming allows the peasant to cultivate far-away fields by establishing provisional shelter on the plot during peak seasons. The importance of commuting time is lessened because of redundant labor and the expanded family's ability to separate into smaller units for seasonal work or prolonged periods. Both the agglomerated and dispersed settlement patterns exist among peasants in Latin America, with a tendency to group in small hamlets or villages. Today's settler may come from either one of these backgrounds.

In the mixed farming stage an array of settlement patterns, representing both agglomerated and dispersed forms, has evolved over time. The mixed farm differs from the subsistence farm in two main aspects: livestock rearing constitutes an integral part of the production system, and an increasing share of the produce is destined for the market. Introducing livestock onto the farm, as well as the diversification of activities, entails the expansion of farmyard installations. Transportation between farmstead and fields becomes a critical point since transportation facilities are usually limited. Distance is one of the main limiting factors during this stage. The mixed farm also requires a more complex system of supply, marketing, and credit than the subsistence farm. This complexity implies the development of a suitable infrastructure and service facilities located within reasonable distances in order to be fully utilized.

Specialized farming usually involves the cultivation of larger tracts of lands, or some highly capital-intensive and land-intensive types of specialization such as greenhouse farming. Many activities on the specialized farm--deep plowing, spraying of pesticides, harvesting, and other operations--become more efficient on a large scale. Large tracts of land necessitate traveling longer distances and there is a greater reliance on supporting services for production inputs and marketing on a regional and interregional scale. The spatial organization at this stage may require further changes in the layout of the settlement. As transportation facilities improve the significance of distance to the fields decreases. In the ultimate stage of specialized farming there is less need for the farmer's continuous presence on his plot and the importance of modern residential facilities is greater. Weitz underlines the advantages of the agglomerated pattern by pointing out that:

> Concentrating the necessary facilities in village centers is therefore both more effective and more convenient than making services available to farms on an individual basis. Very often the people who operate the services also reside within the village, which becomes an attractive social center for the farmer.[10]

While each evolutionary stage of farming can evidently be accommodated with either an agglomerated or a dispersed pattern, difficulties arise in the transition from one farming stage to another with its changing spatial requirements. The changing requirements of agriculture make it difficult to design a workable compromise between the conflicting needs of social and economic development, especially since building a village is a lengthy process involving the construction of physical works as well as community development. During this building process, concepts of social organization, technology, resource allocations, as well as income needs, are liable to change or be modified. Even deciding what land is best suited for a particular crop may involve a long process of trial and error, as exemplified by the United States.[11] The settlement pattern should offer, therefore, maximum flexibility to accommodate current requirements as well as future changes. Such flexibility may not provide the most ideal settlement pattern for a particular stage but should be the most efficient for the developmental process as a whole.

HUMAN AND SOCIAL ORGANIZATIONAL FACTORS

In general, concentrated settlement will be used whenever social criteria are preponderant. The shift to concentrated patterns in Latin American land settlement schemes not only satisfies the desire to maximize social and economic efficiency, but also facilitates the provisioning of amenities, agricultural extension, training, financing, and related infrastructure. In other words, agglomeration is as essential for the efficient operation of the settling agencies as for the settlers themselves.

The advantages of agglomeration raise a question as to the family farm's efficiency as compared to the collective or managed farm based on the separation of management and other types of labor. The latter farm type includes commercial plantations or *latifundia* employing hired laborers and various kinds of state and collective farms, such as the *sovkhoz* and *kolkhoz* in the Soviet Union, the Mexican *ejido*, and the Israeli *kibbutz* or *collective moshav*. The competitiveness of the family farm has been amply discussed on economic as well as on social grounds. Franklin contends that family farms appear to be on the increase, a trend which has given rise to state policies and rural movements aimed at promoting viable modernized farming enterprises.[12] Weitz believes that the family farm has certain attributes that render it more suitable for increasing agricultural production in developing countries than the collective or managed farm.[13] Pihkala notes that the family farm will maximize economic as well as noneconomic welfare,[14] while Hirschman asserts that family-sized farm units lead to a more equitable distribution of income.[15]

In addition to these considerations, agrarian reform and settlement programs in Latin America are generally based on family farming due to the traditional longing of peasants to operate their own farms. This desire is derived from a complexity of economic, social, and psychological motives rooted both in history and in present conditions. Having a feeling of status, purpose, and security, has been described as being as important to the peasant as improvement in his economic situation. The family farm, as conceived of in most Latin American countries, embodies a socioeconomic unit with individual property rights operating within a free-market economy. This concept is implicit in many agrarian reform programs, and is expressed by the Nicaraguan Agrarian Institute in most simple terms: "From the experience of the Institute in other colonization projects it is known that the settler does not adapt psychologically to farming types which are not based on the private property of his holding."[16]

As mentioned previously, the family farm enables utilization of a vast resource of marginal labor for increasing productivity per unit of land with labor-intensive rather than with capital-intensive methods. In a survey in Nicaragua the peasant-farmer's family was found to consist of two work units, or 480 working days per year.[17] In another assessment from a project in Peru the working capacity of an average farm family was calculated as 578 working days per year (Table 3.1) of which an estimated 100 days were spent working in the farmyard. This working potential is especially apparent on the family farm where part-time activities can best be put to use.

Although the family farm pattern has been generally accepted by Latin American institutions concerned with agrarian reform and rural development, several countries have recurrently tried to adopt collective and other associative patterns in their agrarian reform programs. Collective patterns do seem especially applicable in connection with the expropriation of estates or commercial plantations because of the configuration's all-around efficiency in the specialized farming stage. Time and infrastructure costs can thus be saved without changing the physical and operational patterns. Conversion of agro-industrial enterprises into this form may be advisable especially when redistribution would result in extremely small shares. Unfortunately, there has been a tendency to apply similar collective principles to land settlement in general. The inherent risk of a premature introduction of

TABLE 3.1
Family labor capacity in the lower Mayo River area in Peru (in days)

	Husband	Wife	Son
Nonwork days			
Sundays	52	52	52
Saturdays	--	--	52
Holidays	10	10	10
Sickness	10	10	--
School	--	--	171
Absence	10	10	--
Miscellaneous	10	20	--
Total	92	102	285
Work days at home	--	150	--
Total nonfarming days	92	252	285
Total farming days	273	113	64*

Total family farming capacity = 578 (comprising husband, wife, and three sons)

*80 percent efficiency.

SOURCE: Proyecto Específico de Recolonización del Distrito de Cacatachi, Ministry of Agriculture and FAO, Tarapoto, Peru, 1970.

collective patterns will be discussed in light of case studies from Mexico and Venezuela and the lesson gleaned from the Israeli collective moshav.

NOTES

1. August Meitzen, Siedelung und Agrarwesen der Westgermanen und Ostgermanen, der Kelten, Römer, Finnen und Slawen (Berlin, 1895).
2. A. Demangeon, "L'habitation rurale en France: Essai de classification des principaux types," Annales de Géographie, Vol. 29 (1920), pp. 352-375.
3. A. Demangeon, "Types de peuplement rural en France," Annales de Géographie, Vol. 48 (1939), pp. 1-21.
4. Gabriele Schwarz, Allgemeine Siedlungsgeographie (Berlin, 1961).
5. Lipa Kam and Jacob Maos, "Report on Rural Housing and Village Planning in Venezuela," Pan American Sanitary Bureau, Regional Office of the World Health Organization, Caracas, Venezuela, 1964; Emmanuel Yalan, J. Maos, and L. Kam, Land Planning of the Agricultural Cooperative Village, The Rural Building Research Centre, Haifa, Israel, 1963; Emmanuel Yalan, J. Maos, and L. Kam, The Influence of Farming

Rationalization on the Planning of Scattered and Gathered Settlements, The Rural Building Research Centre, Haifa, Israel, 1964.

6. J. M. Houston, A Social Geography of Europe (New York, 1968).

7. C. T. Smith, An Historical Geography of Western Europe before 1800 (London, 1967).

8. Paul Vidal de la Blache, Principes de Géographie humaine (Paris, 1922).

9. Raanan Weitz, From Peasant to Farmer: A Revolutionary Strategy for Development (New York, 1971), p. 42.

10. Ibid., p. 49.

11. Marion Clawson, America's Land and Its Uses (Baltimore, 1972).

12. S. H. Franklin, Rural Societies (London, 1971).

13. Weitz, From Peasant to Farmer.

14. K. U. Pihkala, "The Nature of Agricultural Economics as a Discipline and Science," in Roger N. Dixey (ed.), International Explorations of Agricultural Economics (Ames, Iowa, 1967), pp. 223-229.

15. Albert O. Hirschman, Development Projects Observed (Washington, D.C., 1967).

16. Instituto Agrario de Nicaragua, Proyecto Rigoberto Cabezas: Primera Etapa (Managua, Nicaragua, 1972), p. 72.

17. Ibid., p. 48.

4
Recent Experiences in Rural Development

EUROPEAN SETTLEMENT AS A REAL-WORLD MODEL

The last two centuries of European agricultural development are often looked upon as a period analogous to the transitional stage of rural development in most Latin American countries. Out of a wide range of spatial and social patterns a variety of solutions was assimilated in the New World and juxtaposed on indigenous settlement forms during various periods of colonization. Many of the trends in rural settlement were influential in the pioneer settlement of colonial America. In the long run they produced the present need for far-reaching land reforms.

The shapes and patterns which have evolved, particularly in Central and Western Europe, have been studied in order to formulate a general nomenclature of settlement typology. Several of these studies make it possible to look at the changes that occurred in various land settlement forms over a long span of time. Of special interest are changes from concentrated to dispersed settlement patterns and their underlying causes. It has been hypothesized that outsettlement in Europe, or secondary dispersion, resulted from overcrowding in the village and the congestion of the farmyard, as well as from social changes within the villages. Both phenomena induced the more dynamic or younger farmers to settle outside the village.[1] Throughout the period trends toward improved land use and cooperative methods, as well as associative farming patterns, can be discerned. Presumably these were attempts to arrest the disintegration of the rural community as a social unit. Europe was a breeding place for many such experiments, more so than in the Middle and Far East where patterns remained relatively static.

A study of agricultural development from the viewpoint of land settlement must examine the reasons for stagnation and decline which later brought about the need for extensive rehabilitation measures. In effect, the anatomy of failure may reveal more about the intrinsic strength of a structure, social or spatial, than subsequent undertakings of replanning and resettlement. It seems, however, that in spite of the abundance of historical information the spatial data are too diffused to give a reliable picture of past circumstances. Although spatial forms remain impregnated in the landscape for prolonged periods of time, they are part of an evolutionary process whose exact sequence is not easy to trace. One must remember that, although Europe is usually associated with the advent of modern agriculture leading to the industrial revolution, it was also a place of social and political upheavals, epidemics, and confused migratory movements.[2] A reconstruction of spatial and environmental changes is possible only in broad strokes or in descriptions of temporal situations. The available data concentrate mostly on the economic transition, the termination of patriarchal life styles, and the ensuing need for manpower and mechanization, and less on the spatial forms of rural settlement.

In retrospect, the period of agricultural development in Europe represents a dynamic model with continuously evolving settlement patterns. The forces behind these changes are so diverse that generalization seems futile. Agricultural development was often accompanied by a diminishing rural population and the disintegration of communities, while exogenous factors such as warfare, epidemics, and market conditions also played a role. The Enclosure Movement in England, for example, which brought about the conversion of communal land into individual farms, can be viewed from different standpoints--as the result of agrotechnical innovations, of the modernization of land tenure, or of the response to economic incentives by entrepreneurial farmers.[3] Internal social pressures which caused many communities to disperse, dissolve into urbanization, or disappear entirely, are even more difficult to trace. Attempts to prevent the disintegration of the community as a social entity can be discerned from the layout of many regulated settlements of this period.[4] At what point, exactly, the failure of a settlement pattern occurred is difficult to surmise, save the observation that social processes are often self-destructive and tend to move away from an equilibrium.[5]

An element not fully explored in dealing with this period has been the role of the farmstead in the evolution of rural settlement. The building of a farmstead with dwelling, stables, and other annexes, constituted a vast effort for the single family. Shape and functions were determined by tradition and produced a static framework which could not easily accommodate changes. The family farm situated in the compact village lacked the flexibility and space needed for development, while the isolated small landholder was usually hard-pressed to keep pace with changing agrotechnical requirements. The crisis of this basic production unit may have hindered the development of the village community as an expanded production group. Thus, the disintegration of a settlement was often the result of the malfunction of the intravillage farmsteads--a significant detail often obscured by the impressive achievements in productivity of the isolated farmstead in the United States and Europe. The current success of the dispersed pattern in agricultural production has overshadowed the issue of social inefficiency.

The evolutionary changes of European agriculture do not represent a broad-front development but rather a series of agrotechnical breakthroughs in selected geographical areas favored by certain conditions, mainly in Central and Western Europe. The process bypassed many areas and populations which remained stagnant or declined.[6] Agricultural development did not necessarily improve economic or social efficiency, as can be seen today from the retarded state of many rural areas in Europe where agriculture still remains in an early transitional stage between subsistence and mixed farming. In these areas, farm sites are often crowded together, leaving little space for farm buildings, construction of new premises, or adequate road systems. The fragmentation of land (due to inheritance) continues to increase commuting time and impedes the rationalization of agriculture. European governments are investing great efforts to repair the damages incurred by the deterioration of rural spatial structures through resettlement schemes, consolidation of fragmented lands, and group farming.[7] With distances reduced by modern communications, agglomeration and its resulting advantages in social amenities are considered more important than the disadvantages associated with the separation of holdings and homestead. Jacoby described the general opinion that modern villages are better suited for keeping the younger generation on the land than the isolated farm.[8] The development projects in Italy and Spain (described later in this chapter) are also part of this effort to rehabilitate the distorted rural structures. The magnitude of some of these undertakings is such that they offer useful insights regarding new land settlement.

While the European model throws some light on the problems caused by dispersion and fragmentation, the separate stages of evolution in plan or form are difficult to trace meaningfully. Even those settlements which were originally based on regulated plans underwent changes in their morphology, social structure, and land parcellation to the point that their usefulness as models is extremely questionable. Recent land settlement undertaken in three developing rural regions in Israel, Italy, and Spain, may reveal more clearly the evolution of spatial concepts. These regions also have available more data on plans and visible achievements. While they are not the only areas of recent settlement, their objectives and criteria as well as the basic problems seem relevant to rural development in many Latin American countries. The affinity of conditions in rural areas was probably one of the reasons the Organization of American States entered into agreements for technical assistance from these countries in the early sixties, hoping to learn from the accumulated experience.[9]

A complete comparative study of the three countries is limited because of the different backgrounds and developmental techniques used. However, the common element is the planning of small landholders' settlements and, within this area, specific spatial aspects can be analyzed. This, in itself, makes the study of these real-world models worthwhile.

ISRAEL: COMPREHENSIVE RURAL DEVELOPMENT

Rural development in Israel provides an example of land settlement schemes and the building of services on a regional scale. The basic patterns were based on European experience; however, they developed within a particular sociopolitical context out of which emerged new concepts and approaches. The period of settlement covers nearly a century--a space of time sufficient in length and continuity for settlement models to evolve, yet not long enough for physical features to become blurred by social and structural changes. The criteria which crystallized during this period represent economic as well as social aspects. The objectives in the economic sphere were to rationalize production and supporting services. In the social sphere the aims were to achieve social stability and to improve well being. Both aspects have clear spatial expressions in the Israeli model.

While early colonization at the turn of the nineteenth century was based primarily on private ownership, a doctrine of national rural land was adopted in 1901--a revival of the ancient Hebrew tradition which did not recognize private ownership of land. The social implications of this decision became evident during the period of intensive immigration and consequent need for employment, and the doctrine was later bolstered by a strong labor movement. The national acquisition of land became an important tool in the ideological direction of future land settlement. The census of 1950 showed that only 8.5 percent of Jewish farms in Israel were privately owned. Israel thus occupies a unique position in its rural regional organization and urban-rural relationships, due mainly to the demographic flow of immigrants who were ideologically oriented towards rural life and to the vitality embodied in the rural sector.

There are parallels to this situation in several developing countries where land was originally communal or state property. The settlement of immigrants in Israel, as in Latin American colonization schemes for example, involved transplanting people to unfamiliar ecosystems, an undertaking which required new physical and institutional infrastructures. Similar to the goals postulated in recent agrarian reform movements, the rural development schemes in Israel called for the absorption and assimilation of settlers from diverse backgrounds into the national lifestream. Sparsely populated regions were to be settled as densely as was consistent with their economic potential.

The Israeli cooperative and collective settlement models and their underlying criteria are discussed here, particularly with respect to their spatial characteristics as reflected in the morphology of the settlements. The settlements can be illustrated with the help of layout models which provide useful parameters for analyzing settlement patterns in other countries. The principal settlement forms described here are: (1) the traditional (unplanned) village; (2) early planned "dense" settlement--Moshava; (3) cooperative small landholders' settlement--Moshav; (4) collective settlement--Kibbutz; and (5) collective work settlement--Collective Moshav, or Moshav Shitufi.

The Traditional Village

Most examples of traditional settlements in Israel are Arab villages of ancient origin which evolved in a spontaneous fashion similar to the European-Mediterranean type. Usually located originally on hill tops or elevated sites to escape flooding and disease and for security, some of the villages expanded onto the plains as environmental conditions improved. Dwellings are huddled in compact clusters, with few farmyards or farmland attached. The agricultural plots lie at a considerable distance from the village but most holdings are fragmented due to inheritance customs (see Figure 4.1A). Since reparcellation or land consolidation is difficult, this situation impedes the introduction of rational farming. The expansion of the Arab village is generally "centrifugal"--outsettlement to the plots. Although this outsettlement is accompanied by some improvement in farming methods by individual villagers, there is little cooperation in municipal or production-related activities due in part to the spatial disintegration of the community.

The appearance of Jewish settlements in the traditional rural landscape has accelerated the process of modernization and brought about profound socioeconomic changes. Both the wealthy absentee landlord class and the poor exploited tenant farmer class have mostly disappeared in recent years, while most Arab villages have been incorporated into local and regional frameworks for the provision of municipal and social amenities.

The Moshava (pl. Moshavot)

The oldest type of planned "dense" settlement trans-

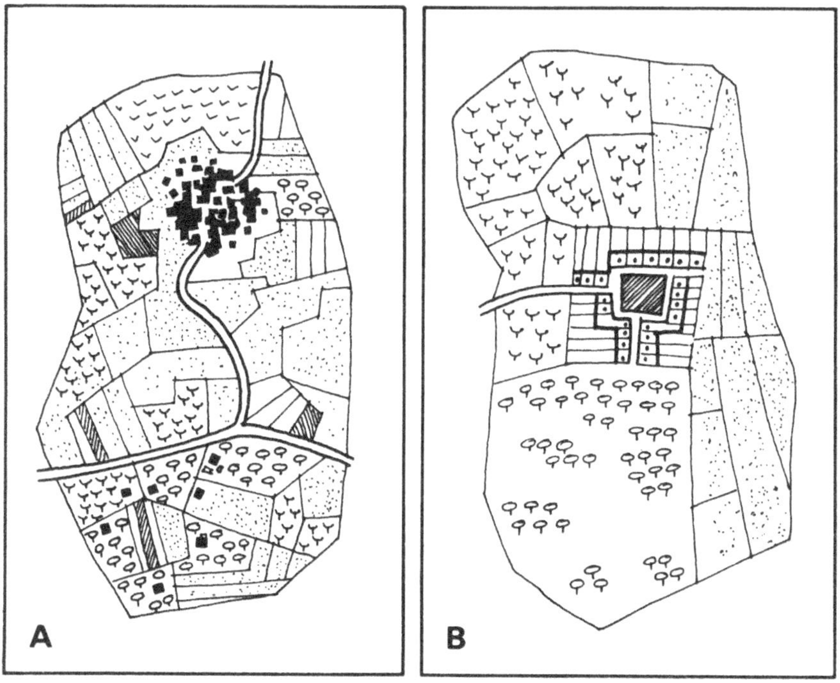

Figure 4.1 Schematic layout of dense nucleated villages in Israel

A. Traditional Arab village: Shaded fields belong to one family. Lower part of plan shows "outsettlement" of individual farmers.

B. Moshava: Farmyards have an area of approximately 800 square meters. Farmyards were sometimes enclosed in a protective wall, depending on security conditions.

planted from Europe at the turn of the century, the Moshava was based on a land allotment system intended for dry farming of fifteen to twenty hectares per family. The land was given in private ownership to settlers who were free to purchase additional land or to use hired labor. With the introduction of irrigation and the intensification of agriculture, Moshavot were considered to be fairly large farms.

The Moshavot on the coastal plain specialized in citrus growing, leading to an influx of salaried labor and to urbanization. Many grew into towns of 20,000 to more than 80,000 inhabitants. The Moshavot in the inner valleys and foothills, generally engaged in the growth of field crops, remained static or declined in population. In some cases efforts were made to enlarge old settlements along the lines of the cooperative Moshav by adding new settlers with holdings of approximately three hectares. However, the difference in production factors (soil and water) and social tensions between the veteran farmers and new settlers slowed down the full integration of these communities.[10]

Figure 4.1B illustrates the spatial arrangement of the Moshava, with dwellings set closely together along a road, farmyard and structures behind them. During the formative years, the living area was often surrounded by a protective wall interfering with the normal development of the farmyard.

The Moshav (pl. Moshavim)

The Moshav was defined as a cooperative small landholders' settlement in which each family worked its separate plot of land, lived in its own homestead, and drew income from the produce of its farm. The governing principles of Moshav life were:

1. national ownership of the land;
2. allotted cultivated areas no larger than the settler and his family could manage alone;
3. no lot division among several heirs or plot enlargement by purchasing additional land;
4. additional labor hired only with the consent of the Moshav authorities--the general assembly;
5. all members obligated to mutual aid and shared responsibility; and,
6. joint marketing of produce and purchasing of farming inputs.

The evolution of this settlement pattern can be discerned by examining consecutive models built in Israel since 1920. The early forms of the Moshav (e.g. Merhavia, or Nahalal) located all holdings in one block attached to the farmstead (Figure 4.2A). Although the concentration

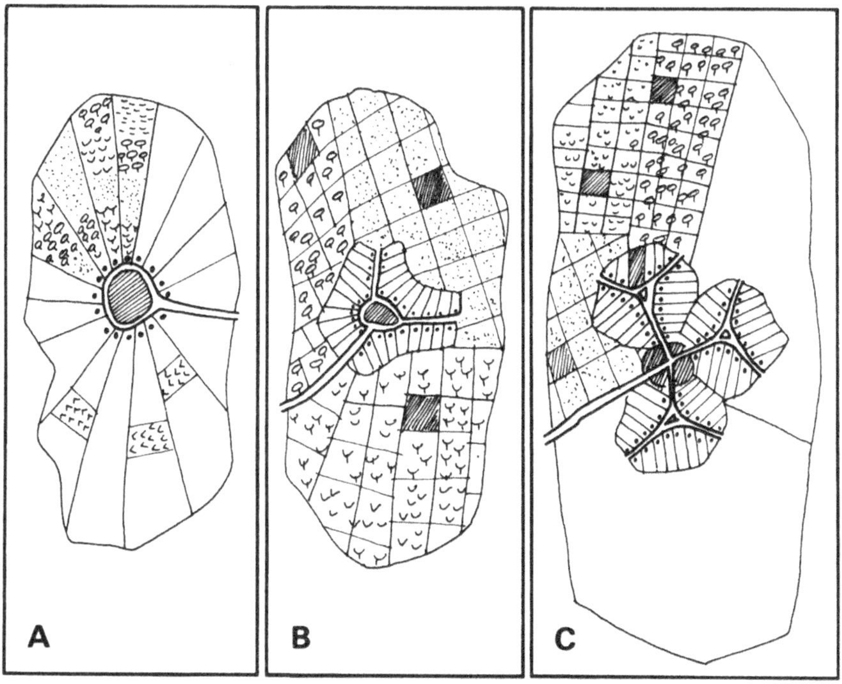

Figure 4.2 Schematic layout of the Moshav

A. Early plan with contiguous holdings. Disadvantages: unequal soil quality and inflexibility in parcellation; fragmentation of crops prevents rational farming methods.

B. Improved plan with homeplots adjoining farmyards and main holdings concentrated in homogeneous cultivation blocks. Equity in land quality and distances to fields is easier to achieve. Parcels can be worked individually or cooperatively, leading to rational farming methods.

C. Multinuclear Moshav with three communities deployed around a common service center. Each nucleus has a village green with kindergarten, communal house, etc., but most facilities are located in the common center, within short walking distance.

of land in one block attached to the farmstead as a homeplot was advantageous from the standpoint of commuting time and unlimited space for farmyard development, several disadvantages became apparent through time. There was an inherent element of inequity in land allotment since soil quality was not always equal in all agricultural plots. This inequality sometimes led to resentment from unfortunate settlers whose land was of inferior quality. The plan also lacked flexibility due to difficulties in adding land to the farms in the same pattern. Another disadvantage involved the fragmentation of crops, preventing large-scale cultivation and creating interferences due to adjacent spraying and irrigation.

A modification of this pattern can be seen in the subsequent developmental phase of the Moshav, planned with farmyards of 0.2 to 0.3 hectares and, attached to this area, a homeplot of about 0.5 hectares. The balance of the farmers' land allotment was divided into one or more plots, each located in blocks of homogeneous soil quality and crops. The resulting two- or three-field system achieved equity in land distribution, both in quality and in distance (by compensating owners of a far parcel in one block with a near parcel in the other block). Moreover, the system made possible the introduction of cooperative methods in specific farming operations such as heavy plowing and aerial spraying (Figure 4.2B). As in the previous model, the family farm usually comprised the farmstead, which included the dwelling area and a farmyard of 0.2 to 0.3 hectares and a contiguous homeplot of about 0.8 hectares. The rest of the land allotment was divided into several parcels, each situated within large blocks of homogeneous cultivation.

Unsolved, as yet, remained the problem of incorporating a larger number of settlers in the village in order to improve supporting services. The solution to this problem was found in the multiunit Moshav (Figure 4.2C), made up of a number of neighborhood units sharing the services of one service center. By increasing the size of population served by this center a greater efficiency and economy could be achieved. Also, the settlement could be located at a greater distance from the regional service center. The separate units, on the other hand, helped to preserve some of the advantages of small size, for communities of sixty to eighty families were found to be more amenable to organization, agricultural extension services, and to social interaction. Small neighborhoods also facilitated physical adaptation to the terrain and provided more flexibility for the incremental execution of settlement programs. An additional advantage of the multiunit settlement type was more efficient mixing of heterogeneous social groups, a serious problem of earlier Moshav-type settlements. Smaller groups of similar socioethnic backgrounds were easier to establish and, by linking several neighborhoods to common facilities, satisfactory progress was noted toward social and economic integration.

Recent advances in agricultural technology and the resulting expansion of production are making more rigorous demands on economic efficiency. The increased use of motorized transportation, drastically altering the significance of distances, has developed correspondingly. Also, a greater awareness of dwelling quality in the village currently exists. The general trend in the physical planning of the Moshav suggests the creation of agroindustrial parks with centralized services and a concentrated residential area with a minimum of storage and farmyard operation facilities. This new pattern is similar to the layout of the Collective Moshav.[11]

The Kibbutz (pl. Kibbutzim)

From a functional point of view the Kibbutz is a large enterprise jointly owned and operated by the workers who reside in its center. The settlement is based on collective and ideological partnership in all aspects of life, including social, economic, and educational activities. Land is communally owned under a national leasehold, and is cultivated according to the most advanced agrotechnical methods available to the community. The layout and interrelationship of dwellings, farmyards, and fields offer a great deal of flexibility and allow for rational development of agriculture.

The Kibbutz is a concentrated settlement whose center of gravity is the dining hall where the community meets several times during the day (Figure 4.3A). The main areas are divided into a residential sector, including dwellings for adults, living quarters for school children, and dormitories for infants, and a work sector for farm buildings such as stables and poultry runs, silos, storage sheds, and garages for farm machinery. The central core contains the dining hall and kitchen complex, administration offices, social club and library, and other communal facilities such as laundry, supply store, and dispensary.

As in the Moshav, land is usually allotted on the basis of a hundred "farm units," calculated for a population of 400 to 500 individuals. This number was regarded to be adequate for the maintenance of productive branches and for stimulating social interaction within the community. Various Kibbutzim, however, strove for improved levels of production and services and managed to increase their membership to 1,000 and 2,000 persons through additional employment in services, processing agricultural produce, and light industries.

The blending of industrial and agricultural enterprises has proven to be easier in the collective settlement than in the individualistic Moshav, since labor is organized on a communal basis. But, the alleged higher productivity is not unequivocal. In contrast to the

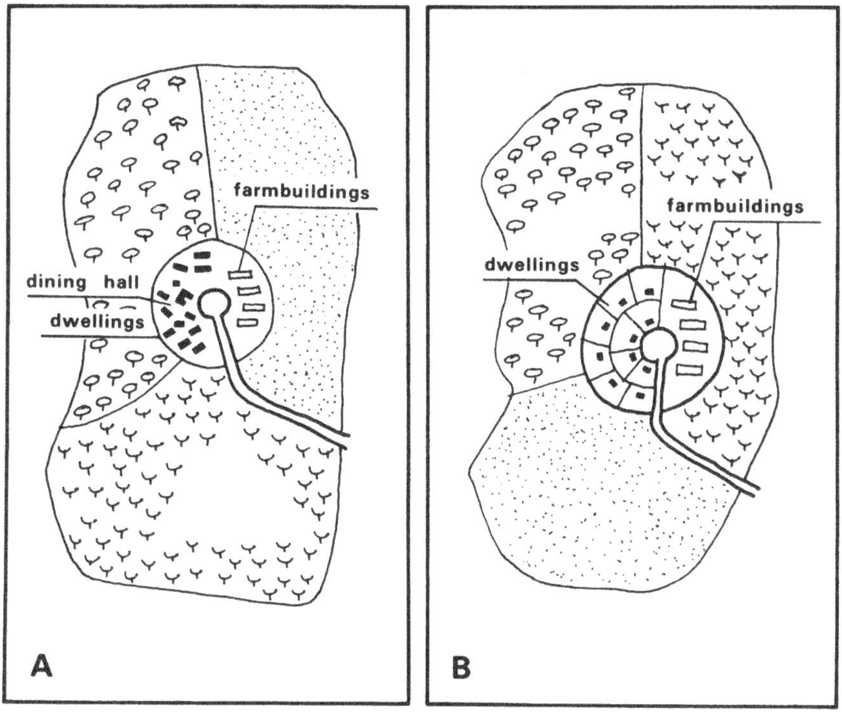

Figure 4.3 Schematic layout of collective settlements, the Kibbutz (A), and the Collective Moshav or Moshav Shitufi (B)

In both patterns there is a complete separation between residential area, work sector (farm buildings, workshops, etc.) and fields. The land is divided into homogeneous cultivation blocks. The center of gravity in the Kibbutz is the dining hall where community members meet several times a day for meals, work assignments, and assemblies. Multiple housing units save space and keep distances to the center to a minimum. In the Collective Moshav each family occupies an individual house and small garden lot.

Moshav, work in the collective settlement must be regimented and will vary under normal conditions from eight to ten hours per day. The difference is aptly described by the following observation: "In the collective settlement a member finishes his work after so many hours, while in the Moshav the farmer finishes working when the job is done."

The Collective Moshav, or Moshav Shitufi (pl. Moshavim Shitufiim)

The spatial arrangements of the Collective Moshav resemble those of the Kibbutz (Figure 4.3B); however, houses offer more privacy and are set in small garden plots. In some cases a somewhat larger plot is attached to the house for kitchen crops or fruit trees. The social organization of the Collective Moshav is a synthesis of the cooperative Moshav and the collective Kibbutz. Simply stated, the Collective Moshav's purpose is to provide joint production while maintaining enough freedom to satisfy individual needs. Work is organized on a communal basis as in the Kibbutz; however, each family lives in its own house as in the Moshav and is free to dispose of its monthly budget according to its own preferences.

The flexibility and relative simplicity of the physical layout, and the possibility of benefiting from economies of scale without colliding with traditional family values or imposing radically different social systems, has appealed to many rural planners. In Israel itself, the idea of a moderate social framework combined with apparent efficiency of production strongly influenced other settlement forms. Yet by 1980 there were only 35 Collective Moshavim in Israel as opposed to 400 cooperative Moshavim and 255 Kibbutzim,[12] a fact which points to some inherent difficulties in this settlement pattern which have not as yet been solved. Many of the Moshavim have applied cooperative methods to various production branches, while in the Kibbutz more amenities are being introduced to enhance the privacy and family life of its members. It is reasonable to assume that in time the contrasting differences between the diverse settlement patterns in Israel will gradually diminish. Occasionally a Collective Moshav reverts willingly to the cooperative Moshav type after a few years of operation. As a precautionary measure, the plans for Moshavim usually anticipate the eventual reparcelling of the village land allotment into individual holdings in order to avoid costly modifications in physical infrastructure. Nevertheless, the conceptual impact of the Collective Moshav on both the cooperative and collective patterns has led to a constant process of change in current settlement forms.

Collective living is undoubtedly a departure from conventional societal forms and entails the selection of candidates professing a particular life style; thus, such settlement forms are restricted to certain groups of people. Cooperative and collective settlement patterns therefore cannot easily be compared equally; social adaptability may, in the final analysis, be the determinant factor in adopting one pattern or another.

The Structure of Services

The structure of services for rural areas was initially based on cooperation between town and village within a framework of small geographical units. Accordingly, the grade "A" Center was to be the community center of a single settlement; the "B" Center was to be a rural service center, with a population of up to 100 families and serving a rural population of four to six villages; the "C" Center, a regional town of 15,000 to 16,000 people, was to be closely tied to the rural area to provide employment and services; and the "D" Center was expected to be a medium-sized city, operating as service center for the provinces and containing administrative planning units. At the top of the ladder were the large urban centers (Jerusalem, Haifa, Tel Aviv, Beer Sheva) acting as district capitals and centers for industry, government services, and a higher range of public and private services. In practice, however, the structure evolved differently. Because the collective and cooperative settlements were already incorporated into independent frameworks for joint marketing and supply (such as the cooperative societies of Tnuva and Hamashbir), the intermediary role of the traditional central place was, to a great extent, eliminated. Planning was generally based on the assumption that a settlement comprising eight to a hundred farming units would be capable of maintaining its basic services unaided. In fact, many settlements did try to set up their own facilities, even though this placed an undue burden on the community and led to redundant services in the region as a whole. This development is exemplified by a group of villages in the Jezreel Valley established in the 1920s (Figure 4.4A). Each one of these villages developed its own services without resorting to existing urban centers. As a result, the services were restricted in quality and relatively costly until the communities could overcome the critical formative period and increase their populations.

Since the Moshav was (and still is) based on the indivisibility of the family holding, only the so-called "continuing son" could remain on the farm. Hence, demographic increase in the Moshav occurred primarily as a result of internal growth and, to some degree, through the addition of families employed in services. Nahalal, one of the first settlements in the Jezreel group, originally consisted of 75 farm families and about 10 "professional" families. During the second phase and transitional period (1924-1947), the village increased to 95 farming families

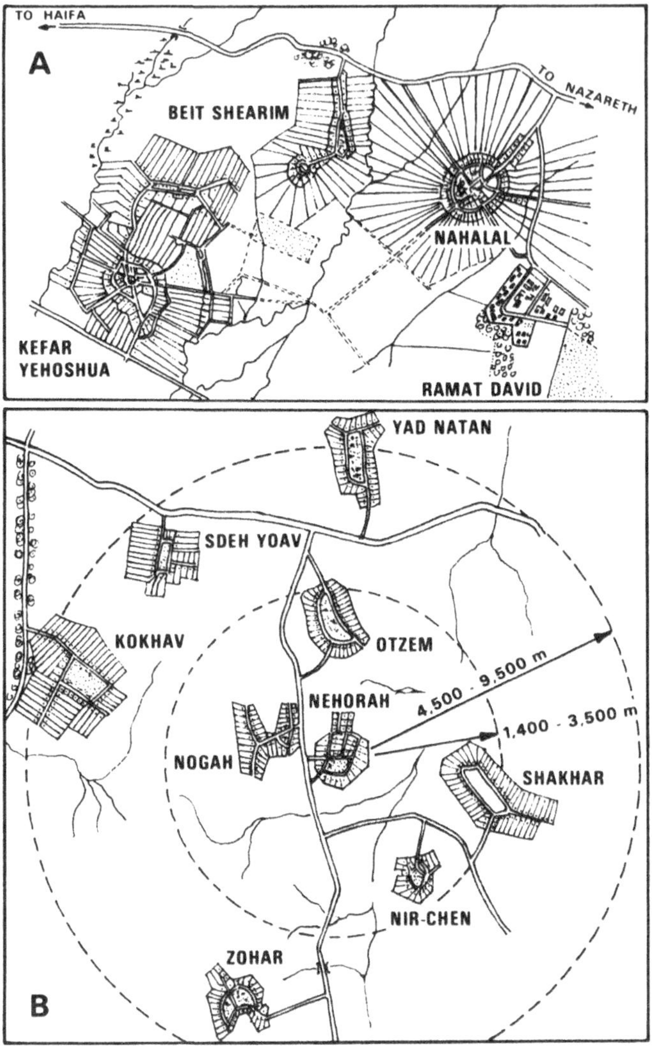

Figure 4.4 Structure of services of rural settlements in Israel

A. The Nahalal group. Independent services located in each village.

B. The Nehora group. A composite rural structure encompassing several settlements, showing effective and ineffective spheres of influence. (Source: E. Yalan, <u>The Design of Agricultural Settlements.</u>)

(made up of the first and second generations) and 25 to 30 families engaged in services. Economic consolidation and specialization in diverse farming branches occurred during the next phase (1948-1959), and the village grew to 130 farm families and 50 nonfarming families. During 1960-1970, further specialization and increasing income levels occurred, and the community grew to 150 farming families and 60 "professional" families, representing three generations working the original 75 farms. At the end of this period the average personal income was markedly higher than the national average. Nahalal showed remarkable ideological and social stamina which enabled it to survive the incipient critical period of small scale and few amenities. Whether new settlements can muster the same vigor of the "pioneer era" is still open to question.

Subsequent settlement models have attempted to correct some of the most apparent shortcomings in the physical plan. For example, the Nehora group of settlements in the Lakish region, developed in the early 1950s, contained eight settlements clustered around a single rural service center. The peripheral villages were to contain basic and daily-frequented services, while the village-group center, Nehora, was to contain those communal services which could not have been run satisfactorily by each individual village, such as the primary school, cultural center, health clinic, cooperative store, and sports and recreation center. Economic facilities unable to maintain profitability in each separate village were also concentrated in Nehora (Figure 4.4B). The resulting functional entity, described as "composite rural structure," was based on the principle of differentiated services. However, the distance of five km and more between some of the villages and the rural center became a serious impediment in this structure. Many communities preferred to develop their own services rather than commute long distances. Because of the smaller number of clientele, services in each village were of a lower standard and the opportunity for broader socioeconomic integration was wasted. Further attempts to reduce distances to the rural service center by planning and developing villages in closer proximity to each other occurred during the same period. Figure 4.5 shows a cluster of four villages in the northern Negev within 1,200 meters of a joint service center. Even this distance proved to be too long and was reduced in other settlement schemes.

The conflict between distance to agricultural plots and distance to communal services was partly resolved by dividing the holding into two main parts: one consisting of the farmstead and a contiguous homeplot, and another comprising the main agricultural plot outside the village. The area allotted for farmstead and attached homeplot was usually about 1.5 hectares. In later plans this size was reduced to 0.9-1.0 hectares in order to allow the farmers' houses to be closer to the center. The continuing search for ways to agglomerate small villages in order to

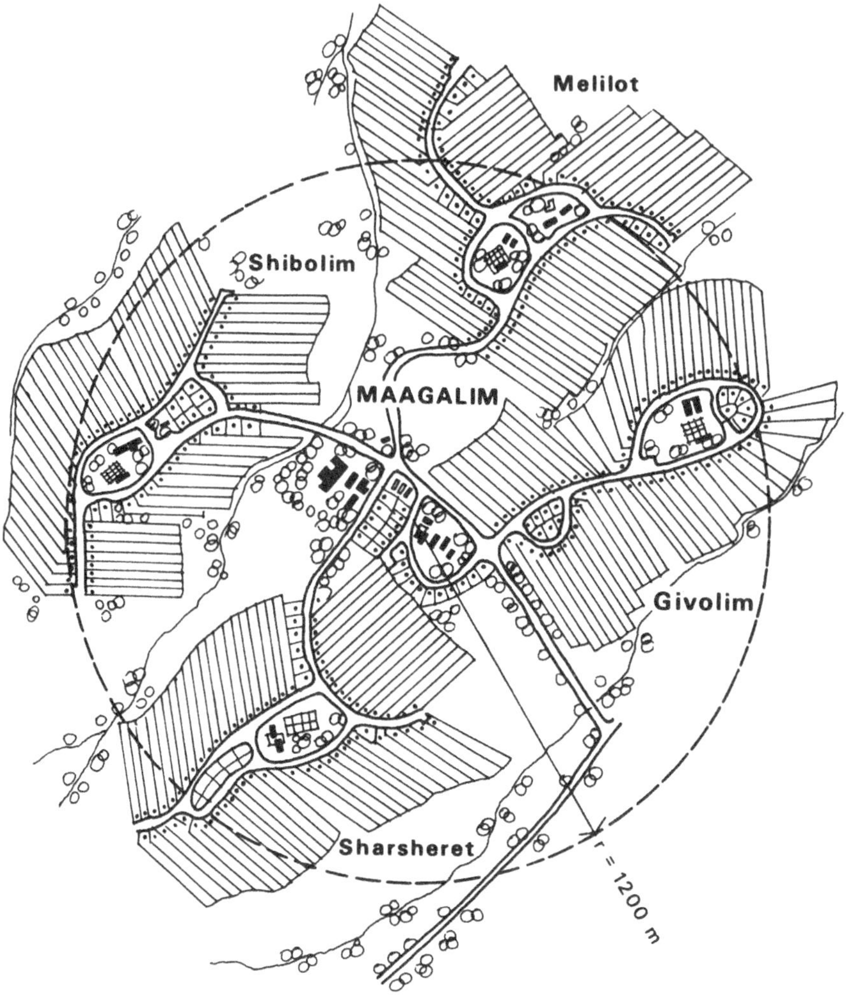

Figure 4.5 The Maagalim group. A cluster of four Moshav-type villages in the Northern Negev, surrounding a common service center. The settlements were built during 1951-1953 and are concentrated within a 1,200 meter radius circle. The distance from the remotest house to the service center is 1,800 meters.

rationalize services culminated in the multinuclear or multiunit village, in which three or four villages were merged into one. The settlement, which assumed the form of a group of neighborhoods, made it possible for each community to retain its individuality while sharing better services. The evolution of this principle in consecutive settlement schemes is illustrated in Figures 4.6 to 4.8. As can be seen, the tendency was to minimize, as much as possible, the distances to the center. An additional advantage of the multiunit pattern was the ability to fuse separate "daily frequency" functions, such as cooperative stores and schools, into one better-equipped service at the center. The individual neighborhoods were left with only those services needed for the youngest and the oldest, such as kindergarten, communal houses, and village greens.

It took, however, considerable shifting toward the common center before individual neighborhoods could overcome the tendency to set up their own services. In two multinuclear villages built in the Jezreel Valley during 1953-1955--Yael (Figure 4.7) and Hever (not illustrated)--the farmstead and homeplot amounted to 1.2 hectares per family. This large farmyard resulted in long distances to the common center--1,600 meters and more--and, as a result, the neighborhoods developed their own services while the center remained idle. In the Omen multinuclear village (Figure 4.8) the farmstead and homeplot area was reduced to 0.9 hectares, allowing the three neighborhoods to converge to approximately 1,150 meters from the center. Only this proximity, it appears, produced the "spark" that linked the communities to one joint service center.

The Israeli experience evidenced a clear tendency to shift to larger units in order to achieve economies of scale, particularly in connection with services. The large diversity in climatic and topographic conditions and the kaleidoscopical pattern of soil types induced the system of block parcellation according to best-suited crops. Constraints such as water scarcity dictated rationalization in the use of land and other resources. Security conditions, on the other hand, were among the reasons for promoting regional organization. However, since land was usually not available in large contiguous tracts, it became necessary to establish small villages. The smaller villages' main chance to overcome limitations of scale was to develop regional frameworks which encompassed numerous rural communities of varying sizes and of differing social patterns.

ITALY: RURAL DEVELOPMENT IN THE MEZZOGIORNO

In cultural heritage, social structure, and even in resistance to institutional change, there are parallels between Southern Italy and many developing regions. The Mezzogiorno,[13] with a population of eighteen million and a

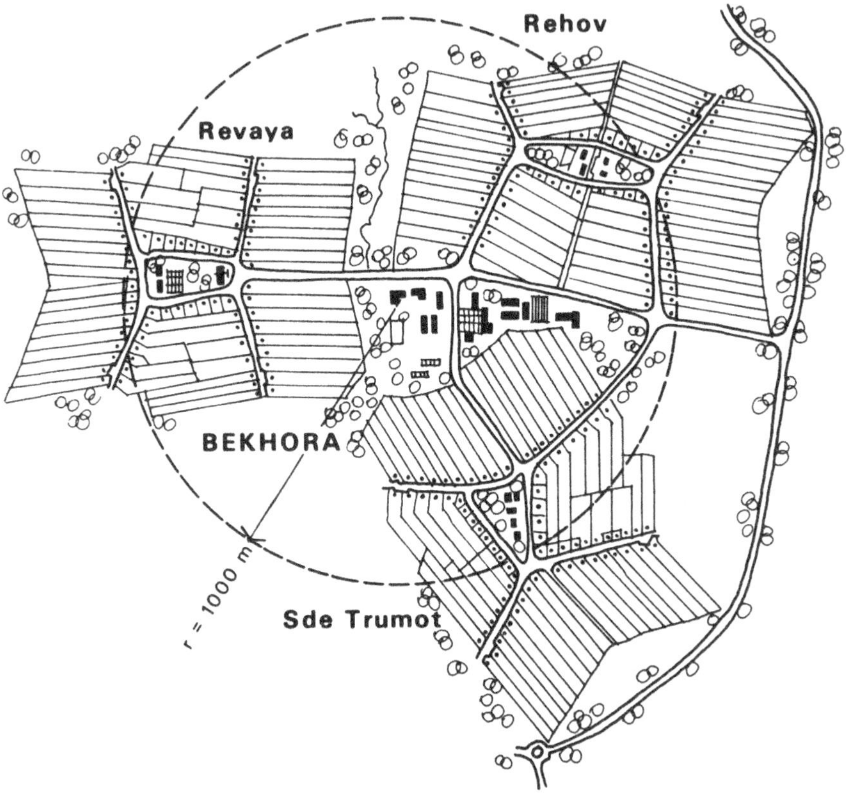

Figure 4.6 Multiunit Moshav Bekhora. A cluster of three Moshav-type villages in the Bet She'an Valley, surrounding a common service center. Each village comprises sixty farmsteads on 1.4 ha plots. The settlements were built during 1951-1952 and are concentrated within a 1,000 meter radius circle. The distance from the remotest house to the service center is 1,500 meters.

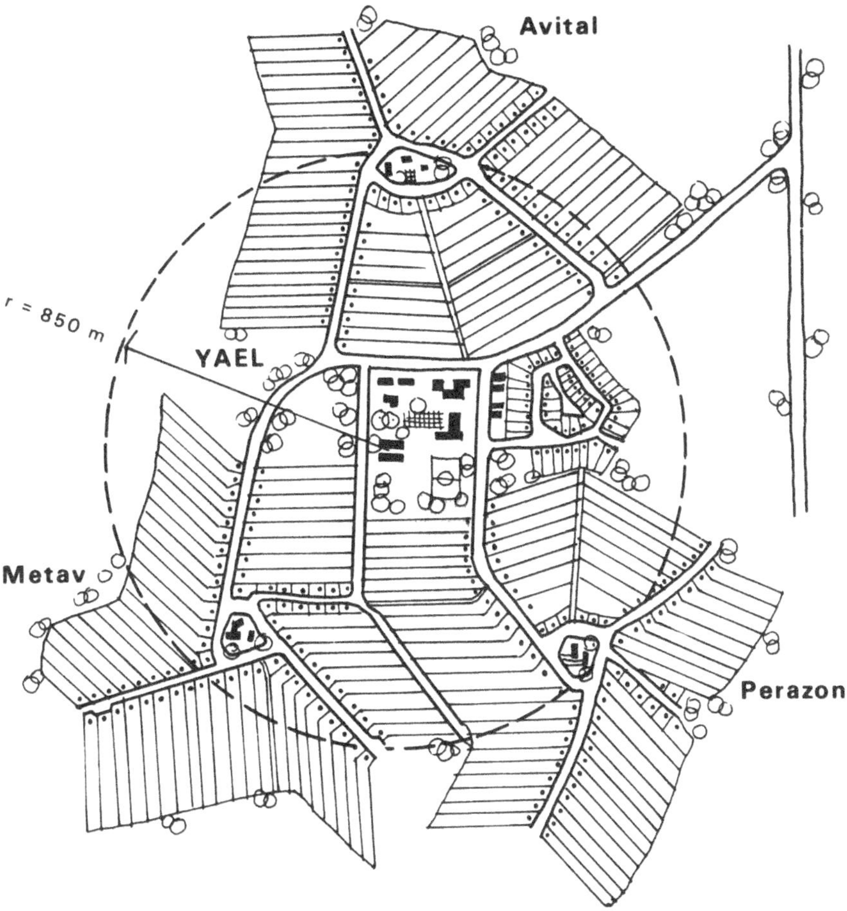

Figure 4.7 Multiunit Moshav Yael. The first of three similar family farm settlements in the Jezreel Valley, built during 1953-1955. Each village comprises sixty farmsteads on 1.2 ha plots. The settlements are concentrated in a 850 meter circle, and the maximum distance from house to service center varies between 1,400 to 1,700 meters.

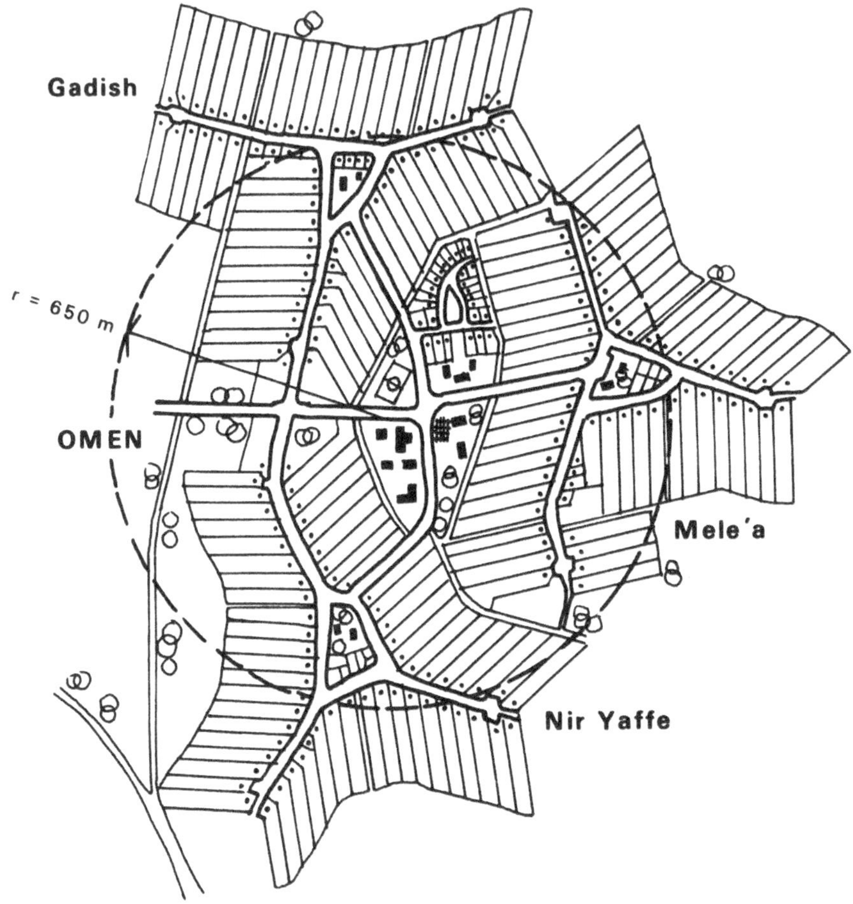

Figure 4.8 Multiunit Moshav Omen. The third of a group of similar family farm settlements in the Jezreel Valley, built in 1956. The farmstead area has been reduced to 0.9 ha. The three villages contain 183 farming families and 52 service families. The villages are clustered more tightly in a 650 meter radius circle. The maximum distance to the service center is 1,150 meters; this distance has proved conducive to the development of joint facilities and social interaction.

separate historical tradition, is a distinct economic entity which in 1964 had a per capita income somewhat below that of the average for Latin America.[14] As recently as 1948 there was still a dense rural population in Italy with 45 percent of all working inhabitants engaged in agriculture. The majority of the villages, however, were poverty-stricken and semifeudal conditions prevailed throughout the country. About 21.5 million hectares of the country's agricultural lands (77.5 percent), belonged to private individuals. Thirty-five percent of the privately owned lands, or about 7.7 million hectares, belonged to 0.5 percent of the landowners. In the southern part of the country thirteen thousand landowners held 4.5 million hectares while almost four million small landholders possessed only 1.0 million hectares.[15]

Planned rural development in Italy began toward the end of the nineteenth century when the prevalence of malaria caused growing alarm. This development consisted of land reclamation and was subsequently expanded to include the amelioration of lands whose economy had suffered by flooding, poor drainage, inadequate land use, and underpopulation. Various land reclamation and amelioration projects were embarked upon before World War II in Tuscany, the Padano Delta of the Po River, the Pontine marshes, as well as in southern Italy, Sardinia, and Sicily. Frequently such projects included the settlement of new farmers, especially from the labor force engaged in public works and rehabilitation of agriculture.[16]

Land reform as a social problem had been a principal issue since the days of Garibaldi (1807-1882). It received new impetus in 1950 with a new law which purported to affect a land surface of over eight million hectares, equal to nearly 30 percent of Italy's territory--seemingly a political move to appease a rural population which was in a state of ferment. The legislation combined land reclamation with expropriation of large estates and their distribution to small landholders, building an infrastructure, and land settlement. The declared objectives were the socioeconomic integration of the rural population and the transformation of the predominantly subsistence economy in the South to modern farming and cooperative methods. In the final analysis, however, only 1.2 million hectares, or 4 percent of Italy's total agricultural territory, were earmarked for expropriation. Of these, less than 770,000 hectares were appropriated and distributed to a total of 113,066 farming families. The average area of new holdings varied between 4.5 and 5.5 hectares in irrigated lands and from 6.0 to 10.0 hectares in nonirrigated and mountainous areas, in accordance with the determined working capacity of the selected families. The average addition to an established holding was 2.4 hectares. Much of this land was in need of additional social capital investment to prepare it for human settlement and cultivation.

The land resources thus obtained were far from

adequate for radically changing the socioeconomic retardation of the South, and in the absence of other resources for rural settlement the coveted transformation could not materialize as desired. The task of attenuating rural plight was relegated to other means such as alternative employment and emigration which, to date, have had only scant success. Most of the efforts of the Cassa per il Mezzogiorno eventually shifted to other sectors such as industry, tourism, and tertiary activities. In agriculture, productivity became the principal objective regardless of conflicting social costs. Nevertheless, even the limited land resources and related improvements in infrastructure represented a vast undertaking in terms of regional development and land settlement, and consequently aroused considerable interest in other developing regions.

The dispersed settlement pattern was apparently considered the most appropriate for rapidly bringing new land into production and for settling farming families. In the plains, where relatively large extensions of land were obtained through the expropriation of latifundia and partly through reclamation, the prescribed method was to parcel the land in a cross-grid pattern observing merely such topographical landmarks as existing roads, streams, irrigation, and drainage channels (Figure 4.9). Farmsteads were located in their holdings, with distances between houses totaling 120 to 250 meters. Wherever possible, three or four houses facing the street were grouped together, thus increasing the interval between such groups to 250 to 500 meters. In areas prone to seasonal flooding a semiconcentrated or "loose" settlement pattern became necessary. The typical settlement usually comprised thirty to fifty houses of settlers with homeplots of 0.2 to 0.3 hectares near the house and the main agricultural plot up to three km away. Such a grouped settlement also contained a service center (Centro di Servizio) for other farming families living on their holdings within a distance of two to five km.

The decision to deploy the settlements in a predominantly dispersed pattern resulted in a cumbersome system of supporting services and infrastructure. Apart from the wish to maximize productivity, the dispersed settlement pattern seems to have been an integral part of the Italian tradition which followed the trends of rural settlement and colonization carried out in Italy and its colonies during the Fascist administration. This, again, seemed to be a repetition of the cross-grid parcellation of land distribution in Roman times (Figure 4.10), remnants of which are still scattered over the Italian landscape. Another influential factor may have been the contemporary settlement pattern of countries such as Denmark, Holland, and the U.S.A., whose achievements in agricultural productivity seemed to confirm the advantages of dispersed family farm settlement.

It may also be assumed that, in view of the people's

Figure 4.9 Typical scattered settlement in the Mezzogiorno region, showing parceled land around Policoro (a former rural town in the Matera Province on the Ionian coastal plain). No village structure is apparent, only a ribbon development of farms along roads leading to the one dominant center in the area. (Source: Land Reform in Apulia, Lucania and Molise, 1964.)

Figure 4.10 Centuriated landscape near Padua, showing existing roads which preserve the Roman grid of 20 x 20 actus squares (776 x 776 yards), i.e. fifty ha. (Source: A. Meitzen, Siedelung und Agrarwesen.)

extreme desire for land and the population's lack of confidence due to continuous procrastinations in rural reforms, the dispersed pattern offered a method of least resistance in planning and implementation. The pattern required no immediate need to create communities, only to select qualified assignees and to leave mutual adaptation pending, with social stress hopefully cushioned by distance. Initial demands by settlers for facilities were modest and could be satisfied gradually. The task of turning the single farmstead into productive enterprises was to be achieved by improved infrastructure and cooperative institutions. The substance of arguments in favor of a dispersed settlement pattern stated that settlers insisted on occupying their newly acquired parcels and that such a pattern was more conducive to higher productivity. Nevertheless, part of the literature from the settlement period proves that planners were not unaware of the difficulties inherent in dispersion.

Attempts to appraise the advantages of diverse settlement patterns were mostly limited to the quantitative aspects of infrastructure costs such as roads, housing, farm buildings, utilities, and other services. Usually, the cost of dispersed settlement proved to be higher than the gathered pattern. A comparison of costs per farmstead in three different types of settlement--dispersed, gathered, and semidispersed (also defined as "open" or "loose") --in the Apulia, Lucania, and Molise land reform area, showed the dispersed type to be over 21 percent more expensive than the gathered pattern.

A similar approach was used in comparing the site plan of an existing dispersed settlement in the Ionian Coastal plains near Taranto with an alternative layout model in a gathered pattern. The settlement, denominated Borgo Perrone, comprised 144 family farms, each with five hectares of irrigated land mostly in horticultural and citrus crops (Figure 4.11). Roads within the settlement, including the Ionian State Highway, measured 10,385 meters. Another approximately 7,905 meters of unpaved roads provided access to dispersed farms. Service roads, parallel to the state highway, would eventually have to be constructed to accommodate the slower-moving traffic from the farms. There were 17,730 meters of power lines and 58 wells for potable water, mostly hand dug. Services were to be built in a centrally located area. In the meantime, the settlers were commuting to the older centers, Conca d'Oro and Marina de Ginosa, lying in opposite directions at a distance of eight and eleven km respectively.[17]

In an alternative layout model of a gathered settlement (Figure 4.12), land allotment was divided into two parts: 0.8 hectares for farmstead and attached homeplot within the residential area of the village, and 4.2 hectares in a plot outside the village. The proposed layout comprised three satellite groups surrounding a common center. The groups accommodated a total of 141 family farms

Figure 4.11 Actual layout of Borgo Perrone in the Ionian coastal plain near Taranto, comprising 144 farmsteads with five ha holdings. Houses are spaced 100 to 125 meters apart. (Source: N. Matarrese, "L'insediamento Rurale.")

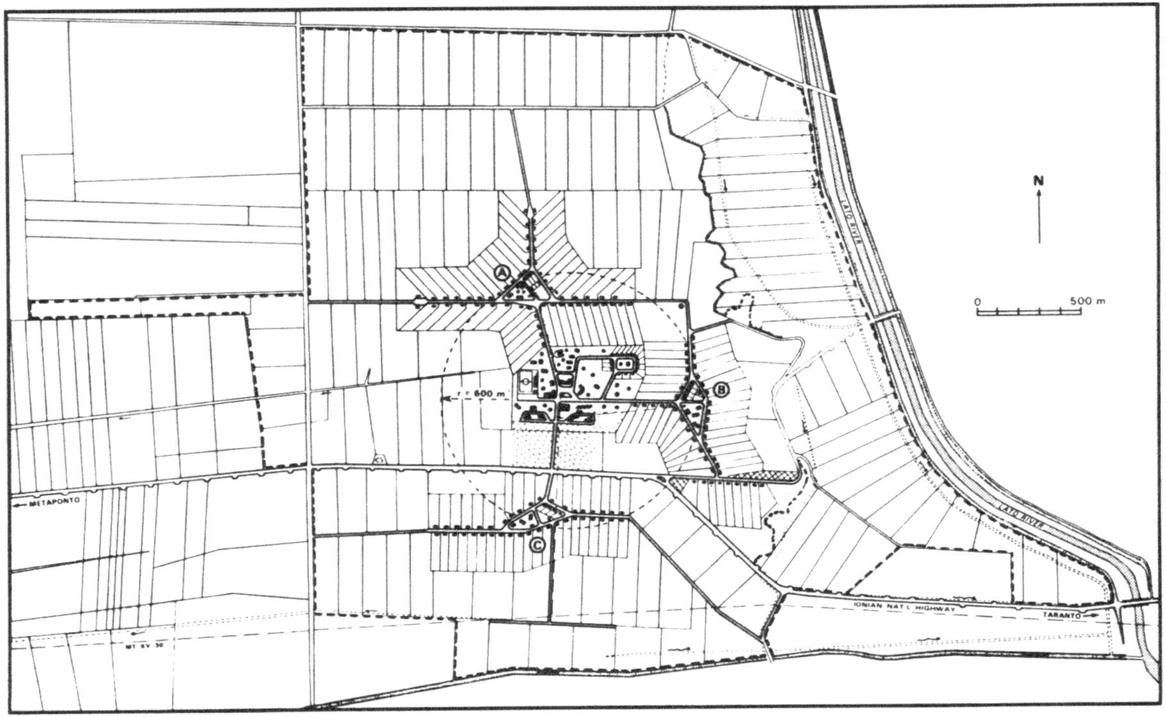

Figure 4.12 Alternative layout of Borgo Perrone, patterned as a gathered nuclear settlement. (Source: N. Matarrese, "L'insediamento Rurale.")

(versus 144 in the existing parcellation), plus 31 families employed in services located at the center. Services were divided into two groups according to frequency of use --those requiring maximum proximity to the houses, and others such as schools, offices, workshops, and stores which were concentrated in the common center. The center was within an average distance of 600 meters from each satellite neighborhood, compared to a maximum of 4,200 meters in the dispersed layout. Distances to the farthest fields did not exceed 2,400 meters.

The comparison between the two alternative layouts demonstrated substantial savings in roads, power lines, and water supplies. However, the contention was also made that a gathered settlement would function better in other respects as well. The claimed advantages of concentrated settlement included: (1) economy in infrastructure costs (roads and utilities); (2) shorter distances to services; (3) better possibilities for family labor in farmyards and homeplots and in extra-agricultural activities; and, (4) flexibility and ease of future reparcellation. The disadvantages were described as: (1) longer distances from farmsteads to fields; and (2) a reduction of 2 percent in total cultivated area. An important element of this analysis is its emphasis on social as well as on economic efficiency. Also noteworthy are some of the criteria used, such as farmyard efficiency, family initiative and labor, and the element of flexibility by anticipating eventual reparcellation needs.

The social isolation of farming families in the dispersed pattern may be harmful in the long run to the economy of the farm. Since many farms in the Ionian plain engage primarily in horticulture, the constant presence of the owner is not imperative and some families prefer to live in their original villages, closer to amenities.[18] Absentee farming is evident in many parts of the region and results in the underutilization of agricultural and human potential.

A more difficult challenge than the settlement of reclaimed lowlands confronted planners in the hilly areas of the Mezzogiorno. As in the plains, there were limited basins of cultivable lands available, interspersed by estates which were not affected by the reform. Holdings were more scattered and fragmented, and expropriation yielded less acreage. The major part of the land at the settlement agencies' disposal was used in consolidation schemes to increase the size of small farms, while only a part was assigned to new settlement development. The smaller scale and accidented topography limited the planners' maneuverability and dictated more concentrated forms of settlement. One result of land scarcity was that many of the newly established villages remained too small to support adequate services. In addition there was a lack of expertise in the physical planning of gathered small landholders' settlements. Planners who were experienced and imaginative in designing urban spaces were not as resourceful when dealing with a rural environment, and often tried either to copy urban patterns or to transfer archaic rural structures to new village plans.

La Murgetta (Figure 4.13) is a typical example of a small planned farming community, also designated as a service center for the farms dispersed in the vicinity. Planned with an urban flair, its houses are surrounded by "green" spaces, but the cramped layout and small area of the annexes make farmyard activities all but impossible. This difficulty became apparent immediately and, consequently, a few of the farmsteads were located outside the planned nucleus in order to provide more farmyard space. This broke up the small community and some of the settlers moved out to their parcels or villages, thus further reducing the size of the community. Since the family farm operates as a system in which functions of residence and production are closely intertwined, these flaws affected not only the residential styles, but also the productive potential of the family.

Planners were not always sufficiently aware of the vital role of the farmyard in the transition from mixed to specialized farming. This lack of knowledge is exemplified in the case of La Martella, a gathered settlement built in 1953 in the Matera Province. Sufficient land resources were available to gather two hundred family farms into one settlement. However, farmsteads were provided with only a 600 square meter area in what can be described as a static approach to the farmyard plan. A two-story dwelling included kitchen and stable on the first floor and dormitories on the second floor. This arrangement was theoretically workable since each farm was to own one milking cow. In practice, however, farmers began to increase their livestock and to expand their cowsheds as well as their homes. The farmyards' narrowness soon led to the congestion of animals and storage space and created stress among neighbors, unconducive to the development of the farmyard. Some of the more industrious farmers or those farmers whose plots were conveniently nearby, settled outside the village, thus starting a process of social and physical disintegration of the village community.

Few attempts to improve the settlement model can be found. An exception would be the gathered multiunit settlement of Borgo Venusio (Figure 4.14), planned for the resettlement of the Sassi di Matera cavern dwellers. These resettled individuals insisted that the new village preserve the community's traditional form of social organization--small family groups. The new village was planned to accommodate about a hundred families which, under the circumstances, seemed adequate for maintaining essential services. Farmsteads, however, were still planned with an area of 400 to 600 square meters, a space too small for developing farmyard activities.

As problems with gathered settlements mounted, some

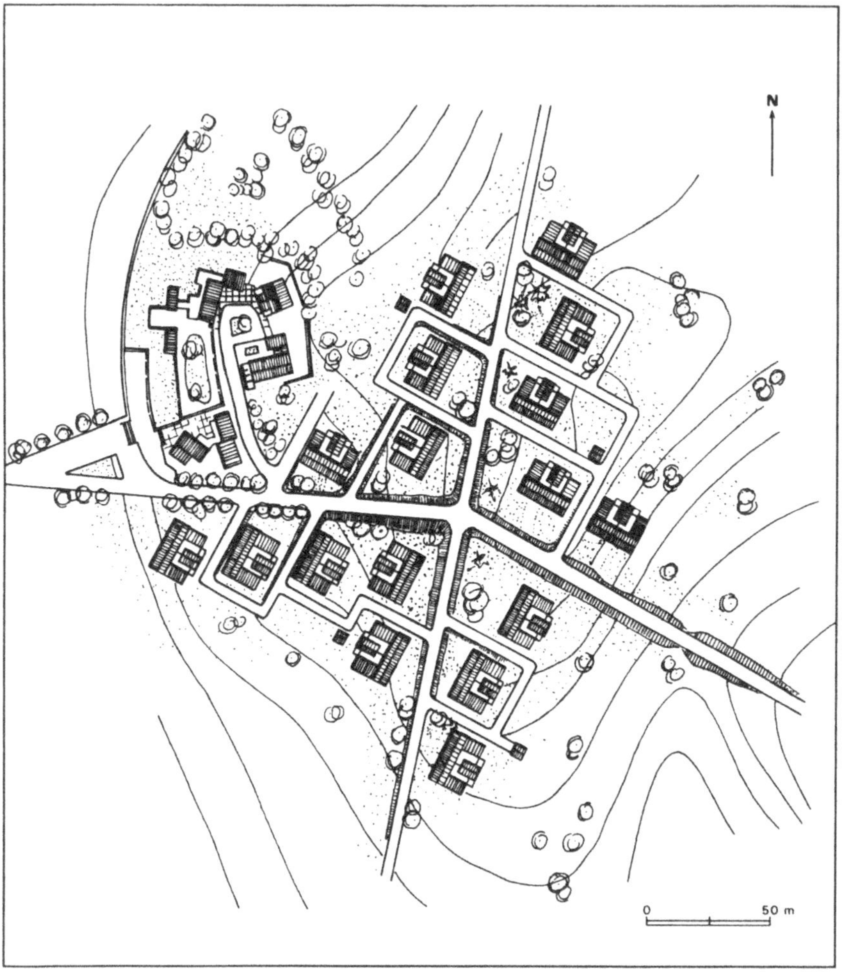

Figure 4.13 La Murgetta, near Gravina in Apulia, a gathered settlement planned for thirty-four family farms. The houses are two-family units with enclosed farm buildings (stable, chicken coop, and piggery) on an area of about 200 square meters. The service core (upper left) contains a school, church, and offices. Only eleven of the planned twin farmsteads were actually built. (Source: Case Coloniche, 1958.)

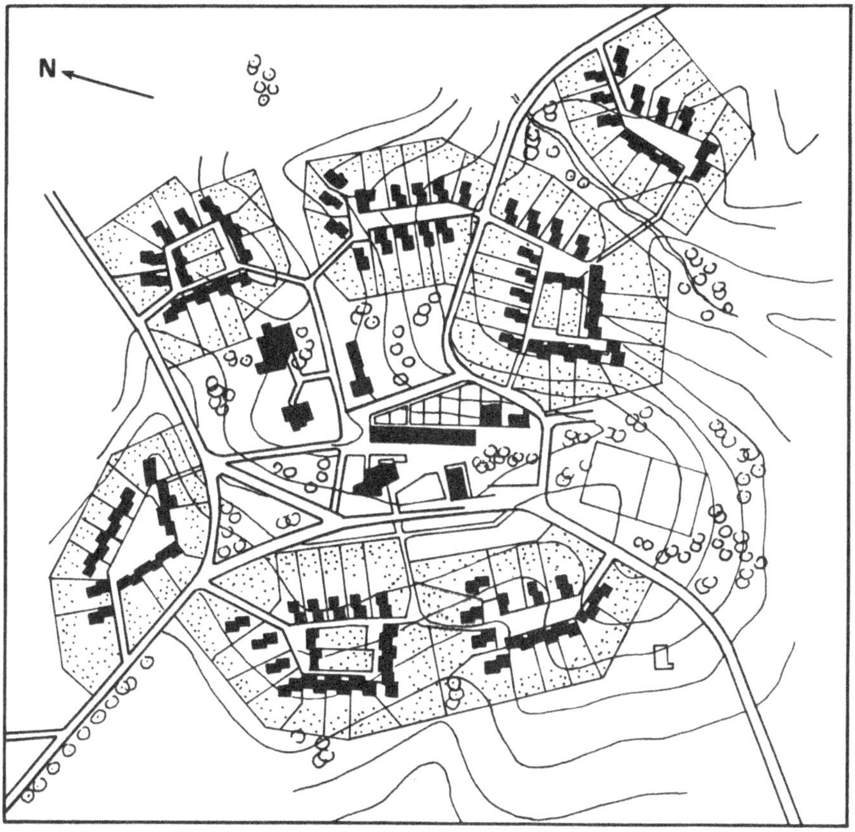

Figure 4.14 Borgo Venusio in the Matera region, a multinuclear village composed of seven neighborhood units, each with twelve to sixteen families. The farmstead area is 400 to 600 square meters. The dwellers of the Sassi di Matera caverns, for whom this village was built, insisted that the new settlement preserve the kinship characteristics of their original neighborhood units (see plan of typical former neighborhood below).

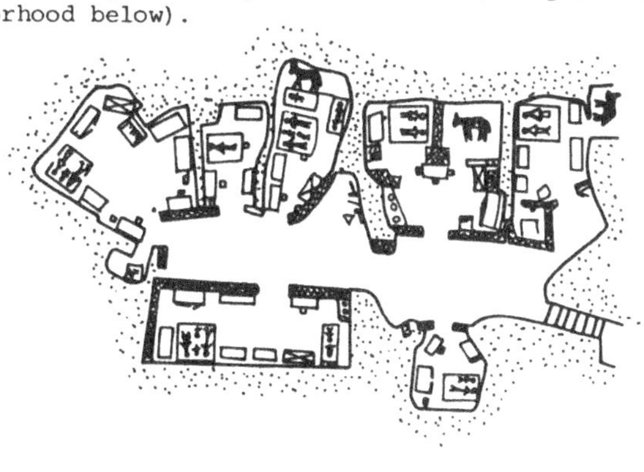

projects were modified while others were not carried out at all. Abandonment and settlers' return to old villages weakened the newly organized communities and burdened the settlement agencies with complicated situations. These problems seemed to favor support for the dispersed settlement pattern, where most of these difficulties did not surface in the initial period and where farmyard efficiency was not hampered by lack of space.

The Structure of Services

The need for services was especially urgent in the new dispersed settlements of the coastal plains which were generally devoid of towns due to past flooding and malaria. The traditional villages were perched in the hills, too far away to provide daily services. Yet, kinship ties were not severed by physical distance and the settlers continued to commute to their old villages on special occasions or resided there intermittently. To respond to these needs, a new major service center (Borgo di Servizio) was built in each of several planning regions. An example of such a center is Gromola in the Sele River plain of Campania (Figure 4.15). The center, which caters to a dispersed population of about 350 families, includes such facilities as elementary, vocational, and agricultural schools, a church, an assembly hall, offices, a cafe, shops, and workshops. Borgo di Servizios were either planned as residential villages, open to private housing development, or, as in the case of Borgo Gromola, as nonresidential villages, designed specifically for service personnel only. An intermediate service center (Centro di Servizio) was established when family farm concentration occurred in areas susceptible to seasonal flooding. An example of such a center is Scanno, a village in the Altavilla area of Campania with ninety families, including thirty farm families with farmsteads in the village area, twenty-five families with auxiliary farms of one to three hectares each, about fifteen dwellings for service personnel, and some private housing. An additional population from some 150 families whose houses are dispersed in the vicinity relate to this Centro di Servizio for their basic needs.

The development of the Mezzogiorno shows no systematic treatment in the distribution or organization of rural services. The general approach seems to have been the establishment of facility sites within a radius of three to five km from the dispersed farms. Other factors which were weighed in the determination of service center location included availability of land, closeness to main arteries, and communications. In regard to schools, however, an exception to the distance criteria was necessary so that their radius of action would be only two km. Additional schools had to be located, therefore, among the

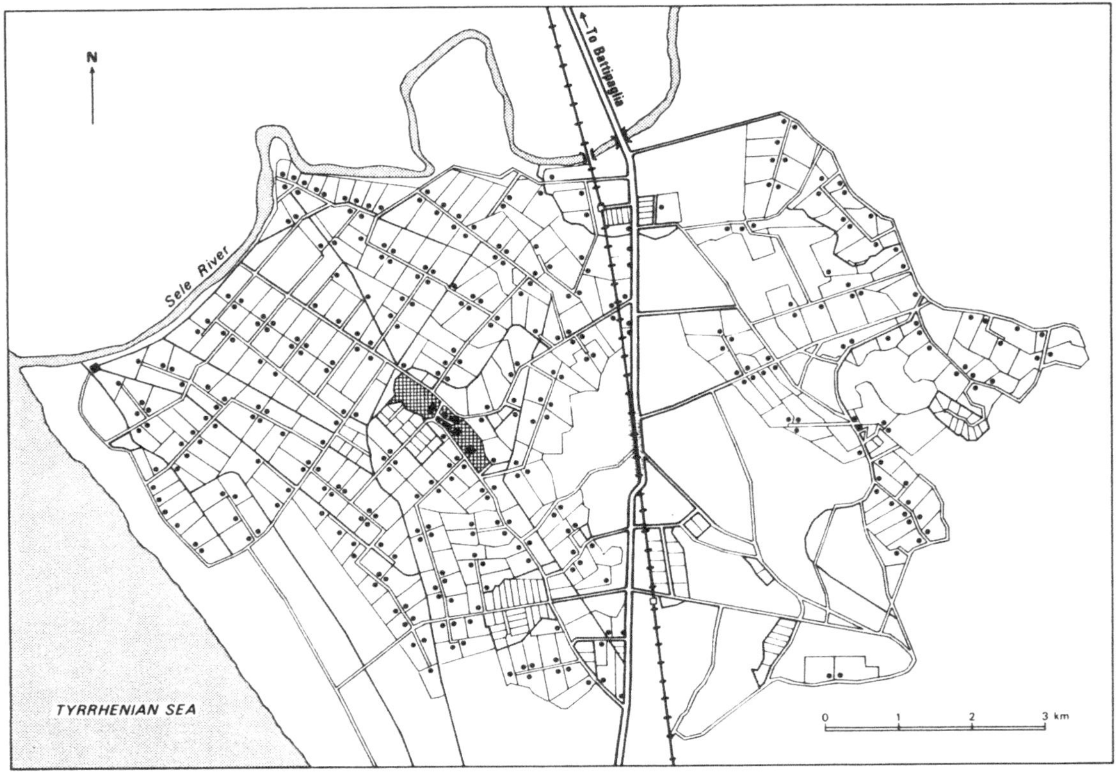

Figure 4.15 Borgo Gromola in the Sele River plain in Campania--a service center catering to a dispersed settlement of 350 family farms within a radius of four to five kilometers. (Source: Borgo Gromola nella Piana del Sele, 1960.)

agricultural plots in order to shorten the walking distance for school children, reducing the quality of the service due to fragmentation of facilities. The lack of contiguous areas of agricultural land for settlement was apparently one of the reasons for deploying facilities on an ad hoc basis. Another reason rested in the dispersed settlement pattern itself, which made a systematic distribution of facilities problematic.

One of the few contiguous areas where a certain hierarchy of services could be developed was found in Sardinia. About 450 farm families were settled in a 9,000 hectare area, with Arborea as a regional center containing municipal, social and cultural, and economic services. Six subcenters were distributed in the area creating an intermediate network of central places. Each of these centers has a radius of action of four to five km, providing lower-range services. As on the mainland, additional school centers with a radius of two km had to be established among the dispersed farmsteads. It appears, however, that many farmers, particularly among the younger generation, preferred to live in the service centers turning them into actual residential villages. As a result, among the dispersed farmsteads in the region there are many abandoned houses. The same phenomenon has already been commented upon by Jacoby, particularly in regard to the countryside in Sweden.[19]

Considerable efforts by regional developing entities have been directed towards establishing an overhead structure in special production areas (e.g. wineries and bottling plants). However, choosing sites for plants and facilities is mainly based on specific locational advantages, rather than on concerns regarding the vitality of new rural centers. In retrospect, it is difficult to separate the spatial organizational aspects from the conceptual framework within which the development of the Mezzogiorno has taken place. While in the early fifties the strategy was to settle a maximum of the rural labor force on farms of a minimal size, today's economic objectives have been changed to creating higher incomes and higher productivity on a regional basis. The Cassa per il Mezzogiorno, for example, established in 1950 and initially funded with American money, was imbued with the current regional planning paradigms. The program followed the theoretically attractive procedure of developing external economies by massive doses of public works, while leaving direct investments in commodity production to private individuals. Accordingly it concentrated most of its efforts on infrastructural, industrial, and tourist related investments. Until 1972 the Cassa programs involved an aggregate commitment of $15,200,000,[20] allegedly capable of stimulating investment projects of over $24,000,000. This program enabled the expansion of fast-traffic highways, local roads, tourist routes, as well as feeder roads in land-reclamation districts. The southern road system, for example, which covered 42,000 km in 1950, covered over 100,000 km by 1972.

In the area of agriculture, the primary objectives of the Cassa, apart from the provision of basic infrastructure, have been the modernization of farming methods through large-scale irrigation, land reclamation and consolidation, providing incentives to farmers for land improvement schemes, supplying technical assistance, and the development of processing and marketing facilities. The Cassa has shifted its efforts to the irrigated and more fertile coastal plains where higher returns on investments can be expected. As a corollary, the interest in rehabilitating the depressed rural areas has notably faded. The chief beneficiaries of these infrastructural improvements have invariably been the bigger and better-endowed farms. On the other hand, capital investments would obviously be less effective in improving the actual structure of the small holding which is further debilitated by its dispersion and fragmentation into inefficient community groups. The wide-scale housing programs of the early settlement period exemplify the difficulty inherent in the implementation of social overhead investments. The housing and farm building program not only strained the Cassas's resources but left many assignees dissatisfied. The program was later changed to a self-contracting system, since many families preferred to build their own homes.[21]

The policy of prioritizing resource allocations to industrial and infrastructural investments over agricultural inputs has been repeatedly debated. Garofalo, who analyzed the effects of investments in agriculture versus other sectors, found that agricultural development compared favorably with industrial projects in respect to value-added and gross savings while yielding considerably more employment, a crucial issue in the Mezzogiorno.[22] Nevertheless, industrial and infrastructural investments prevailed, particularly spurred in light of economic prosperity in Italy during the early sixties and the growing disenchantment with the slow progress in the rehabilitation of rural areas in the South. The subsequent separation of the Cassa from the agrarian agencies further hampered the coordination of southern regional developmental activities. The regional development of the Mezzogiorno involved an overwhelming number of rural population and as such it lacked the fundamental requisite for social and economic advancement: land. The amount of transferred land resources expected to modernize the rural structure was trivial in comparison with the population involved. Consequently, the inertia of economic development in the region has slowed down and the gap between the South and the North has become notably wider.[23]

In spite of its vast magnitude, the southern Italian settlement program did not generate enough momentum for the development of a settlement model. The predominant pattern in the lowlands was and remained the traditional dispersed farmsteads, with a few semiconcentrated combinations of farming communities and service centers. This pattern, when applied to small landholders' settlements, brought about innumerable problems in structuring support services and amenities. In the mountainous areas a greater variety of gathered, nucleated village forms was introduced. However, the brief experience was not continued and the program suffered setbacks such as scarcity of land, lack of planning expertise, and finally, the weakening of institutional aid. The general trend in service organization in southern Italy was oriented toward urban-rural integration. Several of the newly built rural centers, for example, were opened to residential development. The overhead structure, aimed at providing production facilities, has been successful in establishing specialized services for particular production branches. However, while the system has improved the farmers' income levels, it has been unable to extricate them from the problems of dispersion and lack of social amenities. An agglomerated settlement pattern, with a flexible field system, however, may have promoted a more efficient organization of facilities at the village level and more intensive production through cooperative efforts aimed at overcoming limitations in scale.

It appears today that rigidity in the physical planning in the South, resulting in a system of scattered holdings, has proven to be an obstacle in the transition to specialized farming. Many farm units have become too small to provide their owners with sufficient income by nationwide standards. The dispersed pattern of settlement does not encourage the pooling of resources and the introduction of large-scale operations. Insufficient income has resulted in a continuous rural exodus and the abandonment of houses and farm buildings. Facilities representing recent basic investments are unused. It is doubtful that the integration of big farms and small landholders' settlements will stand the test of time. In the absence of alternative economic opportunities, a partial agrarian reform can only be of a temporary nature. The need for future reforms thus becomes practically unavoidable.

SPAIN: LAND SETTLEMENT IN THE BADAJOZ REGION

Rural conditions in Spain are similar in many respects to those in Italy. About 40 percent of the total labor force was engaged in agriculture in 1964,[24] but its contribution to the national income (18 percent in 1968) has been steadily declining. In an otherwise expanding economy, agriculture is considered to be one of the weakest elements, owing to climatic factors, lack of infrastructure, and a primitive peasant society still surviving in many parts of the country amidst historically distorted land-use and tenure conditions.

In the North, holdings are small and fragmented (as

much as twenty-five to forty parcels per farm). In the southern provinces of Andalucia and Extremadura the *latifundios*--large, extensively cultivated farms--are widespread, dating back to grants from after the wars against the Moors. Tenancy continues to be the greatest problem with much of the land in absentee ownership and cultivated by sharecroppers. The inefficiency of the northern *minifundia* and chronic unemployment in the latifundia regions have brought low living standards and poverty, leading to the exodus of the younger and more dynamic sector of the rural population. Rural rehabilitation efforts by the Spanish government have centered on two main areas: consolidation of fragmented holdings mainly in the north, and large-scale irrigation schemes linked with land settlement in the southern dry-farming areas. Land consolidation through grouping and redistribution of fragmented holdings, aided by the formation of cooperatives for joint cultivation, has improved the situation by enabling more effective use of inputs and smaller outlays for machinery per hectare (Figure 4.16). However, 73 percent of the cultivable land is still held in about forty-two million plots, averaging only a little more than an acre each.[25]

The group farming schemes established in connection with the territorial consolidation of holdings in Spain are of special interest to this study. While group farming facilitated higher output per worker and per unit of land (through specialization), and better living conditions were achieved through increased leisure time and the release of family members from farm work, few structural improvements such as higher incomes per family could be attained. Implicit in this situation is the missing link--the farmyard--which could have absorbed the freed labor for the diversification of farming activities, leading to further acquisition of skills, specialization in other branches, and generation of additional income. This spatial unit, however, is almost absent from the densely nucleated Spanish village. Even in newly planned settlements, as will be seen later, the farmyard area has not received its due attention.

Land reform in the dry-farming areas, especially in the southwestern and southern parts of Spain, included construction of large-scale hydraulic works, building irrigation infrastructure, land reclamation, and resettlement of peasants from mountain villages into the irrigated lands. New lands were obtained through the partial expropriation of large estates and paid for in kind with irrigation works. Since the majority of new settlers were *secano* farmers--unskilled in irrigation--their concentration within villages was indispensable.[26]

One of the first large-scale irrigation and resettlement projects undertaken by the National Colonization Institute (INC)--an autonomous authority affiliated to the Ministry of Agriculture--was in the Badajoz region where massive damming and irrigation schemes were begun in 1950.

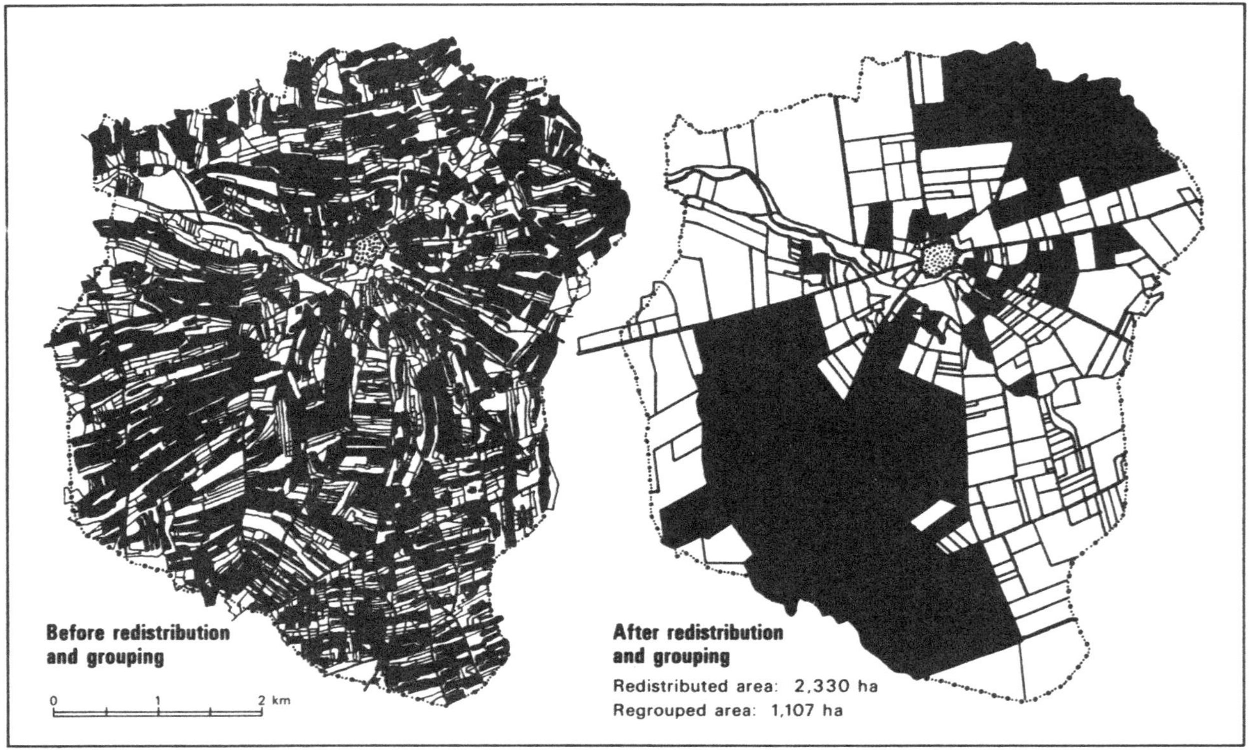

Figure 4.16 Land consolidation in Salamanca, Spain, showing parcellation of holdings before and after redistribution. As a result, eighty-two cooperative members were provided with larger and less dispersed plots. (Source: "Group Farming," 1972.)

By 1972 forty-one new villages had already been built out of the forty-seven planned. The whole settlement area was expected to accommodate about 9,000 farming families. The regulation of the Guadiana River, besides providing other multiple uses, enabled irrigation of nearly 140,000 hectares of land. Of these, some 54,000 hectares were designated for small landholders' settlements while the rest were to stay in the hands of private farmers. A densely gathered settlement with villages for 200 to 300 families was planned, but in many instances village sizes vary according to the amount of cultivable land available in their immediate periphery. About 30 percent of the village population is composed of farm workers who are usually employed on the larger haciendas. Holdings per farm family are four to five hectares, while farm workers receive an auxiliary plot of 0.5 hectares for kitchen crops. Distances to the fields vary within a radius of 3.5 km (the family allotment, though, is in one parcel thereby creating an irreparable inequity in distances). Whenever longer distances are involved, farmsteads are sited on the owner's parcel. Within the irrigation area, 667 such isolated farms have been built.[27]

A problematic aspect of the new villages is the extreme compactness of their site plans. This compactness may have been intentional in order to emulate the traditional setting of the old villages and to save on infrastructure. The farmsteads in the new villages contain an area of 420 square meters and up to 600 square meters in more recent settlements (Figure 4.17). Such sizes may have been suitable for subsistence farming, but are completely inadequate for the requirements of mixed farming. Figure 4.18 shows the village of Valdecalzada, one of the earliest in the project area, built around 1959 for 325 farm families plus 100 farm workers. The compact design and traditionally Spanish wall-to-wall facades entailed additional service roads for rear entrances to the farmyards. In more recent villages such as Palazuelo (Figure 4.19) built in 1969, some improvements in the original site plan can be discerned: the farmstead area is about 600 square meters, and there are front entrances to the yards thus eliminating the need for extra service roads. This particular village comprises 186 farm families and dwellings for 24 farm workers. The farmyard area, however, remains too small for any meaningful activity. The resulting inflexibility of the site plan may grow more problematic as farmers try to introduce livestock and implements for the diverse requirements of mixed farming. While cooperation by grouping land and pooling inputs may be possible when the basic land allotment per family is small, there are few substitutes for the farmyard as a breeding point for initiative, skills, and the continuous rotation of generations in the family enterprise.

Although every farm was provided with a farm building of about 50 square meters (net) for animals and storage,

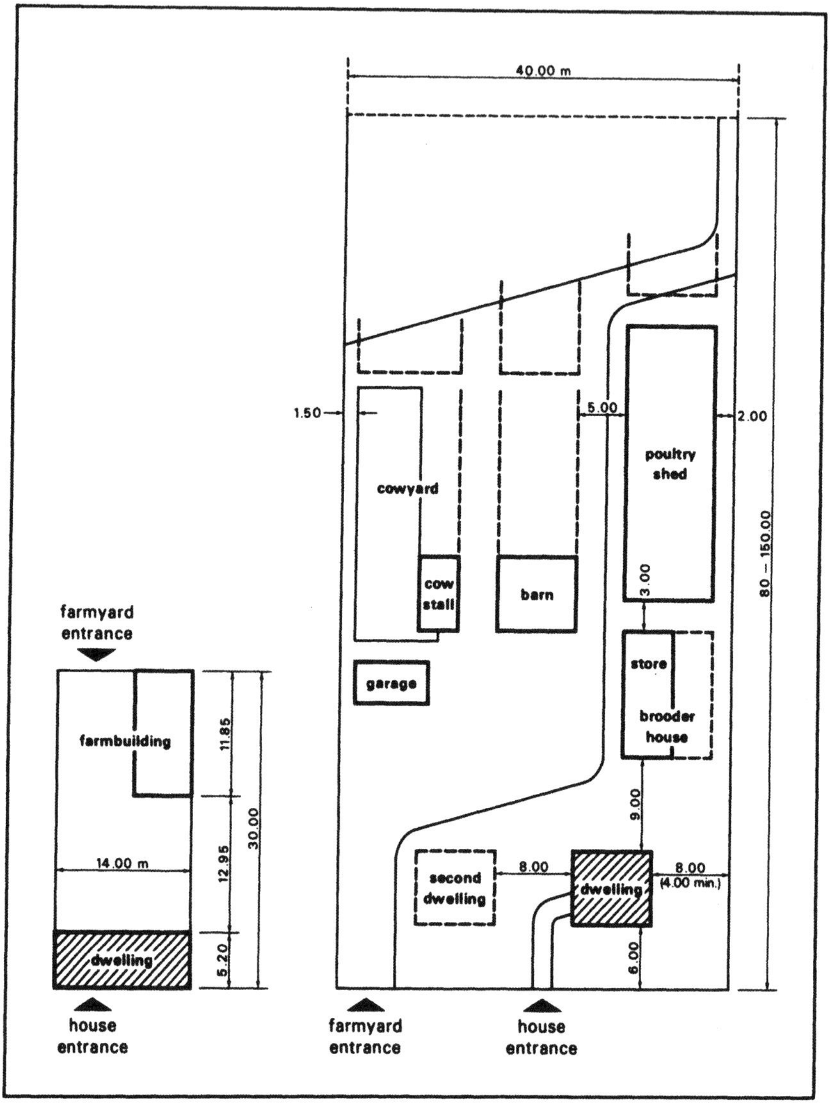

Figure 4.17 Layout and dimensions of "static" and "dynamic" farmsteads

Left: The Badajoz farmstead of 420 square meters (600 square meters in more recent projects). Entrance to farmyard is from rear service road. Lack of space has caused congestion in many of these farmyards, leading to outsettlement on the agricultural plot outside the village.

Right: The Moshav farmstead of 3,200 square meters plus--provides expansion area for second dwelling, farm buildings, and maneuvering space.

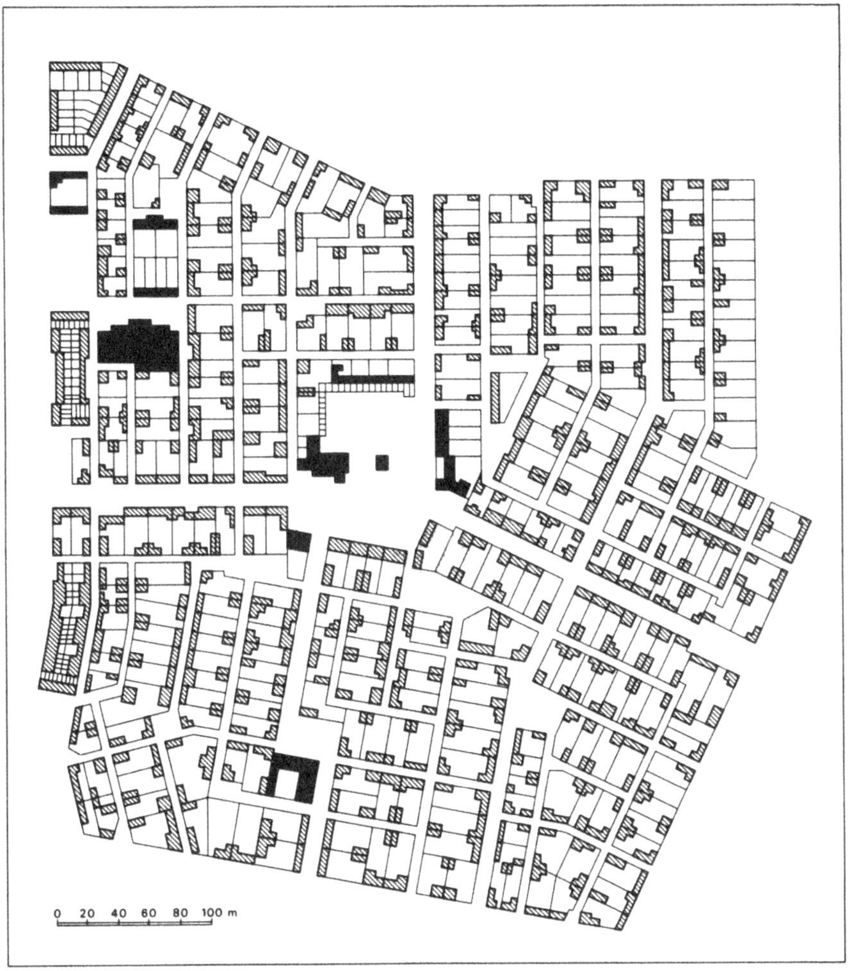

Figure 4.18 Valdecalzada--a planned nucleated village in the Badajoz settlement scheme--built around 1956 for 325 farm families and 100 farm workers' families. Farmsteads have an area of 420 square meters (see Figure 4.17). Yards are accessible through rear service roads. Shaded areas are public and communal buildings.

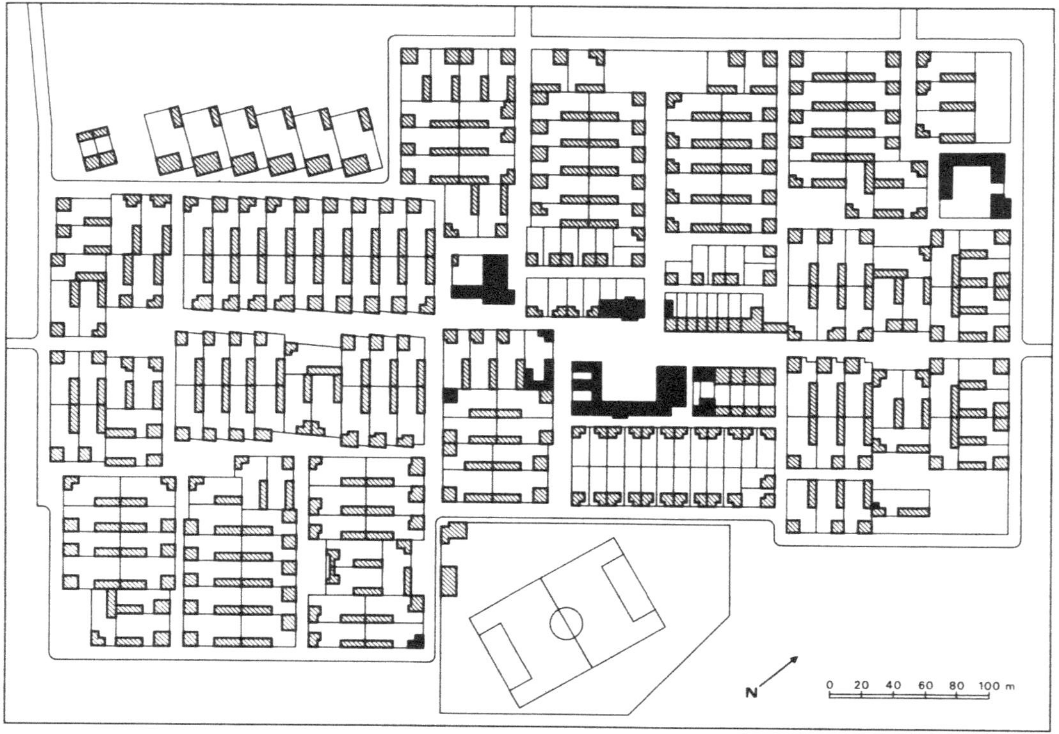

Figure 4.19 Palazuelo--a nucleated village in the Upper Vegas area of the Badajoz settlement scheme--built in 1969 for 186 farm families and 24 families of farm workers. Farmsteads cover 600 square meters each (an increase over the previous 420 square meters). Service roads have been eliminated and entrance to farmyards is from the main street.

they were too small and inadequate in layout. As a result, many yards have already become congested with annexes and structures for livestock, machinery, storage, and other needs while, on the other hand, many of the farm buildings provided in the project are lying idle. Some farmers whose holdings are conveniently nearby have settled out on their plots. The project organizers, who for years had to struggle against the settlers' apathy and lack of collaboration, consider these moves as welcome manifestations of entrepreneurship. This attitude ignores, however, the long-run damages of outsettlement and partial dispersion which may eliminate whatever flexibility is left in the field system and ultimately necessitate other costly reforms.

The Structure of Services

No special hierarchy of services is apparent in the Badajoz settlements. Since the criterion for the deployment of villages was distance to fields (3.0-3.5 km maximum), the new villages were supposed to be self-sufficient in respect to essential services. Each village was provided with a town hall, theater, church, shops, medical dispensary, school, and utilities, and with a cooperative center for farming inputs, repair sheds, and storage. Several villages such as Valdecalzada (Figure 4.18) with 425 families, or Palazuelo (Figure 4.19) with 210 families, may be large enough for efficient services to develop. In villages below the 150 family mark, however, services are liable to perform less efficiently. Higher-range services such as government, administration, commerce, and industry are centralized in the provincial capital of Badajoz.

The government has embarked on an intensive development program for processing industries related to the main agricultural products of the region, including horticultural and fruit produce, textile fibers, and livestock products. Most of these industries belong to the private sector with little participation from the small landholders' settlements, except in the labor force. Badajoz, the largest province in Spain, known for its acute social problems and rural poverty, seems to possess the natural resources that could be utilized to remedy this imbalance. The settlement of small landholders in the irrigation district is part of a multipurpose river basin development which is impressive in its socioeconomic goals as it is in its technological scope. The task accomplished to date, both in land reclamation and settlement, is indeed one of heroic proportions. The purported social goals, however, still remain elusive. There is no doubt that the influx of social overhead capital, as well as increased production through irrigation infrastructure, generation of power, and industrial development, have improved the region's economy. Unlike the Mezzogiorno in Italy, most development efforts in the Badajoz region were aimed primarily at the agricultural sector. However, the main beneficiaries of the project were not the newly settled small landholders, but the private landowners who still retain over 60 percent of prime irrigated land in the district, as well as the industrial and commercial sectors which elaborate and market the agricultural produce. The introduction of private processing industries, for example, has rapidly solved the problems of marketing, but has also preempted future options for increased participation by small landholders' settlements in the elaboration of their products. Such participation could have led to higher incomes and expanded employment opportunities in linked facilities for the region's population. Under these circumstances, the traditional socioeconomic gap can only grow wider unless special measures are taken that can compensate for the accumulated backlog.

Implicit in the structure of services is the classical assumption of urban-rural integration, in which the diverse social classes and economic sectors--small landholders, agricultural laborers, landowners, and the nonfarming population--are amalgamated in a free market economy. However, the original setback of the settlers or farm laborers and the continuing inequities in the allocation of resources may exacerbate the existing disequilibrium of the system.[28] This structural deficiency is reflected in the spatial organization of the Badajoz land settlement. Cooperation--possibly the only resort open to the small landholder to avail himself of bigger scales and economic leverage--depends to a large extent on the spatial arrangement of the settlements. In the Badajoz region services are arranged in fragmented, self-contained agglomerations. The urban amenities so generously provided for the settlers are impressive (there is probably no other settlement scheme that can boast similar accommodations), but they cannot conduce higher levels of regional organization. The mixture of small landholders and landless farm workers, for example, may impede collaboration in areas other than municipal aspects and may hamper cooperation when economic matters are at stake.

The farmstead as conceived of in the Badajoz project epitomizes, perhaps more than anything else, the static nature of the family farm. While considerable emphasis has been placed on the dwelling, the undersized farmyard is practically useless. Evidently, the new villages were planned to suit subsistence farming but not mixed farming since the small farmyards are inadequate for raising livestock on the scale required at the latter agricultural stage. While the spatial arrangements of fields or cooperative production methods are open to improvements and changes (as long as the fields are not distorted by outsettlement), the farmyard itself may turn out to be the most inflexible component and real bottleneck of the settlement scheme.

CONCLUSION

The study of land settlement in the three countries reveals the human element to be the fundamental factor in several different facets of rural development. While in Italy and Spain projects were mainly purported to resettle landless peasants who lived in the region, in Israel it was necessary to introduce people to agriculture who had never before been farmers. The emphasis in the Israeli settlement program was, therefore, on social and educational aspects as a corollary to economic development.

The opportunities for large-scale settlement in Italy and Spain were not used in developing new rural settlement models. With only a few exceptions traditional models were applied, often wrapped in attractive urbanistic forms which contributed little in terms of integral rural solutions. In Italy as in Spain the villages emulate urban development. The reason for this trend is that in the static village, where economic possibilities terminate with the agricultural process, farmers have to search for other occupations as an outlet for their full potential. In Israel settlement patterns evolved on the principle of concentration, but without sacrificing farmyard space. The provision of an adequate farmyard encouraged diversification and also facilitated the expansion of economic activities beyond the village limits. This expansion opened the way for the amalgamation of rural settlements into a larger system of regional cooperation. It follows that regional cooperation is based on a dynamic concept, not bound to rigid physical boundaries but only to the capacity and energy of the settlers. Likewise, an increased participation of the farming families in the productive cycle can best be achieved in the concentrated settlement pattern with adequate space for farmyard activities.

Of particular interest to developing regions is the service structure in the Israeli model, in which rural settlements developed their own independent system with services including the most complex production facilities. The resulting returns from scale, both in economic and social areas, have generated new sources of employment for the younger generation, thereby counteracting the universal trend of depopulation that follows the rationalization of agriculture.

NOTES

1. Gabriele Schwarz, Allgemeine Siedlungsgeographie (Berlin, 1961).

2. Wilhelm Abel, Die Wüstungen des Ausgehenden Mittelalters (Stuttgart, 1955).

3. Vernon W. Ruttan, "Induced Technical and Institutional Change and the Future of Agriculture," in The Future of Agriculture: Theme

Papers (Oxford, 1973), pp. 16-33.

4. Glenn T. Trewartha, "Types of Rural Settlement in Colonial America," The Geographical Review, Vol. 36 (1946), pp. 568-596.

5. Gunnar Myrdal, Economic Theory and Underdeveloped Regions (New York, 1971).

6. S. H. Franklin, Rural Societies (London, 1971).

7. "Group Farming: A New Experiment in Co-operation between Farmers," OECD Observer, No. 56 (1972), pp. 31-33.

8. Erich H. Jacoby, Land Consolidation in Europe (Wageningen, 1959).

9. Angel Palerm, Observaciones sobre el desarrollo agrario en Israel, Estudios y Monografías, XIII, Panamerican Union, Organization of American States, Washington, D.C., 1964.

10. Emmanuel Yalan, J. Maos, and L. Kam, Land Planning of the Agricultural Co-operative Village, The Rural Building Research Centre, Haifa, Israel, 1963.

11. J. Maos and D. Pelley, "Agricultural Settlement Planning in the Specialization Era: New Approaches to the Physical Planning of the Moshav," GeoJournal, Vol. 5.3 (1981), pp. 269-276; A. Sharon, "Collective Settlements in Israel," Town Planning Review, Vol. 25 (1955), pp. 225-270.

12. Statistical Abstract of Israel--1981, No. 32 (Jerusalem, 1981).

13. The Mezzogiorno is the traditional name for Southern Italy, including Apulia, Lucania and Molise, Calabria, Campania, Sicily, and Sardinia. The Cassa per il Mezzogiorno is a special development agency for this region.

14. Hollis B. Chenery, "Development Policies for Southern Italy," in J. Friedmann and W. Alonso (eds.), Regional Development and Planning: A Reader (Cambridge, 1964), pp. 668-700.

15. The agrarian problems in southern Italy are described, among others, by Abraham Granott, Agrarian Reform and the Record of Israel (London, 1956), Chapter VIII; Giuseppe Medici, "Pulverization and Fragmentation of Landed Property in Italy," in Roger N. Dixey (ed.), International Explorations of Agricultural Economics (Ames, Iowa, 1964), pp. 153-163; and, Decio Scardaccione, Land Reform: Experiences in Apulia, Lucania and Molise (Bari, 1965).

16. Giuseppe Tassinari, Ten Years of Integral Land Reclamation under the Mussolini Act (Talura, Italy, 1939).

17. Nicola Matarrese, "L'insediamento Rurale di Centri Satelliti," Annals of the Faculty of Agronomy, Vol. 18 (1963).

18. This statement is based on my impressions during a visit to the area in 1973. Many of the houses were uninhabited although the fields seemed to be well tended.

19. Erich H. Jacoby, Land Consolidation in Europe (Wageningen, 1959).

20. United States dollars.

21. Case Coloniche, Sezione Speciale per la Riforma Fondiaria in Puglia Lucania e Molise, Bari, 1958.

22. S. Garofalo, "Investimenti netti e progresso tecnico nello sviluppo dell'agricoltura meridionale," Rivista di Economia Agraria, Anno 25, No. 2-3 (1970), pp. 209-232.

23. Artur Glikson, Planned Regional Settlement Projects: Comparative Study; Background, Experience, New Trends (Jerusalem, 1970). See

also, Russell King, Land Reform: The Italian Experience (London, 1973); and A. B. Mountjoy, The Mezzogiorno (Oxford, 1973). More recent appraisements include: Russell King, "Italy," in Hugh D. Clout (ed.), Regional Development in Western Europe (New York, 1981), pp. 119-149; and Klaus Rother, "Das Mezzogiorno-Problem: Versuche des italienischen Staates zu seiner Lösung," Geographische Rundschau, No. 4 (1982), pp. 154-162.

24. Economic and Social Development Program for Spain: 1964-1967, Prepared by the Commissioner for Economic and Social Development Planning, Spain (Johns Hopkins University Press, Baltimore, 1965).

25. Peter Enggass, "Spain," Focus, Vol. 20 (1970), pp. 1-8; and "Land Reform in Spain," Focus, Vol. 20 (1970), pp. 9-12.

26. John Naylon, "Irrigation and Internal Colonization in Spain," Geographical Journal, Vol. 133 (1967), pp. 178-191; and "Iberia," in Hugh D. Clout (ed.), Regional Development in Western Europe (New York, 1981), pp. 359-387.

27. Zonas Regables de Badajoz, Ministerio de Agricultura, Dirección General de Colonización y Ordenación Rural, Instituto Nacional de Colonización, Madrid, 1972.

28. A detailed evaluation of the Badajoz settlement scheme is included in Olivier Balabanian, Les Exploitations et les Problèmes de l'Agriculture en Estrémadure Espagnole et dans le Haut-Alentejo, 2 vols., published doctoral thesis, University of Clermont-Ferrand, 1980.

5
The Latin American Context

THE HISTORICAL BACKGROUND OF SPATIAL ORGANIZATION

The study of social and economic retardation in Latin American rural areas has taken into account the events which followed the Spanish Conquest some four centuries ago. Assumedly, the preColumbian indigenous population knew only collective or communal land tenure. Under more advanced cultures, as in Mexico or Peru, such collective tenancy was bound within a rigid sociopolitical system. However, the majority of the population did not deviate from the tribal concept of universal patrimony. One of the profoundest changes, therefore, was the transition from collective land tenancy to private ownership and the consequent socioeconomic stratification of the population. This confrontation of radically different concepts of tenancy may explain the singular relationship between conquerors who took possession of territories with relative ease and native populations.

The span of time beginning with Spanish colonization is characterized by four periods, summarized as follows:

1. The original urban period (sixteenth to seventeenth century)--Cities for defense purposes and strategically located settlements with adjacent farmlands for food supplies were founded. The overall emphasis was on mining, with animal husbandry assuming increasing importance. The <u>encomienda</u> marked the advent of big estates on the American rural scene and the consequent domination of lands.
2. The rural period (seventeenth to eighteenth century)--The hacienda became the main economic growth pole, the town serving as government and church seat. Poor subgroups in search of land squatted on the fringes of the big estates, thereby consolidating the latifundia boundaries and becoming part of a paternalistic system.
3. Rural-urban transition (mid-eighteenth to nineteenth century)--The creation of rural towns as an

intermediate administrative link between city and country opened new possibilities for small trade. The concurrent relaxation of monopolistic controls attracted the immigration of merchant classes from Europe, terminating in the emergence of a new power group by a coalition of hacienda owners and traders. With the appearance of rural towns a new urban relationship was created as the towns absorbed part of the rural unemployed. The abolition of the encomienda system towards the end of the eighteenth century resulted in diverse conditional land tenure forms such as share-cropping, corporal services arrangements, etc. The encomendados, renters, and small landholders were absorbed by the latifundia because of illiteracy, poverty, and habituated paternalism.

4. The urban period (mid-nineteenth century to date)--Accelerated development of urban centers and relative stagnation of rural areas occurred. Infrastructure, mostly access roads and railways, were built in spatial enclaves of mining and agriculture engaged in primary exports. Normally the enclaves used as their base existing towns whose centripetal forces provoked the first rural exodus. The economic benefits derived from these developments were rarely reinvested into the rural sector but spent on urban-located enterprises or channeled out of the country. The backwardness and social ferment in rural areas stirred the concern of some governments and led to the first irrigation and colonization programs; however, the investments into related infrastructure often consolidated the dualistic latifundia-minifundia structure which is the only known developmental model.[1]

URBAN VERSUS RURAL GROWTH IN LATIN AMERICA

Both the rate of population growth and the increase in urban sectors in Latin America are known to be among the highest in the world.[2] Current demographic studies indicate that in mid-1981 the continent contained a population of 369,500,000.[3] About 64 percent of this population was estimated to be living in urban areas, a percentage which is expected to grow to nearly 75 by the year 2000.[4] If present trends continue, some Latin American cities will be true "megalopolises" of the type currently identified with highly urbanized and developed countries; however, the per capita income in the Latin American countries would be only 20 percent higher than it is today and, consequently, far below the average per capita income in the United States or Europe. Even the countries which will not contain cities of more than a million inhabitants will nevertheless have urban centers of more than 100,000 inhabitants. Of these cities, the capital city in each country will also constitute a metropolitan zone with all the problems of traffic, housing, basic services, and squatter settlements (proportionate to their size) that characterize life in the gigantic conurbations.

While urban expansion in Latin America has spiraled at an unequaled rate, the belief is still widespread that economic development is associated with city rather than with rural life. The notion that rapid urbanization is inseparable from human progress is deeply ingrained. Agglomeration is considered the natural outcome of industrialization; urban blight an unavoidable social cost. Characteristically, many planners and decision makers subscribe to the classical concept of spatial concentration of economic activities as a rationale for drastically changing the regions' settlement patterns and forming large urban agglomerations. According to this concept, settlement patterns tend to change in the wake of rapid economic growth as urban employment increases with new capital investments which, in turn, provide external economies for other enterprises. The subsequent social overhead investment and higher levels of public services and amenities increase the comparative advantages of urban centers for industrial location. Consequently, significant proportions of income generated in the periphery are channeled to the center, attracting the migration of the best skilled labor in the periphery. Both the demographic and economic concentration increases the political gravity of the urban centers, enabling them to draw an increased share of both public and private resources. As more employment and increased personal incomes stimulate diversification and expansion of the tertiary sector, more employment and higher incomes are generated leading to the continuous broadening of internal markets within the centers. Consequently the basic infrastructure at the national level is shaped by an economy which revolves around centrally located activities which, again, favors the process of concentration.[5]

The supposed advantage of metropolitan growth is marred, however, by the harsh reality of the urban situation which reveals a constantly growing gap between the modern and traditional sectors, also described as "development dualism."[6] To date no clear policy on urban development has emerged. In addition, concepts borrowed from conventional regional science seem unfit for many incipient situations. It is also increasingly apparent that the rapid urbanization now taking place all over the underdeveloped world has its origin less in urban economic opportunity than in the disruption of rural life. The change is not a transfer in economic function, but a shift from disguised unemployment in agriculture to open unemployment in the so-called shantytowns, _favelas_, _barriadas_, etc.[7]

Some planners admit that the unbalanced growth of

urban areas is an end product of rural stagnation and that the forces at work are different than those usually dealt with in urban science.[8] Nevertheless, the dynamics of agglomeration continue despite their negative effects in the national sphere. Most cities were expected to double their 1970 population by 1980, and urgent action is necessary to deal merely with the environmental impacts of this increase. It is doubtful whether any planning solution in the cities themselves will prevail against the explosive urban growth generated almost entirely by refugees from rural poverty. Slowing down rural migration may therefore become the sine-qua-non of urban survival and for further economic development. Such a decrease in migration may eventually be achieved by shifting the priorities in resource allocations from urban to rural areas.

While the percentage of population in rural areas may be declining in relation to urban areas, it is increasing in absolute numbers in most Latin American countries. The generally primitive living conditions of the rural population are well known and documented. Lack of amenities, desolation, health deficiencies, and waste of human potential have tended to accelerate the rural exodus. At the heart of this situation are commonly held notions: rural migration is inevitable, it accompanies the modernization of farming, economic growth entails industrial rather than agricultural development, and finally, urbanization is necessary for social and economic development. Many planners are resigned to the fact that migration to the urban centers is an irreversible process, and maintain that it should therefore be guided into constructive developmental channels instead of being allowed to impede national growth. Although some of these notions seem historically true for some of the economically advanced nations, they have led to erroneous conclusions when applied indiscriminately to other developing countries. In many cases more damage has been wrought by diverting attention away from depressed rural areas, thereby resulting in a migratory movement swamping urban centers. A United Nations interagency team which studied the situation in Colombia pointed out that the unidirectional migration flows, resulting from the lack of economic opportunity (land, employment, income) and social infrastructure (education, health, housing), contributed to a deterioration of the rural situation as the growing--and politically more significant--problems of the towns claimed increasing attention.[9]

AGRARIAN REFORM AND SETTLEMENT

Agrarian reform, as a process, first manifested itself in Mexico and extended to numerous Latin American countries with varying degrees of efficiency and success. Although aimed at transforming socioeconomic structures and not at the mere redistribution of land, many of these efforts have been thwarted by the cumulative effect of urban-rural imbalances and administrative managerial incapacities. Moreover, as redistribution of agricultural resources was not always compatible with the sociopolitical aims of the establishment, some programs paid little more than lip service to agrarian reforms. The basic problems of overpopulated versus underpopulated areas, fragmented and dwarfed holdings, and the structure of intermediary elements in credit and marketing have similarly remained unsolved. In the face of pressure on occupied lands, new settlement projects have become a means to amplify the governments' involvement in land reform and, at the same time, to consolidate national territories through human settlement. Settlers are mostly drawn from the subsistence sector, and thus settlement becomes a form of wealth distribution which is synonymous with agrarian reform and socioeconomic development.

In most Latin American settlement schemes the family farm is the core element, and communities of small landholders constitute the organizational pattern. Cooperation, broadly defined, is considered a means for achieving economies of scale in production services and social amenities. From the land settlement point of view, tenancy is no more the crucial issue since many lands are publicly owned. However, titles are usually expected by the beneficiaries of the reform, and landed property is still the most powerful incentive for settlers. Ownership on a leasehold basis has been considered in several instances by agrarian reform entities but has seldom been put into practice.

Land ownership is a problem that may emerge at some future point, but is currently dwarfed by many other difficulties besetting rural development. One of these difficulties is the marginal quality of lands at the disposal of settlement agencies. Most of the land is in need of clearing, irrigation, drainage, or other infrastructure before production can begin. In many respects the countryside, burdened by centuries of upheavals, spontaneous colonization, and sporadic developments, is frequently found in a state of disarray. In addition, although the agrarian reform can be perceived of as a spatial process unfolding on a national scale, it rarely operates in a territorial "tabula rasa." Population density in Latin America is notably low; yet, even where sparsely populated, most regions bear evidence of existing settlements, hamlets, small rural towns, etc. Many of these settlements remain unaffected by land reform and do not change spatially. Medium-sized and large farms, though curtailed in area, continue to coexist and exert their influence. Reform often means the beginning of a prolonged administrative process which brings a disrupting uncertainty to the settlement areas. Urban-rural relationships depict a dichotomy which occurs between the smallest rural town and its periphery. Efforts to inject amenities into depressed areas may have little effect because of the accumulated backlog of destitution.

Early attempts at planned settlement related to agrarian reform programs retained many spontaneous characteristics. Projects were usually begun by building roads in an area and settling the families in a linear pattern along the road. Innumerable small farms and shacks, planned or improvised, are strung today along Latin American highways and roads in this fashion. To some extent road arteries serve as a link between consumers and services. However, long distances constitute weak links preventing the development of the support system needed to raise the existing rural structure to higher social and economic levels. Examples from early settlement experiments in Venezuela illustrate some of the spatial problems involved. Las Guaduas, on the western shore of the Maracaibo Lake in Zulia State, is a planned linear village which was established in 1964 and stretches along a road over twenty-five kilometers in length. Dwellings are located on holdings of ten hectares with about 200 to 250 meters of frontage on the main road. For many families, facilities such as the rural school or store are from five to ten kilometers away. The costs of installing utilities such as electricity, water supply, etc., are prohibitive and maintenance is problematic. Community participation--indispensable for the social and economic advancement of a family farming village--is severely hampered.

Another agricultural settlement, Capitanejo, in Barinas State (Figure 5.1), is similarly strung along a road some seventeen kilometers long, originally constructed as a penetration route to a petroleum drilling site. The length of the road was divided into twenty hectare parcels with 250 meters of frontage for combined pasture and arable farming. Two rural schools are located at different points along the road. A store and rural dispensary were built at another point. Some services are located in a small hamlet near the old drilling camp and in a bigger village on the other end of the road at the junction with the Barinas Highway. The farming population is divided between the village, hamlet, and several houses and shacks built on the holdings, resulting in a dispersed and fragmented community with redundant, inefficient services.

An attempt to agglomerate settlers into a compact village provided with facilities was made in Zipayares, another agricultural settlement in Zulia State, Venezuela. The village was planned for three hundred farming families, but the agricultural plots were some fifteen kilometers from the village dwellings and hardly accessible. Consequently, many of the houses built by the Venezuelan National Agrarian Institute (IAN) remained empty. Other houses were abandoned when families moved (with certain logic) to shacks which they built on their allotted plots. These extreme, but by no means isolated, cases are taken from one of the first countries to engage in land settlement

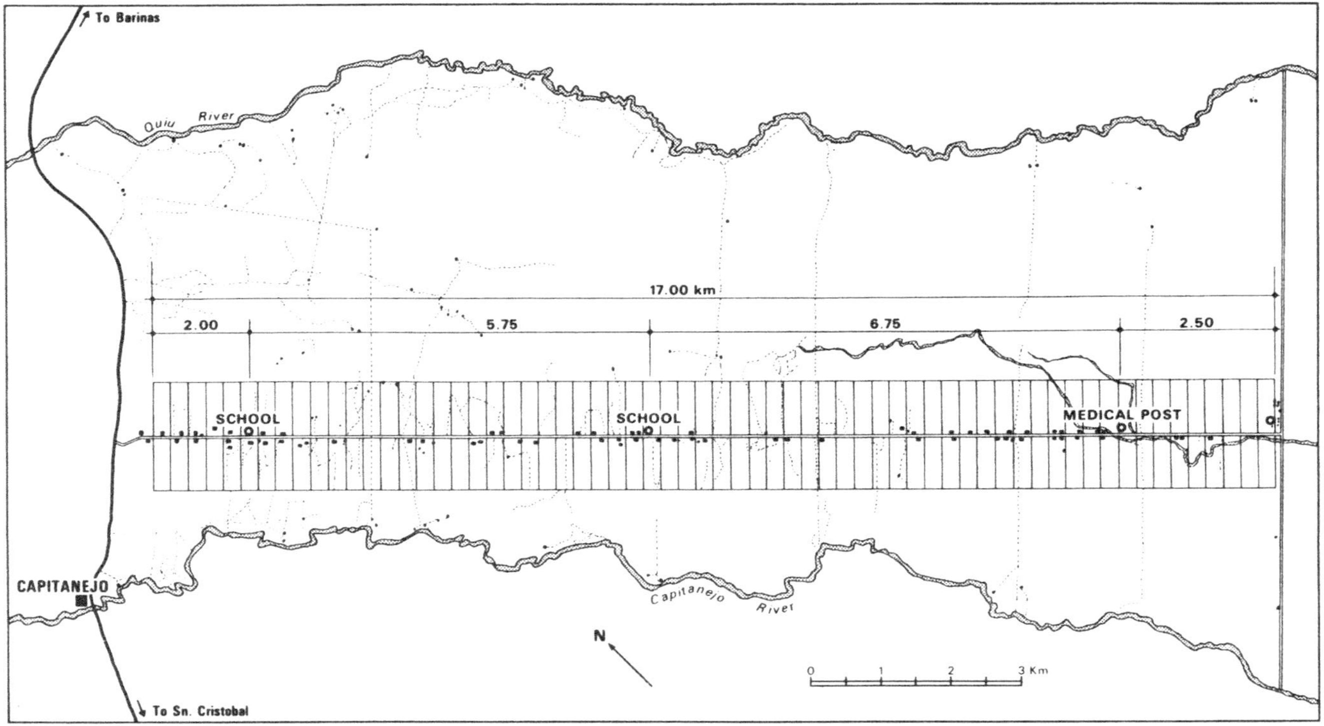

Figure 5.1 Ribbon development of family farms land settlement in Capitanejo, Barinas. (Source: J. Maos (ed.), Course on Rural Architecture.)

in a pragmatic way. They exemplify the fact that the mere choice of pattern, gathered or dispersed, is not enough to establish a settlement.

Irrigation projects on a different scale were initiated during the 1950s and 1960s in Venezuela, Peru, Mexico, and other countries. In many cases, farmers were selected on the basis of financial ability. New settlements were laid out in a dispersed pattern with medium-sized holdings of two hundred hectares per family. Services were to be provided by existing towns in the area. The results were mixed: while farm size was large enough to afford good incomes and distances could be overcome by motorized transportation, the projects contributed little toward easing the rural poor's hunger for land. Mounting pressures caused many of the projects to be restructured to absorb larger numbers of farm families with smaller holdings, a planning task which turned out to be tedious and costly.

The search for better settlement procedures brings this study to bear on earlier periods of rural settlement in Europe. However, while settlement patterns in Europe evolved over centuries through a process of slow as well as cataclysmic changes, rural development in Latin America is generally guided by pragmatic planning. Thus, the evolution of planning models conforms to the conceptions of planners who evaluate experiences and compare alternatives in light of changing conditions. These conceptual images are often influenced by the alleged virtues of historical settlement patterns and the theory that indigenous communal tenures predispose peasants to collective farming. The ease of spontaneous--nondirected or semidirected--colonization, an undertaking which thrives on the popular craving for land, is tempting. The planner is consequently attracted by the Utopian image of collective settlement which combines large scale (economic efficiency) with equity in income (social justice), and allows for a high degree of flexibility in physical planning. The planner's judgement is also attracted by the high productivity of dispersed farms in the U.S.A. and in other advanced countries. Yet, the evidence suggests that collective farming has been unsuccessful because of drawbacks which may be more pronounced in Latin America than in other places. On the other hand, focusing on productivity through the individualization of agriculture disregards the crux of the problem in developing countries and the long-run social costs involved in this approach.

A considerable amount of planning and implementation has taken place prior to and after the inception of agrarian reform programs. The accumulated experience contains, understandably, a vast list of errors and omissions which in themselves could form a detailed manual on how to embark on land settlement projects. However, evaluation of past efforts is seldom attempted, as already affirmed by several authors. Consequently, this vast treasure of experience is often wasted. Many settlement projects constitute isolated experiments. Errors of a similar nature recur in neighboring countries or regions at different points in time, yet the lessons go unheeded. Improvements in the settlement model occur only when projects are carried out successively in the same region, provided there is continuity in the planning staff and its policies. Spatial aspects, as already pointed out, are only a few of the many vital components in the land settlement process. However, the results of spatial decisions are often the hardest and costliest to correct.

NOTES

1. Soublette E. Browne, "Planificación Física para Reforma Agraria," in Seminario Interamericano de Planificación Física Rural, Instituto Interamericano de Ciencias Agrícolas de la O.E.A., Bogota, Colombia, 3-9 December 1972, pp. 42-58.

2. United Nations, Centre for Housing, Building and Planning, Global Review of Human Settlements (Oxford, 1976), p. 12.

3. World Population Estimates, The Environmental Fund, Washington, D.C., 1981.

4. United Nations, Statistical Office of the Department of Economic and Social Affairs, Global Review of Human Settlements: Statistical Annex (Oxford, 1976), p. 54.

5. "Some Regional Development Problems in Latin America Linked to Metropolitanization," Economic Bulletin for Latin America, Vol. 16 (1971), pp. 57-90.

6. T. R. Lakshmanan, "Integration of Physical and Economic Planning," Paper presented to the U.N. Group of Experts on Integration of Economic and Physical Planning, Ref. ESA/HBP/AC.10/4, August 1973.

7. Charles P. Kindleberger, Economic Development (New York, 1965).

8. See for instance: John Friedmann and Mike Douglass, "Agropolitan Development; towards a new strategy for regional planning in Asia," in F. C. Lo and K. Salih (eds.), Growth Pole Strategy and Regional Development Policy (Oxford, 1978), pp. 163-192.

9. United Nations, International Labour Organization, Toward Full Employment: A Programme for Colombia (Geneva, 1970).

6
Case Studies of Land Settlement in Latin America

Several case studies based on real-world situations in rural development can serve to illustrate specific points. In some Latin American countries there has been sufficient continuity of settlement history to produce an evolution of spatial concepts. In Mexico, one of the first countries to embark on a wide program of agrarian reform, large-scale land settlement was undertaken. In Venezuela, the policy of "plowing the oil back into the land" has generated similar rural development and settlement projects. The countries from which the case studies are drawn are by no means the only ones engaged in land settlement, but they enable the review of problems which, with variations, are common to most settlement projects: (1) a noted absence of systematic evaluation; (2) paternalism in settlement schemes; (3) excessive land allotment and farm size; and (4) difficulties in establishing a support system. As will be shown, there has been a marked shift from dispersed to concentrated settlement patterns. The importance of this transition is elucidated by the experience of several rural development projects. Another aspect of this shift which invites the planner's attention involves the utilization of collective settlement patterns purported to facilitate planning and implementation.

VENEZUELA

In the past thirty years Venezuela has been transformed from a poor and backward society into a rich industrial country. This transformation has occurred as a result of plowing back oil revenues into urban and industrial development and, to some extent, into agricultural development and agrarian reform.[1] There has been sufficient continuity in Venezuela for the crystallization of certain development concepts; or, in the terms used throughout this work, for the evolution of a land settlement model.

Some of the earlier Venezuelan experiments in planned

settlement and attempts to agglomerate largely dispersed peasant families have been described in Chapter 5. Several colonization schemes were designed based on land allotments of as much as 250 hectares per family. These schemes usually included four-hectare subsistence farms for low-income families expected to supply the labor for larger farms. The Guarico and Majaguas irrigation schemes, for example, were originally intended to benefit middle-class farmers, but were later converted by the Agrarian Reform institutions to incorporate farm families with holdings of ten to fifteen hectares. Rural development connected with land settlement and agrarian reform often assumed the shape of large-scale capital-intensive irrigation projects, with a technological carry-over from similar schemes in the United States.[2] As will be seen, such projects were hardly adapted to the needs of small family farm settlements. Moreover, they were built with technical and engineering aspects foremost in mind. Many such irrigation schemes, however, continue to be developed today under the direction of the Venezuelan Ministry of Public Works.

The Majaguas Irrigation Project

Las Majaguas (Figure 6.1) is one of the major irrigation schemes located on the western Llanos in Portuguesa State, and its settlement with family farms was begun in 1963. Of the 90,000 hectares planned for irrigation, 19,000 hectares are already covered by a network of canals. About 1,700 farm families, and an additional number of service families, were to be incorporated into the first developmental stage. Two main zones were defined according to soil quality, one for arable farming with ten-hectare holdings, and another for dairy-livestock farming with fifteen hectares per family. Because of the need for access to pasture, the dairy farms were built in a dispersed pattern with farmsteads located on the agricultural parcel. The arable zone was planned in an agglomerated pattern, based on communities of sixty to a hundred farm families. Four settlements related to a service center, or service village, located within a distance of three to four kilometers. Higher level services were to be provided by a regional center located in the existing rural town of Agua Blanca. The distance between the farmer's house and his agricultural plot was not to exceed 3.5 kilometers.[3]

The project had a particularly difficult gestation period. Adjusting the region's peasants to modern irrigation farming was in itself a tedious task, and there were added problems in the selection and social adjustments of the settlers as well as lags in the introduction of essential services. The region has generally poor soils, a problem which was compounded by the destruction of much of the fertile topsoil while leveling the land required for

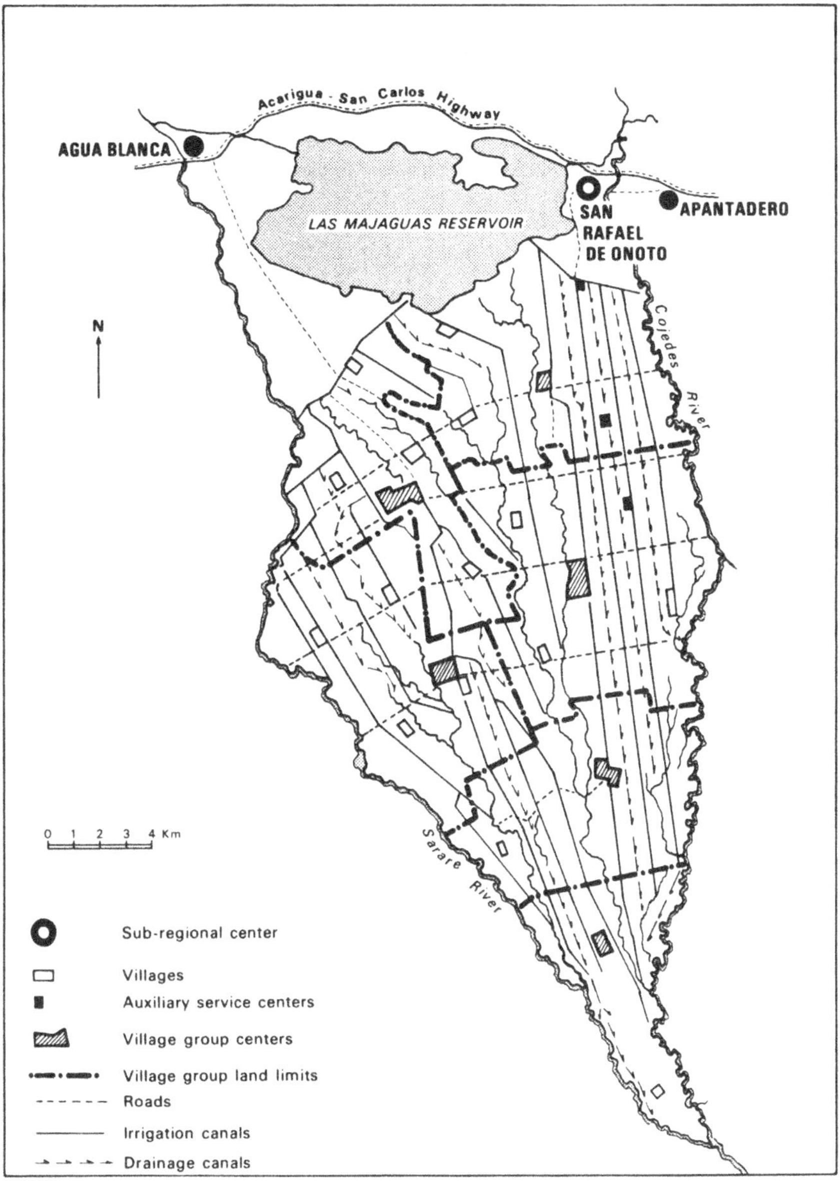

Figure 6.1 General layout of settlements and service centers in the Las Majaguas Irrigation Project, Portuguesa, Venezuela. (Source: H. Pedregal and H. M. De Pedregal, Principios Generales.)

surface irrigation. The initial adjustment of dairy farmers, provided with producing herds, was smoother than that of the arable farmer since a cash crop in milk deliveries could almost immediately be generated. The dispersion of the dairy farms was offset to some degree by small subservice centers designed to provide daily services. Basic utilities, however, like potable water drawn from individual wells, were often unsatisfactory.

Land allotment for the arable farmers, who were concentrated in villages, was in the form of one single plot per family. This decision would later interfere with the introduction of large-scale cultivation. Grouping plots for joint farming was initiated in some instances by the farmers themselves, but did not become a general practice. Farmyards in the village were planned with 2,040 square meters (34 x 60 meters), providing space for annexes and a second house; however, little guidance was given for the utilization of the farmyard area. The main shortcomings of the physical plan are that the villages are too small to support adequate services and that distances of five to six kilometers to the designated village-group service centers are too long (Figure 6.2). The accelerated shift from traditional farming methods to a full-fledged commercial agriculture was done at exaggerated costs and at the expense of a paternalistic system which today is difficult to extricate and continues to tie up valuable managerial and professional staff.[4]

The Boconó Irrigation Project

This project, initiated in 1964, is situated on the eastern slopes of the Andean Cordillera, some fifty kilometers southeast of the town of Guanare. Located on good soils with high agricultural potential, the plans included the irrigation of 220,000 hectares and production of hydroelectric power.[5] The first stage involved clearing the land and irrigating 9,200 hectares for the settlement of 485 farming families in four villages of 150 to 200 families each, with holdings of ten hectares per family (Figure 6.3). As in the Majaguas project, the Ministry of Public Works was the executive agency that coordinated the inputs of the Ministries of Agriculture (MAC) and Health (SAS), the Agrarian Institute (IAN), and the Agricultural Bank (BAP).

The physical plans called for a noteworthy increase in community size per planned village (Figure 6.4) resulting in somewhat longer distances to the fields (up to 3.5 kilometers, with the exception of one village where distances reached 5.0 kilometers). Farmsteads measured 0.2 hectare and were designed, as in the Majaguas project, to provide space for farm buildings and a second house for the farmer's son. Two adjacent rural towns, La Veguita and Sabaneta, were selected as service centers for the

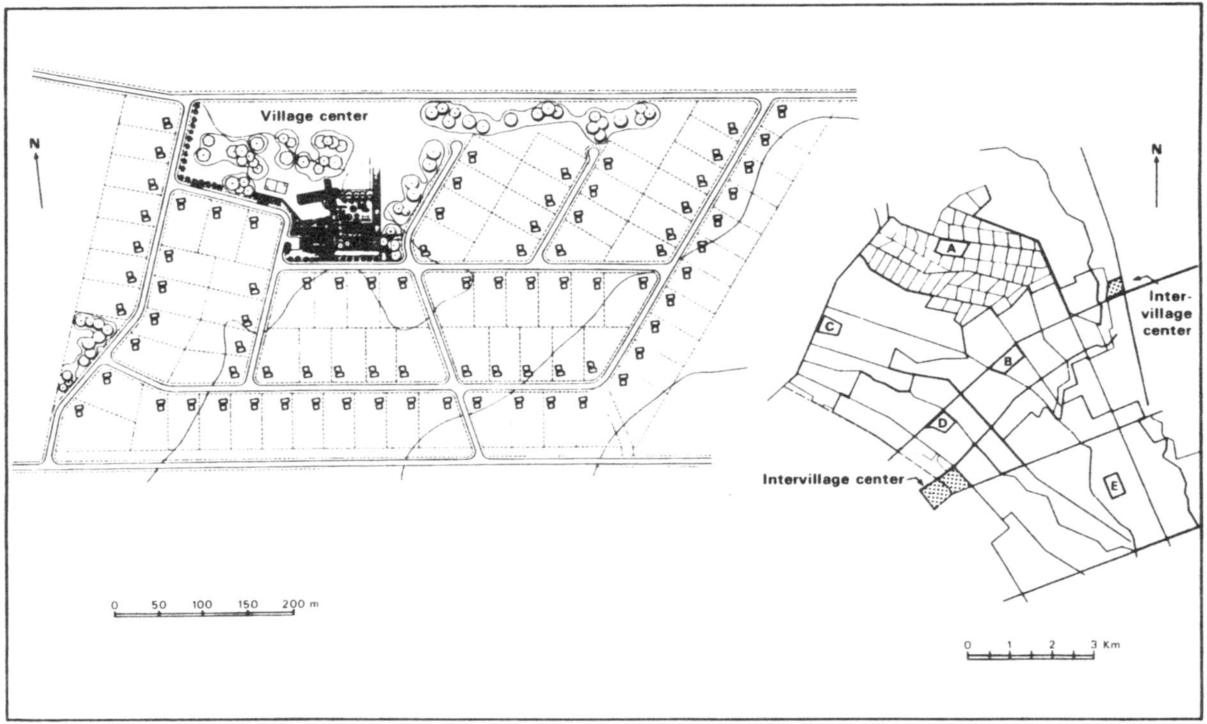

Figure 6.2 Plan of village in the Majaguas Irrigation Project. The village ("A" in location plan) comprises eighty-three farm families, each with a 2,040 square meter farmstead, and is situated in the midst of its holdings. Distances to village-group centers are five to six kilometers. (Source: H. Pedregal and H. M. De Pedregal, <u>Aldeas Agrícolas en Venezuela</u>.)

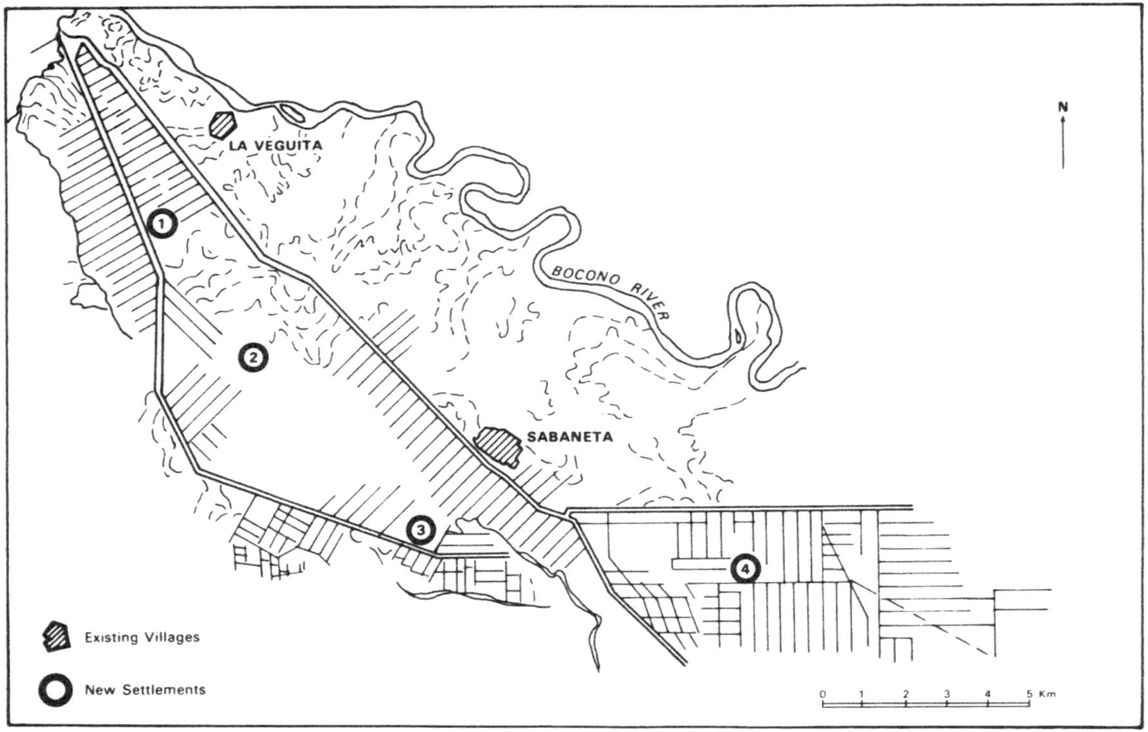

Figure 6.3 General layout of settlements and service centers in the Boconó Irrigation Project, Venezuela. (Source: H. Pedregal and H. M. De Pedregal, Aldeas Agrícolas en Venezuela.)

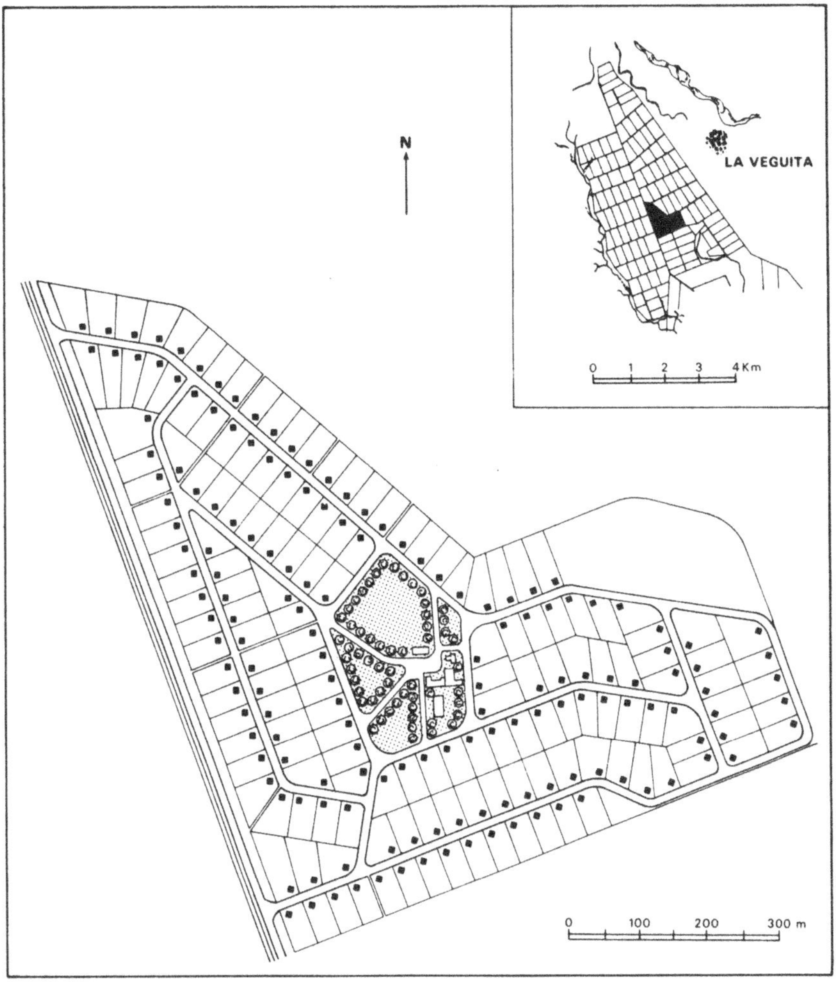

Figure 6.4 Plan of village no. 1 in the Boconó Irrigation Project. (Source: H. Pedregal and H. M. De Pedregal, Aldeas Agrícolas en Venezuela.)

provision of facilities unavailable in the new villages. The Ministry of Public Works supplied technical assistance, mechanized farm operations, seeds, fertilizers, and other inputs. Credit and marketing facilities were administered by the Agricultural Bank.

An evaluation carried out by an especially appointed interministerial committee sheds more light on the project's gestation period during the years 1964-1967, and reveals some typical aspects common to many irrigation and land settlement schemes. According to the committee's findings, 4,200 hectares of land had been cleared and cultivated toward the end of 1967 and over two hundred assignees had been incorporated into the project. Yet, many of the settlers continued to plant subsistence crops to which they were accustomed on part of their plots, thereby interfering with the overall agroeconomic plans. The report also noted that there was a lack of facilities for drying grains and storage, causing delays in harvesting and marketing operations. In addition, the introduction of services was not keeping up with the needs of the settled farming families. In its conclusions, the committee suggested the suspension of further settling activities until the necessary facilities were installed. The report underlined the need to slow down the development of the project in order to correct mistakes, but at the same time the committee recommended that production be accelerated to offset the high developmental costs of the project. It was expected that increased production would stimulate the establishment of local processing plants and generate regional economic activities.[6]

The approach used in the Boconó project is typical of many other land settlement schemes in Venezuela. The combination of agrarian reform objectives with high-cost land development caused economic return to be a predominant factor. Such an approach usually entails the rapid adjustment of the peasant-settler to specialized farming methods, as well as the construction of infrastructure for irrigation and mechanized land clearing to quickly prepare the land for cultivation. Centralized project management and state-financed production credits are essential for achieving high levels of production and for maintaining these levels. The settler's labor contribution remains relatively small and his participation in management is minimal.[7] The recurring difficulties encountered in this approach suggest that the transition from subsistence to specialized farming should be brought about gradually, making it possible for the settler to adjust to his new role as decision maker and producer within radically different conditions. It is significant to note that in the Boconó Irrigation Project the farmers continued to raise subsistence crops in spite of the programmed cropping schedule backed by technical and financial assistance. While the review committee recognized this problem and suggested a slower pace, it also made the conflicting demand that production be accelerated.

By 1971, over four hundred farm families were already housed and engaged in agricultural production under the management of the Ministry's professional staff. The fields were properly tended and the villagers seemed content and prosperous. The negative side of this picture of success was that many hundreds of peasant families had flocked into the region and were squatting on the area designated for the project's expansion. These squatters reflected both the hunger for land and the desire to receive a stake in the good fortune that had befallen the settlers selected by the administration of the project. The contrast between landless peasants and a paternalistic settlement system casts many doubts upon the wisdom of concentrating the benefits of heavily subsidized development on a relatively small group of people.

Another difficulty laid in the fact that the farmyards, which were designed to supplement family incomes, remained mostly in disuse. The evident reason for this disuse was that the earnings realized after a short time were higher than the settlers' income expectations. The problem, when considered in light of spatial and social organization, points to a number of solutions. For example, more space for the family farmstead in the village area may have encouraged settlers to grow traditional subsistence crops near their homes and not on the main agricultural plots. The undisturbed production of commercial crops, in addition to the already enumerated advantages of a spacious farmyard, would have more than made up for the loss of the small irrigated area. Furthermore, by initially allotting only a fraction (e.g. one-half) of the planned acreage per family, more labor-intensive cultivation methods might have been used. Smaller land allotments, on the other hand, would have enabled a proportionate increase in the number of settlers, with only a marginal increase in expenditure on infrastructure. In this way, both the production goals and minimum income conditions could have been met through more intensive inputs of labor (with a more efficient utilization of the family's marginal manpower), and a gradual increase in income levels. When additional land was needed after a number of years an additional tract in the project area could have been opened. The incorporation of additional lands as well as the additional distances involved would not ordinarily present special problems after a period of adjustment and transition to an advanced stage of mixed farming. The experience accumulated during the initial period of intensive farming would thus pave the way for the introduction of socially and technically more advanced cultivation systems. Over-providing the settler with resources, as exemplified in Boconó and other settlement schemes, not only prevents the spread of benefits over a larger proportion of the region's population, but may also have the inverse effect of thwarting independence and deadening incentive.[8]

The Structure of Services

The initial experience in Venezuela proved that agglomeration is an essential prerequisite for the introduction of amenities and the organization of production. The Israeli model of cooperative Moshav seemed to be remarkably well suited for this purpose and also adaptable to local conditions, and thus became the prototype for many new land settlement schemes. The organization of rural space was designed along similar patterns featuring three basic levels: the farming village, the village group center, and the rural town. Four to eight villages, each comprising 80 to 120 farm families could be clustered about a village group center. Several such centers, in turn, surrounded a planned regional center or existing rural town.

Although many settlement projects in the Venezuelan program were of considerable magnitude and scope, the development of rural service centers was not always sufficiently coordinated. Even the provision of essential facilities often lagged behind the actual arrival of the settlers. The main effort was directed at technological and physical aspects such as irrigation canals, access roads, and housing (the latter because of the active interest of the Ministry of Health and Social Welfare which realized the significant opportunity to extend the coverage of its health services). Rural planners dealt mainly with the urbanistic aspect of the village proper--its housing development and related services. As a concept, however, the service structure was an integral part of the planning process. The village was planned at first to be a self-sufficient entity in respect to services. Later, the service functions were to be differentiated and higher service levels--the village group center and the regional service center--were to be defined. The responsibility for these services was usually assigned to existing villages and rural towns where some of the needed facilities were already available. This differentiation of services was also expected to revitalize the economy of the traditionally stagnant rural localities.

At the microlevel, the single village proved to be too small for efficiently supporting its own facilities. Also, gravitation towards the village group center did not occur due to excessive distances (five to six kilometers). The need for a workable compromise between the production process and efficiency of services led to the development of bigger villages with somewhat longer distances to the fields, and to the multiunit village which offered the advantage of more consumers per service and better possibilities for phased development. The principle of the multiunit settlement was applied whenever physical conditions and land resources were adequate.

It is worthwhile to point out that the Israeli model of rural spatial organization underwent a further development as the Israelian rural communities became economically and socially consolidated. A higher level of support services evolved which was specifically geared to the needs of the rural settlements. This rural system, unlike the conventional rank-size hierarchy of central places, developed quite independently of the urban system. In the Venezuelan settlement program this latest development has not yet taken place. Although generously endowed with resources, the professional and managerial manpower has not been great enough to deal with the vast rural hinterland to a similar degree. The main emphasis of professional development continues to lean heavily on urban, rather than rural aspects. The existing institutional framework concerned with rural problems is minuscule in comparison to the size of the task. A dwindling in the ranks of rural planners has occurred because of the lusterless work in remote areas, as reflected by the lack of public interest and lower priorities in national plans.

Another problem in establishing specifically rural support services is the lack of a specialized settlement agency and difficulties in coordination among entities involved in land settlement, hampering the development of a rural organic structure.[9] Conceptually, there is no spatial framework which will successfully combine individual land use with a genuine cooperative enterprise. In Venezuelan land settlement schemes, planners sometimes attempt to steamroll the subsistence sector into the specialized farming phase with little regard for the spatial and social organization that such transition entails. This situation may eventually lead to a retrograde process in rural planning areas. One corollary is the recurrent effort by planners to "squeeze" new settlement schemes into collective patterns. The prototype of this pattern is embodied in the Collective Moshav, which combines collective production with individualized domestic life, providing economies of scale in production with efficient services through compact urban-like living (see Chapter 3). The attractiveness of the collective patterns is increased by exasperation with the slow pace of rural progress and, at times, by sincere desire for profound social reform. A number of material arguments easily "sell" the collective-production idea to policy makers. One such argument propounds the relative simplicity of the physical layout and the returns in scale from concentrated services and the joint cultivation of large tracts of homogeneous crops. Projects are sometimes programmed to shift rapidly into specialized farming and this shift seems to obviate the need for the individual farmyard. The possibility of dispensing entirely with the farmyard by concentrating production branches in separate locations looks attractive from an economic, as well as from a hygienic and aesthetic point of view, but is misleading functionally.

A recent example of this trend can be found in a rural development project now under way in the western Llanos of the Venezuelan Andean region. Living conditions in this region were described as precarious. Over 60 percent of the rural population is illiterate; lack of basic health services result in high morbidity and infant mortality. The young age group (0-20) exceeds 50 percent of the total population. A survey of agricultural resources indicated the possibility of establishing twelve settlement units in the region. The first unit, comprising 573 farm families, was planned for a 5,850 hectare area, equivalent to some ten hectares per family. The social and economic organization was defined as a "collective settlement, which optimizes the use of resources and income, resulting in a reduced investment per settled family and equitable conditions for production and provision of adequate services."[10] The first of the twelve units, denominated Modulo I, is described in Figure 6.5. It is composed of three neighborhoods, each with its own basic services and a common service center. Residential plots are 450 square meters (15x30 meters) per family. Farmyard activities are separated from the residential area. The mode of operation of the settlement is only vaguely indicated, except that it purports to agglomerate the region's population in order to provide adequate amenities which cost will be offset by returns from agricultural production. The settlement pattern appears to be a unique type of Collective Moshav, initially operated as an administrated farm.

Unfortunately the Modulo I plan lacks the individual farmyard area which would have enabled the full utilization of family manpower and a gradual transition to mixed farming activities. The size of the settlement itself, although efficient from an urbanistic point of view, may be too large to handle. The project represents a positive evolution of the settlement model toward larger villages; however, both the social and economic efficiency of this scheme are yet to be tested. Collective patterns in land settlement are not easy to induce. They best result from the voluntary decision of people inclined to live and work together and accustomed to ironing out problems as they come along. Imposed collective systems, though problematic, can eventually be advantageous when the same concepts are shared by the mainstream of society. Casting a previously neglected rural population into new social dies for presumed socioeconomic efficiency, however, is even more difficult than providing the costly short-cuts from subsistence to specialized farming. The uncalculable risks in such social experiments are evident from the experience with the ejido in Mexico, in Venezuela itself, and in Israel where the Collective Moshav has remained an exception rather than the rule. Problems in running collective enterprises may be attributed to the human element in the settlements or to the administration of the settling

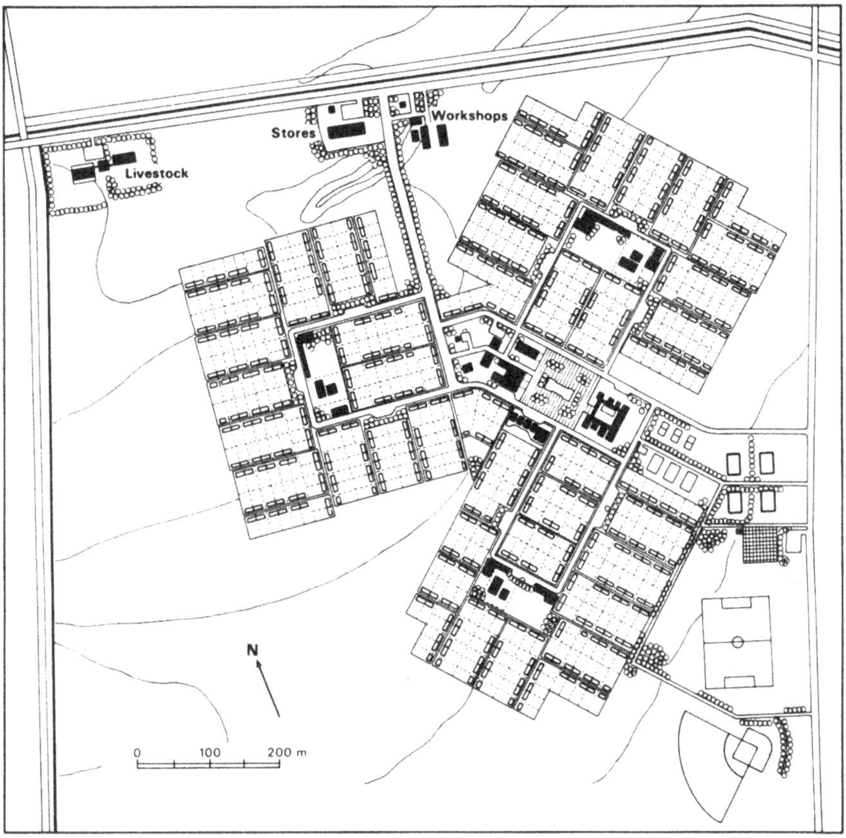

Figure 6.5 Layout of "Modulo I"--a nuclear settlement in the western llanos of Venezuela--consisting of 573 farm families and 57 families employed in services. (Source: H. Pedregal and H. M. De Pedregal, Aldeas Agrícolas en Venezuela.)

bodies which, as yet, are too thinly spread for efficiently assuming a social task of this magnitude.

THE DOMINICAN REPUBLIC

The Dominican Republic has been notable among Latin American countries for its attempts to colonize new lands, due in part to the need to bolster its sparsely populated frontier against infiltration (a motive which exists with variations in many other Latin American countries), and the need to integrate its rural population.[11] In contrast to other West Indian territories, the country has an overall density of some 66 persons per square kilometer--one of the lowest in the Antilles; but, the most desirable lands in terms of climate and accessibility have already been preempted. The land tenure structure in the country represents an unhealthy division between large farms and small holdings. The number of holdings less than one hectare increased by 250 percent from 1950 through 1960, reflecting the growing pressure on available land exerted by population growth. On the other hand, there still exists a pattern of underutilized cropland and the concentration of agricultural lands under a few owners.[12]

The Dominican Agrarian Institute, on the basis of a census carried out in 1960, estimates that some 300,000 to 350,000 small landholders live in poverty. Of the 140,000 hired rural laborers registered in the census, at least another 50,000 to 70,000 live in similar conditions. This estimate implies that 350,000 to 400,000 families or some two million persons live in precarious circumstances, a situation which can only have deteriorated since 1960.[13] The open border policy and the need for settling frontier areas which began since the late twenties, have created a certain conscientiousness regarding rural development. Lessons from earlier failures in land settlement due to inaccessibility and sporadic rainfall have created a national interest in irrigation and transportation. However, even this movement, hampered by political and institutional problems, has not been able to overtake population growth.

The specific subject of this case study is the El Sisal settlement scheme in the southern arid part of the island near the town of Azua, some 120 kilometers west of Santo Domingo. The Azua Valley contained approximately 40,000 inhabitants in 1965 distributed in twelve villages in the vicinity of Puerto Viejo, a derelict harbor village. The basic goal of the plan was to revive the region through social and economic development of agricultural settlements, the establishment of service centers, and the eventual rehabilitation of the harbor. The project envisaged four gradual stages of development, two of which (the settlement of 331 farm families in four neighborhood units) were already in full operation by 1972.[14] Another village group comprising 316 farm families was established by 1976 and, with the recent completion of the Yaque-del-sur irrigation canal, a third settlement which is to accommodate up to 280 farm families is being incorporated into the project.[15]

The site plan of the first settlement is illustrated in Figure 6.6. The land allotment per family is composed of two parts: a 0.5 hectare homeplot of which 0.3 hectare is irrigated, and a main irrigated plot outside the village area of 3.8 hectares. The maximum distance from the farmers' houses to the village group center is 1,200 meters. The distance from the village to the fields can total up to 3,250 meters. The plan follows the familiar form of cooperative villages in a loosely gathered pattern, with some significant differences. First, there is an emphasis on the homeplot for traditional and supplementary crops, aimed at better utilization of the family's marginal manpower. Second, the two villages built so far, one with 331 and the other with 316 family farms, with the additional number of families employed in services, constitute "big" villages--a fact which is apparent in the efficiency of services. To some degree such village size was possible because of the smaller-than-usual land allotment meticulously tailored to the working capacity of the average family (about 500 working days per year) and a target income of $1,500.00 per year.[16]

The Structure of Services

The influence of this relatively small project (involving some 1,000 farming families or 6,000 people in the final phase) on the traditional rural landscape with over 40,000 inhabitants is already evident in the dissemination of agrotechnical innovations and the further expansion of development projects in adjoining regions.[17] An additional impact upon the surrounding rural area can be expected from the support services generated by the new settlement. Table 6.1 shows the main service functions of each service center and their distribution at distinct settlement levels. Four service categories are identified: (1) the village center, serving 80 to 120 farm families; (2) the intervillage, or village-group center, shared by 200 to 350 farm families; (3) the subregional center, serving over 1,000 families; and (4) a regional center, in this case Azua, the capital of the province, for typical urban facilities.

The salient element in this structure is the subregional center which functions would complement the production process generated by the new settlements and at the same time provide social amenities to both the new and old villages in the area. Thus, the subregional center, which would usually provide services only for the El Sisal project, assumes broader functions because of the relatively

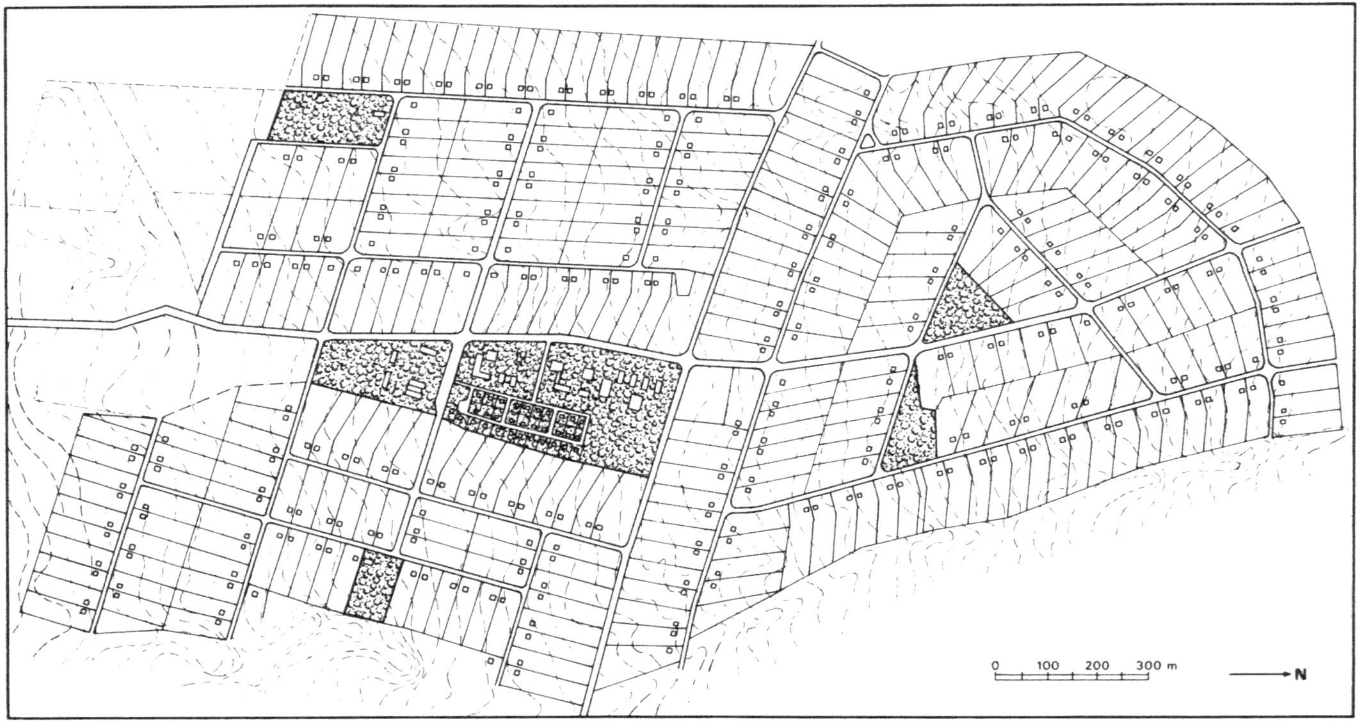

Figure 6.6 Layout of El Sisal multiunit settlement in the Azua Valley. The four neighborhood units comprise altogether 331 family farms, each on a 0.5 ha lot, of which 0.3 ha are furrow-irrigated. (Source: Instituto Agrario Dominicano, Proyecto El Sisal.)

TABLE 6.1
Functional distribution of services and activities in the El Sisal settlement area

Services	Village Center (80-120 families)	Intervillage Center (200-350 families)	Subregional Center (Over 1,000 families)	Regional Center (Azua)
Maximum distance	500-600 meters	1,500-2,000 meters	5-15 kilometers	20 kilometers
Mode of travel	Walking	Walking	Motorized	Motorized (public)
Administration, Commerce, and Stores	--	Administration and accounting office Cooperative shops and stores	Administration and accounting center Regional committee Post office Bank branches Irrigation district office Transportation office Technical office Experimental farm and agricultural extension Stores (apparel and domestic appliances) Cafeteria Artisan shops Handling, sorting, and storage of agricultural products	
Education and culture	Kindergarten Playgrounds Village green (Future development: Communal club)	Primary school (with library, multiple-use rooms, meeting hall) Cultural club Church	Secondary school (agricultural or technical) with multiple-use rooms Sportgrounds and swimming pool	
Health	--	First aid station Maternity guidance center (one nurse)	Medical post (physicians and dentist) Pharmacy	Hospital
Mechanical center	--	Agricultural machinery park Maintenance facilities Spare parts stores	Central workshops: mechanical, carpentry, electrical, gasoline station, tractor station and farm machinery park (2-3 ha)	
Industry	--	--	Processing of agricultural produce	Industry

SOURCE: Azua Valley Regional Plan, Dominican Agrarian Institute, Santo Domingo, 1971.

dense rural population already living in the region. Some lower-range services have evolved over time in the traditional villages and have also been planned and built into the new multiunit settlement, but the middle-range services of the subregional center constitute a new element which must be created from scratch and adequately located. Three alternative proposals for the location of the subregional center were considered by the Agrarian Institute planners (Figure 6.7). One proposal suggested a central location in the El Sisal settlement area and in the geographical center of the region. Another suggestion proposed locating the subregional center at the road junction leading from Puerto Viejo to Azua. A third alternative envisaged the location near the southern fringe of the settlement area adjoining Puerto Viejo, which already possessed important facilities such as storage sheds from the old Sisal plant as well as the shipping dock which could be used to export farm produce.

There are locational advantages and disadvantages to each of these proposals. Attaching the subregional center to the new El Sisal settlement (Figure 6.7, location 1) would enable the gradual expansion of existing facilities and attract further services because of the large concentration of family farms. Such a location, however, would assign excessive weight to one single settlement in the area and, furthermore, might produce undesirable traffic from the populated flanks--part of which would move through the cultivated fields and across a topography interrupted by irrigation and drainage channels. While the initial development would be a welcome addition to the El Sisal settlement, it would increase the disparity between the new and the older villages. It might also interfere with the subregional center's normal function as an agricultural village and lead to congestion and uncontrolled urbanization.

The location at the road junction to Azua (Figure 6.7, location 2) in the demographic center of the region would not interfere with the agricultural areas of the El Sisal settlement but, on the other hand, would serve only a part of the scattered population and require additional infrastructure. Such new development is questionable especially in a depressed area which would invite uncontrolled urban sprawl. This location would also discriminate against the population on the western side of the valley, remote (10-15 km) from these facilities.

The Puerto Viejo location (Figure 6.7, location 3) appears to be more equidistant in terms of road access from the new settlement area and the existing villages in the valley. Although close to the old port, it remains within the southern limits of the project area, outside the municipal jurisdiction of Puerto Viejo. It enables the utilization of abandoned buildings and sheds from the former Sisal plant for storage, processing, and packing for export by sea as well as for land transportation via

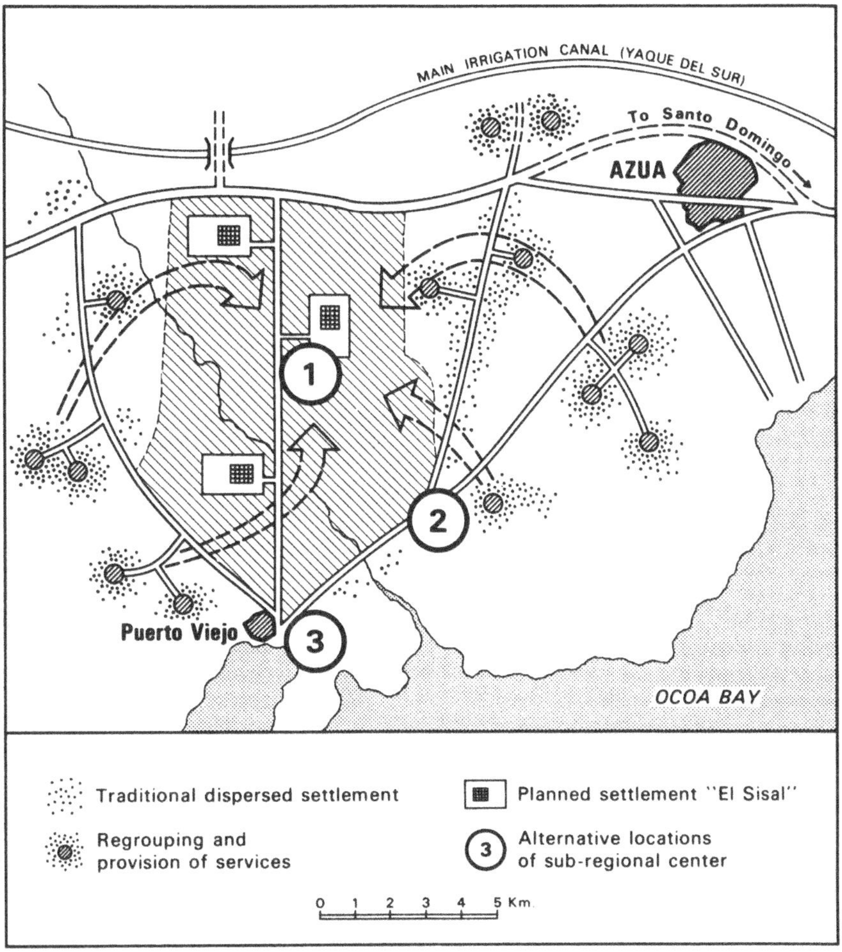

Figure 6.7 Schematic map of the Azua Valley, showing alternative locations of subregional service center in El Sisal settlement area. (Redrawn from: Instituto Agrario Dominicano, "Plan Regional del Valle de Azua No. 1.")

Azua. Two factors allow for the increase in distance to the subregional service center near Puerto Viejo: first, the El Sisal settlements are already endowed with a fully equipped "B" center; second, the increased economic activities and clientele served by the more central and accessible location near Puerto Viejo should lead to the development of better facilities which, in turn, will justify longer distances. The proximity of the subregional center to the town may have a revitalizing effect on this locality in terms of infrastructure and employment--a mutual advantage. These facilities, as well as the urban development, might also benefit the depressed fishing and other rural villages in the western part of the valley.

The broader socioeconomic development of the whole Azua valley undoubtedly entails partial concentration and resettlement of the dispersed population into villages provided with better services, the development of new lands through irrigation, and the incorporation of government plantations. A further intensification of agriculture in the area can be expected with the building of the Yaque del Sur irrigation scheme.

MEXICO

Mexico carried out one of the best-known land reforms after the revolution of 1910. Since then, the country has accumulated long experience in collective farming, and in recent years has engaged in multiple large-scale land settlement. A review of this experience should be of interest when studying current trends toward collective and other associative forms of settlement in Latin America. Examining a settlement model that has evolved through successively improving patterns would be of specific interest.

The main achievement of the agrarian reform in Mexico was in changing the pattern of land tenure. Nevertheless, concentration of land ownership in a few hands has not yet disappeared and there is still large disparity in incomes. By 1950, 0.25 percent of landowners in Mexico still held 40.0 percent of the entire land area under cultivation. Nearly twenty million rural populace were estimated to be outside the market cycle. The lag in development of human and institutional infrastructures may be among the reasons the reform did not achieve its main objectives. The Banco Ejidal, for example, serves only 10 to 15 percent of small farmers who are still exposed to middlemen, merchants, and moneylenders.

The establishment of the collective ejido movement was a logical step toward the creation of human and institutional frameworks which would enable the rationalization of the kind of agriculture practiced by the small landholder. The first cooperative ejidos--a collective village association which owned all the land of the village and engaged in all farming-related activities--were established in the 1930s when about 800 collectives out of 20,000 ejidal settlements were instituted. The number of cooperative ejidos has now fallen to between 400 and 500 and many have lost their collective characteristics. Some of these ejidos were successful in increasing production but collapsed because of intolerable internal friction, while others showed poor economic results yet survived because friction was less acute. The success or failure of the ejidos has been aptly described as a function of two conflicting elements: the economic advantage of scale against the social disadvantage of friction.[18]

Wilkie studied a collective ejido, San Miguel, in the Laguna region.[19] The ejido, established in 1936 for a group of 150 members with four hectares per ejidatario, has since grown into a population of 1,200. An increased disparity in income and living standards between the select charter group and the rest of the inhabitants has occurred, and a clear trend of decollectivization and individualization in important aspects of the economy, including property rights and working methods, was observed. Few opportunities exist for the bulk of the population to fit into the economic structure, nor is there work outside the community to accommodate the growing labor force. Social difficulties can often be attributed to spatial factors, as exemplified by land distribution in the Laguna region. This distribution fragmented farming units into an intricate mosaic of holdings, since land was usually divided among claimants on an equitable basis instead of assigning potential peasants to spatially and economically well-defined units of production.[20] The disintegration of the ejido has also been attributed to lack of political and institutional support and the consequent weakening of the regional organization.

One of the factors that impeded rational development of both the collective and the small landholders' ejido was incompatibility between the spatial organization and the existant phase of farming. The lack of a farmyard area in the traditional village, whose occupants were previously engaged on the hacienda, was a serious drawback. In the typical old village few farmyard activities were undertaken since most of the village area was filled with dwellings. The nonexistence of a farmyard area, which proved an obstacle in attempts to diversify employment on the family farm, became a frequent planning mistake in new settlements. Farmsteads were sometimes planned too closely together and too small in area for auxiliary structures. The overriding concern was to establish large villages in order to maximize service efficiency. Today this layout seriously hampers the transition to mixed farming as farmyards are too small and distances to the fields are too long for keeping livestock. Many farmers who wish to raise livestock or to intensively cultivate their land move out of the village and establish new farmsteads on their plots. The dissemination of farming skills and techniques, so vital during these transition phases, is hindered by this trend to disperse.

The La Chontalpa project is typical of many irrigation-settlement schemes in the country. The project, situated on the coastal plains of Tabasco in southeastern Mexico, was started in 1966 as part of a multipurpose river basin development by the Grijalva Commission, a semi-autonomous agency under the jurisdiction of the Secretaria de Recursos Hidraulicos. It included the damming of the Grijalva River with a reservoir of 39,000 square kilometers and a storage capacity of thirteen million cubic meters, installation of a 360,000 kilowatt hydroelectric plant, and flood control for the agricultural development of 270,000 hectares of land. A prior pilot project, El Limon, was begun in 1958 and involved draining and irrigating 72,000 hectares to be allotted for intensive farming to 6,200 families, part of which were already living in the area. This project was later expanded and renamed La Chontalpa, and in its final form will include 4,800 farm families.[21]

La Chontalpa's initial land allocation of ten hectares arable plus two hectares communal pasture was later increased by another three hectares in pasture or plantations which were to be run as corporate enterprises.[22] The physical plan represents a rectangular block pattern of about twenty new settlements which include families relocated from several old ejidos in the area. Each village consists of two neighborhood units with a total of about 270 farm families, plus housing for personnel engaged in administration and services (Figure 6.8). Farmsteads each occupy an area of 900 square meters and can be divided into two parts for a second house. Altogether the village contains a population of some 2,000 inhabitants, a number which can be doubled with the development of the village's expansion area and the subdivision of farmyards (leaving an area of 450 square meters per family). Family holdings total ten hectares, resulting in maximum distances of four to five kilometers to the fields. An additional allotment of five hectares per family is contained in a communal plot.

The administration of the Chontalpa project organized a self-aid building program which increased the involvement of the new settlers in the project and also offset to some extent the high costs of housing. Settlers were also attracted by eventual benefits in improved amenities, easier to find in big urban agglomerations. Nevertheless, the reduced size of the farmyard and the urban character of the new villages indicate that the dual function of the farmstead as dwelling and working place has not been sufficiently recognized. The settlement is neither a collective nor administrated farm--forms which may have justified the separation of dwelling and production functions--nor is it in the advanced stage of specialized farming which could fit certain urban patterns. On the contrary, the majority of the relocated ejidatarios from the project

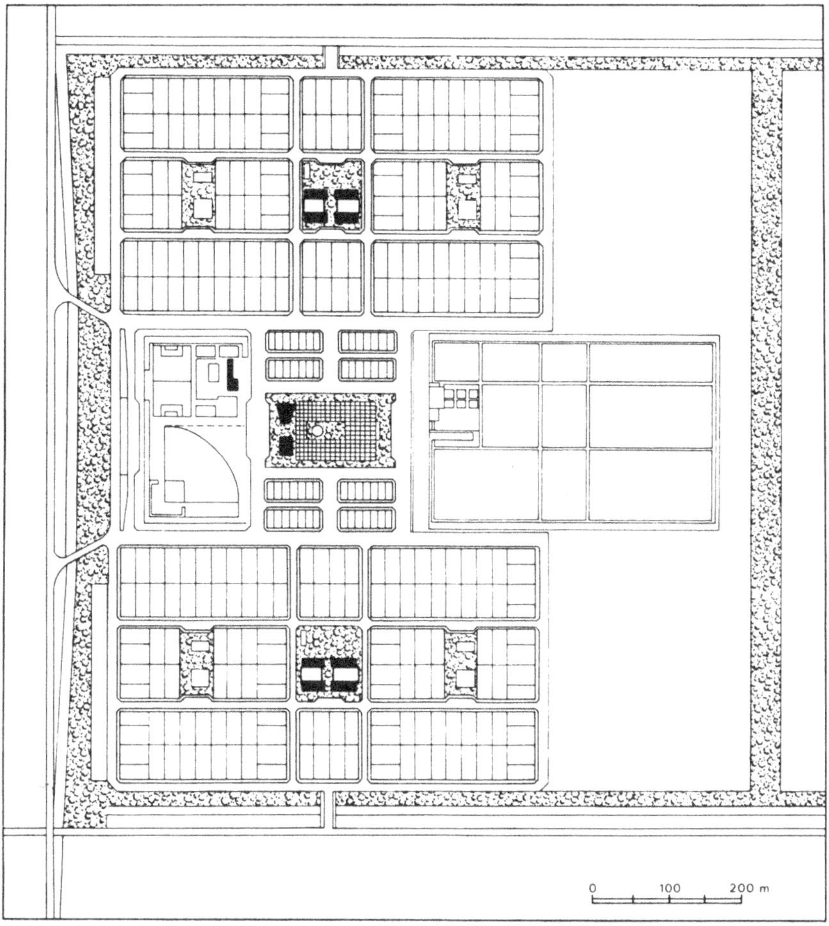

Figure 6.8 Typical layout of settlement in the Chontalpa Project. The village is formed by two neighborhoods flanking a joint service center. Each neighborhood consists of 136 family farms on plots of 900 square meters each, which can further be subdivided in two. (Redrawn from: Proyecto Piloto el Limón.)

area, as well as the settlers brought in from elsewhere, originated from a typical peasant environment. There are no indications that industrial or any other economic development will take place in the immediate vicinity, and most of the hydropower generated by the Malpaso Dam is likely to be used outside the region.[23]

Several aspects about the spatial organization of the Chontalpa project can be pointed out at this stage. First, the diminutive size of the farmyard, and its further reduction into two residential plots, preempts an indispensable phase in the transformation from subsistence to mixed farming and impedes the full utilization of the family's labor and initiative. Second, the growth of a salaried labor force and a nonfarming population in the villages may lead to conflicts of interest, inequity in incomes, and the individualization of important economic issues. Third, the excessive size of the village invites future difficulties in the settling operation and the management of the community as an efficient production unit.

In economic terms the feasibility of such capital-intensive projects is still ambiguous. Even their regional impact remains controversial. But, aside from its unique economic traits, the project testifies to the vital role of the human factor in the success of land settlement. The experience in the ejidal movement and other rural settlement in Mexico indicates that economic and social efficiency are interdependent and must be dealt with in an integrated manner. In the Chontalpa project a premature urban approach was used for the planning of the agricultural villages. While the project management has been expedient in construction and settling activities it has also taken a paternalistic stance toward the settlers. These circumstances, taken together with the problematic physical layout of the villages and the growth of a heterogeneous social structure, may forestall human and institutional development, crucial prerequisites for diversifying and deepening the settlers' economy and, in the long run, for providing new sources of employment.

PERU

Like several other Andean countries, Peru has a long history of colonization and land settlement and has been particularly active in promoting new land development. Since 1958 the government has undertaken a series of resource surveys designed to lay the foundations for development and settlement of economically viable new lands, both in the tropical Andean piedmont and the coastal arid but fertile desert. The three projects chosen here as case studies demonstrate past experience, current problems, and planning for the future. A precise comparative study is difficult since both the spatial and sociopolitical environment is different in each case.

San Lorenzo, the first case study, represents an early attempt at wide-scale settlement within agrarian reform measures which set a new pattern by allotting land to relatively small family farms and by granting credits and technical assistance to small landholders. The project, however, had to overcome the opposition of big landowners and, furthermore, as an irrigation scheme it posed special problems in the planning of infrastructure and the deployment of farmsteads. The second project, Tingo Maria-Tocache-Campanilla, is a tropical land development now under way and is bound up with the Marginal Forest Highway (Carretera Marginal de la Selva). The third project, in the Central Huallaga, is also a tropical land development comprising irrigated and nonirrigated farming, now in the planning stage. There are a number of common elements in these projects since all are based on family farming and all have basically the same spatial problems, making it worthwhile to examine them in detail.

The San Lorenzo Project

The project situated in the Peruvian northern coast near Piura, envisaged the irrigation of 50,000 hectares of quasi-desertic lands by diverting the waters of the Quiroz River toward the elevated plain lying between the Piura and Chira Rivers. Actual settlement began in 1963, several years after completion of the irrigation infrastructure. Altogether, about 30,000 hectares, or 24,000 hectares net of irrigated land, and some 1,300 settlers were incorporated into the project. The landowners, from whom part of the land was expropriated, were given the option to preferentially purchase irrigated land up to a maximum acreage, whereupon the remaining parcels were offered to the inhabitants of the area. This action resulted in an heterogeneous social structure of former landowners and small landholders in an array of farm sizes varying from six to sixty hectares.

The irrigation district was divided into seven sectors, each with its own service center and facilities including schools, offices for irrigation control, technical assistance, medical posts, and social assistance services. Two towns situated on the periphery of the irrigation area, Tambogrande and Las Lomas, with populations of 12,000 and 3,300 respectively (in 1968), were directly affected by the development activities; however, with termination of the construction works the towns relapsed into stagnation. There has been little social or economic integration with the settlement, even though employees of the project live in Tambogrande and some services such as schools and health centers are shared with the farmers.

The fact that small landholders could have been incorporated into a project of this kind at all is in itself a remarkable feat, considering the sociopolitical situation prevailing at the initiation of the project.[24] However, from the vantage point of hindsight one is reminded that the capacity of the project to absorb farming families could have been tripled with a more equitable land allotment of six to eight hectares per family. Although the benefits of the development project could not be expected to spread indefinitely, such redistribution would have solved more problems of the region's landless and unemployed, difficulties which are reflected in the violent contrast in living conditions between the population of the project and those who have remained in its periphery. In addition, a social problem was created by the system of selection and preferential sales used in the project. While such strategy may be sound from a purely economic point of view, by facilitating the recovery of investments, it may bring back the same conditions that called for a costly reform in the first place.

This distribution problem is clearly illustrated in the San Lorenzo project, where over half of the irrigated area is contained in relatively large farms of twenty hectares and more (see Table 6.2). The amorphous structure of the farming population is evident in the social and economic disparities--a situation which is aggravated by the dispersed pattern of settlement and the isolation of houses located on parcels. The dispersal made it necessary to deploy service centers in each sector within six kilometers or two hours walking distance from each farmer's house. The larger landholders, however, were able to live in the towns and employ day laborers, thus creating a system of small haciendas.[25] The long distances to services and a clientele of a lower economic status thereby reduced the efficiency and growth of services in the rural area.

The dispersed pattern of settlement and inequitable land ownership are evidently among the major obstacles to broader cooperation and amenability. These factors may have hampered the project management's efforts to diversify the farming economy by introducing crops other than cotton--a monoculture which may expose the smaller farms to unexpected risks. Another result of the socially stratified and spatially dispersed pattern is the difficulty in organizing viable communities which may assume the control and management of irrigation, organization of production, administration of credits, and marketing. Although the project has generated considerable expertise during its existence, much of this capability has remained immobile due to the chronic paternalism exercised by the authorities. Ultimately the solution to the problem of the landless and underemployed in the region may depend on another agrarian reform that will achieve a better distribution of wealth and generate a greater variety of economic opportunities.[26] While further reforms may be necessary to remedy the social and economic retardation of the region's population, it must be clear that in order to obviate the need for further "reforms of the reform," the

TABLE 6.2
Number of colonists and area according to size of lot, San Lorenzo Project, as of 1 May 1968

Size of Lot in Hectares	Irrigated Area in Hectares	Number of Parcels
Up to 8	3,087.3	458
8-13	2,398.1	211
13-20	4,337.3	266
20-40	5,390.5	193
40-60	3,695.2	74
More than 60	2,081.5	30
TOTAL	20,989.9	1,232

SOURCE: C. L. Dozier, Land Development and Colonization in Latin America: Case Studies of Peru, Bolivia, and Mexico (Praeger, 1969).

fundamental weakness of this initial project must be overcome. This experience suggests that spatial and social factors, such as dispersion or a heterogeneous social structure, may impede the formation of viable communities.

The shortcomings of the San Lorenzo project have been corrected in other land settlement programs based on irrigation, such as La Joya in Arequipa, La Yarada in Tacna, and others. The high costs of the San Lorenzo project may be justified in part by its value as a pilot project. Its problems seem to point to the need for shifting emphasis from the physical to the human and institutional infrastructure. This implies a gradual transfer of leadership and administrative functions to the settlers, and the promotion of local and regional initiative so that settlers may assume full responsibility as the settlement agency phases out its professionals in order to tackle new assignments.

The Tingo Maria-Tocache-Campanilla Project

The project area stretches along the Huallaga River for about 200 kilometers, following the Marginal Forest Highway which has become the focus for many government-sponsored settlement activities. The construction of the Huanuco-Pucallpa Highway during 1931-1940 gave impetus to various spontaneous, foreign, and privately organized settlements. In 1938 a law was passed reserving a 10-20 kilometer strip of land on either side of this highway (about 800,000 hectares) for settlement. Estimated requirements for land in the tropical regions of the country by 1990 have reached 1.7 million hectares.[27] Consequently, these areas have received renewed attention.

A study of natural resources including about 290,000 hectares was conducted from 1961-1962 and identified some 96,000 hectares suitable for agriculture. Of these, 10,500 hectares were already cultivated, supporting a rural population of 19,000. It was estimated that there were about 4,800 colonists in the project area, 1,220 with firm titles, 1,410 with applications pending on fiscal lands, and 2,150 without rights. The study also indicated that full development of the area over twenty years (1962-1981) would result in a rural population of 118,000, including local population growth and more than 10,000 immigrant families. On the basis of this study a twenty-year plan was prepared which, in its final form, was to rationalize the tenure and resettlement of 2,150 existing subsistence settlers onto 30,000 hectares. A further 55,000 hectares of new land was to be opened for the settlement of 3,000 colonists forthcoming from the highlands and other overpopulated areas.

By 1970 about 2,000 families had already been resettled or reorganized within the framework of the project which followed the construction of the Marginal Forest Highway to the north of Tingo Maria. The physical plan was basically a dispersed settlement. The bulk of families already settled along the Marginal Highway were to be incorporated into the project. New holdings were parcelled out along feeder roads in a Waldhufendorf-type pattern which penetrated the cultivable pieces of land on the two margins of the Huallaga River. The consecutive developmental phases of the project are schematically described in Figure 6.9.

The 10-15 hectare land allotment per family was divided into one main parcel of 10 hectares, with the rest contained in a communal plot. Since the experience of previous schemes had raised serious doubts regarding the efficiency of scattered settlement, an attempt was made to concentrate the population in so-called Urban Units (<u>núcleos urbanos</u>), each planned for eighty to a hundred families and located on small plots of approximately 400 square meters. The Urban Unit (comparable to an "A" service center) was to include a school with one or two classrooms and some utilities. A further number of Basic Service Units (<u>unidades básicas</u>) was planned along the highway to serve both the settlers in the Urban Units and those dispersed in the project area. These centers, comparable to the "B" service centers, included offices and dwellings for the extension workers, a store for production inputs, a school with two classrooms, a medical post, and a small water supply system. Most of these centers were to be inhabited only by the personnel directly employed therein. The Basic Service Units were spaced twenty to thirty kilometers apart, but these rather long distances made it necessary to distribute a school every six

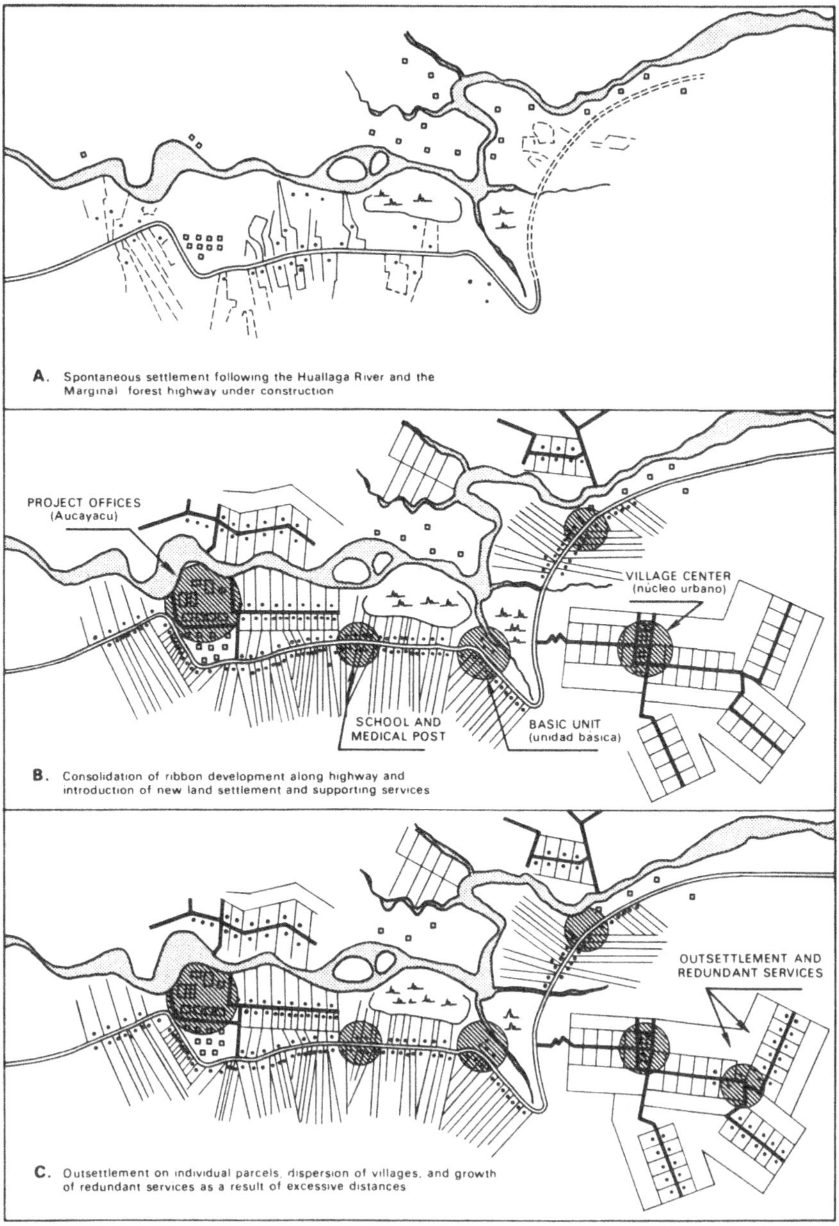

Figure 6.9 Schematic plan of the Tingo Maria-Tocache Project, showing changes in settlement patterns and distribution of services.

to seven kilometers at more or less regular intervals, and a medical post combined with a primary school every fifteen kilometers. The administrative center of the project, situated near the village of Aucayacu about fifty kilometers north of Tingo Maria, has practically become a subregional "C" center and contains, besides the project offices, various installations belonging to the cooperatives organized in the area. When highway construction progresses beyond Puerto Pisana (where it will connect with the northern section of the Marginal Highway in the Central Huallaga Valley) the establishment of a second administrative center may be contemplated for the vicinity of Tocache, 120 kilometers further north of Aucayacu. This will become another "C" center with a higher range of services.

The linear development of the project has posed special problems for the introduction of services. In the settlements developed along the feeder roads, the Urban Units were sited so that distances to parcels would remain within 2.5 to 3.0 kilometers (except for parcels of extensive pasture that could be located at a distance of 10.0 km and more). However, the Urban Units offered only a minimal residential lot of 400 square meters and many settlers preferred to build their houses on their individual parcels since growing subsistence crops and raising animals outweighed the advantages of the few services offered in the Urban Units. The settlers thus began dispersing to their individual parcels, making contact exceedingly difficult to establish. Although the project has been relatively saturated with extension officers and social workers, several programmed activities, such as supervised credits or planting commercial crops, were severely hampered or could not be initiated at all. The conflict between distances to parcels versus distances to services results in the inevitable appearance of unplanned, redundant services for very few families at intermediate points along the feeder roads (see Figure 6.9C).

From the viewpoints of internal organization, project management, and further developmental activities, the bulkiness of the project produced serious difficulties which in part could be directly attributed to the shortcomings of its physical plan. The project was consequently restructured in 1970, especially formulated to change settlement patterns by forming larger concentrated villages with sufficient capacities to support adequate services. The new villages were also provided with farmyards to counteract the rampant outsettlement tendencies. Plans were prepared for new settlement groups, several of which were organized as production cooperatives. This social pattern made it possible to concentrate on the village infrastructure rather than on costly access roads to remote forest plots. Although the production cooperatives proved more efficient in forest clearing operations and farming, the nuclear villages were planned with farmsteads of 0.8-1.0

hectares to enable utilization of the family's working potential. A survey in the Tingo Maria area and other projects showed that while most settlers considered production cooperatives appropriate for the initial period of colonization and development, many thought of it as only a transitional form which would later revert to a cooperative village of individually owned farms.[28]

The Central Huallaga Project (Proyecto Integral de Reordenamiento y Asentamiento Rural del Huallaga Central, Ministry of Agriculture, Tarapoto, Peru, September 1971)

This is one of several specific projects[29] dealing with rural settlement and spatial organization in the Huallaga River Basin. It is based on one of the most elaborate and integrated resource surveys undertaken in the humid tropics of Latin America--a seven-year FAO/UNDP program which covered an area of 33,600 square kilometers in the Peruvian northeastern tropical forest.[30] The project area is a continuation of the Tingo Maria-Tocache development project (see preceding case study) which occupies the upper part of the Huallaga River, extending along the central part of the Huallaga basin between the Huayabamba River near the township of Juanjui and the lower Mayo River. The biggest town in this region is Tarapoto which is connected to the Atlantic by the Amazon River passing through the river port of Yurimaguas some 100 kilometers away. The economic integration of the region will be further aided by the completion and upgrading of the Marginal Highway which will improve connections with Lima by way of Tingo Maria and with the northern coast by way of Chiclayo.[31]

The original survey indicated that the region could potentially support 10,000 new settlers; however, further studies suggested that, at an average of fourteen hectares per family, little land would be available for new settlement since the best lands had already been identified and occupied. While controversy rages over the size of holdings per family and the optimal intensity of land use in tropical soils, many tropical regions have undisputably depressed human living conditions, a situation which often calls for costly relief programs. Tarapoto itself has experienced several invasions of squatters revealing the same symptoms that have caused the rural exodus from the Sierra regions.

Recent studies tend to confirm that more intensive exploitation of tropical lands is feasible for the economic and social development of the region.[32] The objectives of the project have accordingly been constructed to: (1) rationalize the existing land tenancy and land use; (2) achieve the organized participation of the campesino in the regional economy; (3) increase productivity and production of essential commodities for the national market;

(4) ensure the adequate exploitation and conservation of natural resources; and (5) provide the farmers with essential infrastructure. Within this framework the project intends to: (1) consolidate the settlement of 19,350 campesino families (16,120 in farming and 3,230 in services), 65 percent of which are already living in the region mostly as squatters; (2) incorporate 223,200 hectares of land for arable and livestock farming; and (3) raise the living standards of approximately 96,800 inhabitants. The town people, about 50 percent of the total population in the region, are expected to benefit indirectly from the project. The project encompasses three distinct phases: a short-term phase of two years for resettlement; a second medium-term settlement phase of three years; and a third long-term phase covering fifteen years of reorganization and settlement.

Three types of land allotment are contemplated in the project: cooperative, individual, and a combination of the two. All allotments are based on a family unit, with the size of holdings designed to yield equal returns in each particular project area and to enable the optimal exploitation of land under given agroecological conditions. This principle resulted in the following farm sizes:

1. Arable unit under irrigation = 3.5 ha for intensive cultivation plus 1.0 ha of reserve area;
2. Nonirrigated arable unit = 7.0 ha for extensive cultivation plus 1.0 ha of reserve area;
3. Pasture unit = 40 ha for extensive grazing plus 2.0 ha of reserve area.

A concentrated settlement pattern was chosen for all types of arable farming in order to minimize distances between houses and to keep distances to the fields within reasonable limits.

The diverse planning elements are defined as follows:

1. The family farmstead, described as the basic spatial unit and comprising the dwelling, a small garden area for kitchen crops (panllevar) and fruit trees, maneuvering and parking space for medium-sized vehicles (pick-up truck, wheeled tractor, farm implements), workshop, storage structures, livestock and poultry sheds, and expansion area for the dwelling or for another house for a family member. An area of 0.4 to 1.0 hectare is considered adequate for these purposes.
2. Village or rural community, an agglomeration of 80 to 120 family farms clustered about a village green of 1.5 to 2.0 hectares, within a maximum distance of 500 meters from the houses.
3. Village center, a center for basic noncommercial services designed to draw together the neighbors and to stimulate social interaction. It includes

a kindergarten, meeting hall, sportsyard, and playground.

4. Village group, a group of two, three, or four communities comprising 200 to 300 families and their respective production areas, within an approximate range of three to five kilometers.
5. Common center, destined for the daily communal services related to production, culture, health, security, commerce, and technical assistance. When the center is part of a multinuclear village distances to the farmers' houses will usually be within 600 to 1,600 meters. When catering to a group of small single villages the radius of action is about five kilometers.
6. Subregional service center, a complex providing specialized services of production as needed by the farming area to which it is assigned. The radius of action is eight to twelve kilometers.
7. Regional service center, the grouping of facilities, installations for storage and handling of produce, transportation and communication services, and premises for technical and administrative staff. Some of the existing townships were found adequate for providing these functions (e.g. Juanjui, Saposoa, Bellavista). Their radius of action is estimated to be ten to twenty-five kilometers.
8. The main urban center, the town of Tarapoto has the characteristics of a developmental pole, and the necessary facilities, infrastructure, and interregional connections (highway, airport, and waterway) to serve as a center for such higher-range services.

The criteria for the establishment of services are detailed in the project as follows:

1. Location--radius of action, interconnection, and availability of facilities or feasibility of their installation.
2. Capacity of services--number of families served and production area served.
3. Residential conditions--preferably nonresidential, except for watchmen. When existing settlements or townships must be used, special regulations will be prepared to prevent uncontrolled development.[33]

A schematic description of the planned rural structure, including settlement population capacity and distances between settlements, is shown in Figures 6.10 and 6.11. The hierarchy of services, in ascending order, exists as follows:

1. Rural community of 80-100 families with its village center for basic services (equivalent to the

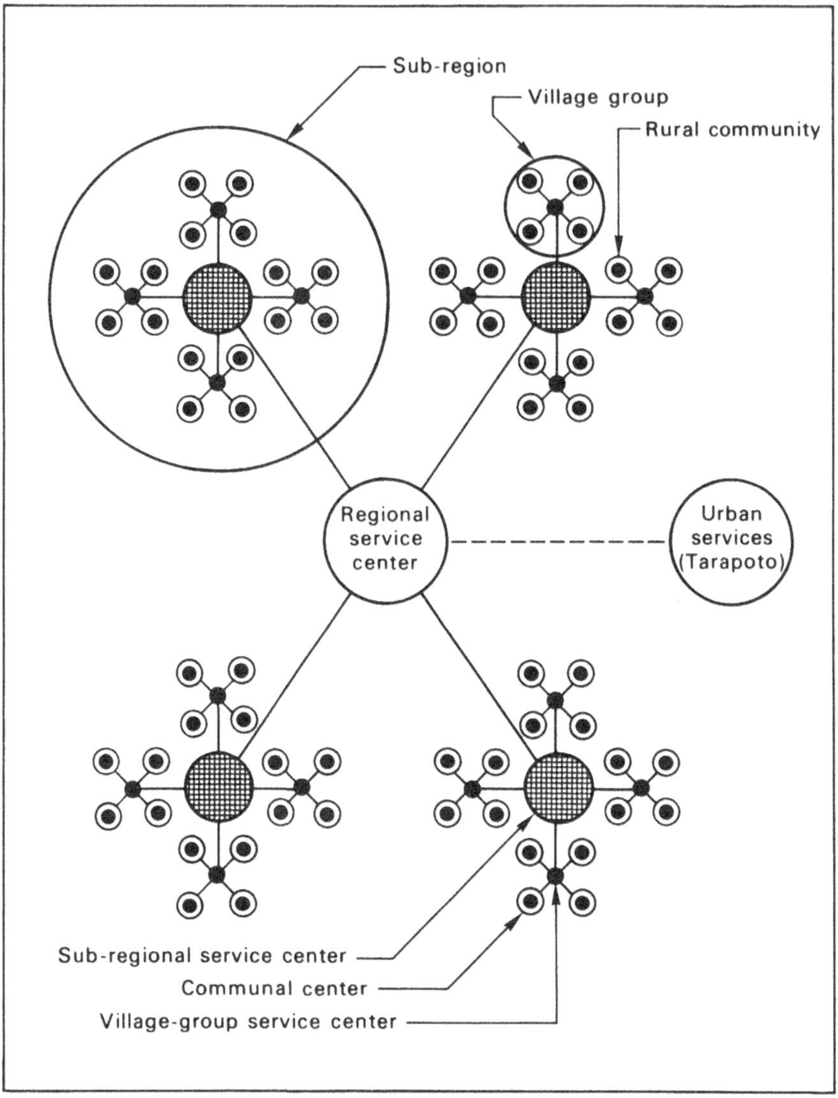

Figure 6.10 Structure of settlements and service centers in the Central Huallaga Land Settlement Project. (Source: Proyecto Integral de Reordenamiento y Asentamiento Rural del Huallaga Central.)

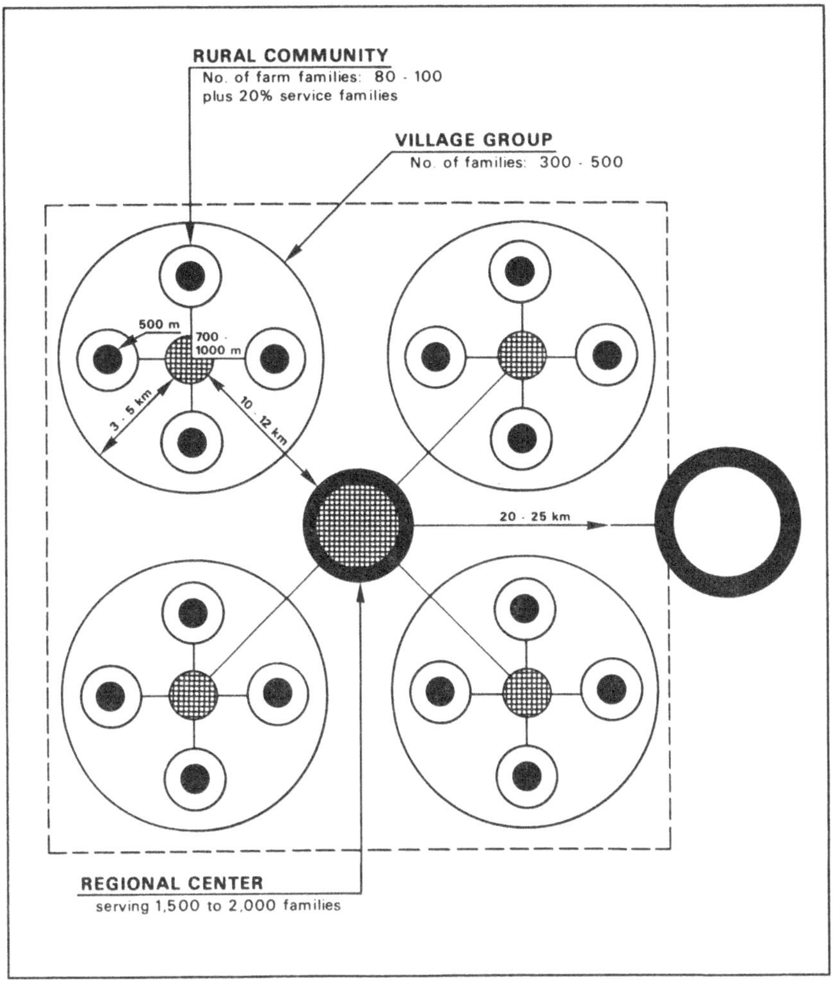

Figure 6.11 Scheme of distances and settlement capacity in the Central Huallaga Project. (Source: Proyecto Integral de Reordenamiento y Asentamiento Rural del Huallaga Central.)

"A" center, as categorized in Chapter 7). Several such communities compose a rural settlement.

2. Rural settlement (núcleo rural or centro poblado), either a multiunit settlement with a common service center (equivalent to the "B" center) or a group of single villages surrounding such a center and within a radius of five kilometers. Several of these settlements are served by a subregional center.
3. Subregional center (centro subregional, equivalent to center "C"), for specialized production services as needed by the predominant farming types, as well as administrative, commercial, educational, and health services. A number of such subregions relate to a regional service center.
4. Regional service center (centro regional de servicios), or "D" center, for storage, handling, and processing agricultural produce.

Urban facilities are provided by the town of Tarapoto, categorized as a higher center due to its geographical location, existing facilities (airport, hospital, vocational schools, commerce and banking, ministerial offices), and other infrastructure.

The spatial organization of settlements in the project area and their integration with existing villages and towns is illustrated in Figure 8.12. It is interesting to note that the structure preserves a high degree of independence by retaining most facilities in the settlement area. Only at the regional level is the location of the "D" centers identical with existing towns that can serve as bases for the development of higher-level facilities. But even at this level there seems to have been concern about the eventual "urbanizing" effect of the service center, a danger which the plan attempts to stave off by recommending special land-use regulations.[34] The same urbanizing effect has presumably prompted the planners to underscore the principle of the "nonresidential service center." Experience from previous projects indicates that squatters attracted by construction and public works can be detrimental to future community development (e.g. San Lorenzo) by flooding a family-sized economy with cheap labor. The influx of squatters may generate a process of socioeconomic stratification, countering thereby the efforts toward rationalization and cooperative enterprises and undermining the success of the project.

AN APPRAISAL OF SETTLEMENT MODELS

Despite the differences between settlements described in this study, it is possible to point out certain common denominators in distances to fields and services, as summarized in Table 6.3. Two categories of settlement are

TABLE 6.3
Summary of spatial factors in agglomerated smallholders' settlement projects

	Built or Planned	Number of Family Farms	Farmstead Area (ha)	Total Land Allotment (ha)	Max. Distance to Center A (meters)	Max. Distance to Parcel (meters)
SINGLE-UNIT VILLAGES						
Majaguas (Venezuela)	1963	60-100	0.20	10.00	500	3,000
Boconó 1 "	1964	160	0.20	10.00	750	3,500
Boconó 2 "	1965	178	0.20	10.00	750	4,000
Boconó 3 "	1967	152	0.20	10.00	750	4,000
Badajoz (Spain)	1968	186	0.06[a]	4-5.00	600	3,500
Boconó 4 (Venezuela)	1968	215	0.20	10.00	1,000	5,000
La Joya (Peru)	1968	100	1.25	8.25	1,300	2,500[d]
MULTIUNIT VILLAGES					Max. Distance to Center B	
Maagalim (Israel)	1951	240	1.00	4.00	1,800	--[e]
Behora (Israel)	1952	180	1.40	4.00	1,500	--[e]
Yael (Israel)	1953	180	1.20	4.50	1,400-1,700	--[e]
Omen (Israel)	1956	183	0.90	4.50	1,150	--[e]
Borgo Perrone (Italy)	1958	141	0.80	5.00	1,000	4,200
Chontalpa (Mexico)	1966	272	0.09[a]	15.00[b]	700	--[e]
Cojedes (Venezuela)	1967	231	0.40	10-15.00[c]	1,300	--[e]
Central Huallaga (Peru)	1972	500	0.40	4.50	1,600	--[e]
El Multinacional (Ven.)		214	0.06[a]	10-15.00[c]	500	6,000[e]
Modulo I (Venezuela)	1973	537	0.04[a]	10.00	550	13,000[f]

[a]"Minuscule" farmyard.

[b]10 ha field plus 5 ha in communal parcel.

[c]3-5 ha irrigated parcel and 7-10 ha "dry" parcel.

[d]Approaching a two-field system.

[e]Distances balanced through multi-field system.

[f]Production cooperative based on mechanized transportation to fields.

listed in chronological order: single-unit villages in which the settlement is situated in the midst of its agricultural lands (e.g. Majaguas, Figure 6.2), and multiunit villages in which several village neighborhoods are grouped around a common service center (e.g. Cojedes, Figure 8.8).

In the single-unit villages the main design criterion appears to be limiting distances to parcels (usually 3.0 to 3.5 km), thus limiting the total number of farm families in the village.[35] The general trend in the projects listed here was to increase the number of farm families in the village, resulting in longer distances to the fields. Most of the single-unit villages are relatively compact with small farmyards, and all have a one-field system, except for La Joya which has a big homeplot of 1.25 hectares apart from the main parcel of 7.0 hectares.[36] Because of the long distances to higher-range services (usually over five km), the single-unit village must provide essential facilities (e.g. school, shops, health, social, and administrative services) for a relatively small population which is unable to support such services efficiently. In other words, the "A" center assumes higher-range functions --a redundancy which, in turn, weakens the services of the "B" center by depriving it of a larger clientele.

Another noticeable trend in these settlement projects is the diminution of the farmstead, both in the single-unit and the multivillage settlement. In Israel, for example, cooperative Moshavim were established initially with family farmsteads and adjoining homeplots of ten hectares (e.g. Nahalal, or Kfar-Jehoshua, 1920-1924), a size which was gradually reduced in consecutive plans to 0.9 hectares and less (e.g. Omen, or Ramon, 1956-1964). Attempts to maximize the efficiency of services and to minimize infrastructure costs have led in some cases to minuscule farmyards, stripping the area of its usefulness (e.g. Badajoz, Spain, or El Multinacional, Venezuela). In villages with individual holdings this small size has created a bottleneck which may undo the socioeconomic goals of such projects through outsettlement and social disintegration. Villages with nonparcelled agricultural lands still retain the option to either replace family initiative by farmyard activities on a communal scale or to designate special plots outside the built-up area of the village for family enterprises.

The case studies described in Table 6.3 confirm the trends toward:

1. Concentration of population--through the planning of bigger villages, leading to improved amenities; and,
2. Increased flexibility--by multiblock parcellation, by allotting part of the land in communal plots, and through production cooperatives. These measures may lead to the pooling of resources and to centrally managed operations, enabling the

introduction of rational and modern farming methods.

For the future, the production cooperative seems to offer more planning flexibility. However, the related problems of human and social organization have not yet been satisfactorily resolved and may offset the advantages of collective production. More crucial than these social problems is the transition from subsistence to the more advanced stages of mixed and specialized farming. This is a dual problem of social and agrotechnical transformation. The process depends on a myriad of factors and is necessarily a gradual one. Even in China a transitional period lasting several years was planned during which peasants were to be organized into producers' cooperatives in preparation for ultimate collectivization.[37]

In Peru, as in many other Latin American countries, the family farm is the socioeconomic unit upon which agrarian reform and land settlement are based. Spatial patterns must, accordingly, be adjusted to employ the full potential of family labor. For this purpose an adequate farmyard, adjoining or close to the dwelling, seems to be an indispensable component. The optimal size of such an area fluctuates around 0.5 hectares, depending on local circumstances. As shown in the following models this farmyard size makes it possible to meet most other requisites of concentration and distances to work and services, and in addition, does not foreclose the possibility of converting to more associative forms of production in the future.[38]

NOTES

1. Doreen Warriner, Land Reform in Principle and Practice (Oxford, 1969). See also, P. Cox, Venezuela's Agrarian Reform at Mid-1977, Land Tenure Center Research Paper No. 71, Madison, Wisconsin, 1978; and E. H. Moscovitch, "Urban-Rural Investment Allocation in Venezuela," unpublished Ph.D. dissertation, Massachusetts Institute of Technology, 1966.

2. W. C. Thiesenhusen, "A Venezuelan Agrarian Reform Settlement: Problems and Prospects," in R. D. Stevens (ed.) Tradition and Dynamics in Small-Farm Agriculture (Ames, Iowa, 1977).

3. H. Pedregal and H. M. De Pedregal, Principios Generales para la Planificación Física de Aldeas Agrícolas, Ministry of Health and Social Welfare, Caracas, Venezuela, 1968; and Aldeas Agrícolas en Venezuela, Ministry of Health and Social Welfare, Publication No. 73-03, Caracas, Venezuela, 1973. A review of implemented settlement schemes is given in Robert C. Eidt, "Agrarian Reform and the Growth of New Rural Settlements in Venezuela," Erdkunde, Vol. 29 (1975), pp. 118-133.

4. The introduction of modern inputs and their acceptance by

traditional farmers is treated in Yitzhak Abt, "Types of Agricultural Projects Used in Developing Countries," in R. Weitz (ed.), *Rural Development in a Changing World* (Cambridge, MA, 1971), pp. 391-405.

5. *The Economic Development of Venezuela*, Report of a Mission Organized by the International Bank for Reconstruction and Development, The Johns Hopkins Press, 1961.

6. "Informe Técnico sobre el Desarrollo del Sistema de Riego Boconó--Edo. Barinas," Comisión Especial: MOP, MAC, IAN, BAP, SAS, CIARA, Caracas, Venezuela, October 1967.

7. Michael Nelson, *The Development of Tropical Lands: Policy Issues in Latin America* (Baltimore, 1973).

8. Craig L. Dozier, *Land Development in Latin America; Case Studies of Peru, Bolivia and Mexico* (New York, 1969).

9. Warriner, *Land Reform in Principle*, p. 368.

10. Pedregal and De Pedregal, *Aldeas Agrícolas*, p. 62.

11. John P. Augelli, "Agricultural Colonization in the Dominican Republic," *Economic Geography*, Vol. 38 (1962), pp. 15-27; R. Symanski and N. Burley, "The Jewish Colony of Sosua," *Annals of the Association of American Geographers*, Vol. 63 (1973), pp. 366-378.

12. Peter Dorner, et al., *Agrarian Reform in the Dominican Republic (The view of your consultants)* (Madison, 1967); W. F. Buck, *Agriculture and Trade of the Dominican Republic*, U.S. Department of Agriculture, Washington, D.C., 1972.

13. Instituto Agrario Dominicano, *Proyecto El Sisal*, O.A.S.--Israel--B.I.D., Santo Domingo, 1969.

14. Avi Lahav, *Proyecto El Sisal--Etapa C, República Dominicana: El Sistema de Riego y de Agua Potable, y la Planificación Física* (Jerusalem, 1972); Joseph S. Zalmanov, *El-Sisal Development Project* (Rehovot, 1973); J. Cesar Becerra de la Flor and Shlomo I. Abarbanel, *Proyecto de asentamiento campesino "Alexander Dothan" (El Sisal) Prov. de Azua, República Dominicana*, OAS, Lima, 1974.

15. Santiago de la Fuente García sj, *Geografía Dominicana* (Santo Domingo, 1976), pp. 244-247.

16. Instituto Agrario Dominicano, *Proyecto El Sisal*, O.A.S.--Israel--B.I.D., Santo Domingo, 1969.

17. *Proyecto de Planificación Región Sur República Dominicana*, Fundación David, Publicaciones sobre Desarrollo Rural Integrado, No. 1, Rehovot, 1981.

18. Warriner, *Land Reform in Principle*.

19. Raymond Wilkie, *San Miguel: A Mexican Collective Ejido* (Stanford, 1971).

20. Shlomo Eckstein, "Collective Farming in Mexico," in R. Stavenhagen (ed.), *Agrarian Problems and Peasant Movements in Latin America* (New York, 1970), pp. 271-299.

21. Banco Interamericano de Desarrollo--Secretaría de Recursos Hidráulicos, *Sinopsis del Informe sobre el Proyecto Piloto El Limón* (Mexico, 1963); Angel Basols and Gloria Gonzales, "Acerca de la Colonización en México y del Plan Chontalpa," Instituto de Investigaciones Económicas, Universidad Nacional, 1974.

22. Michael Nelson, *The Development of Tropical Lands: Policy Issues in Latin America* (Baltimore, 1973).

23. D. Barkin and T. King, *Regional Economic Development; The River Basin Approach in Mexico* (Cambridge, 1970).

24. Albert O. Hirschman, *Development Projects Observed* (Washington,

D.C., 1967).

25. Dozier, Land Development in Latin America.

26. New approaches to socioeconomic and physical planning aspects have been applied in recent development projects. See for instance, Y. Arbel, D. Freeman, and J. Maos, Proyecto de Desarrollo Rural Regional Integral de Chira--Piura (Perú), Settlement Study Centre, Rehovot, 1980.

27. Estevam Strauss, Reestructuración del espacio económico latinoamericano (Santiago, Chile, 1969), p. 47.

28. Colonización Majes; Lineamientos para Determinar los Tipos de Asentamientos y Formas de Organización, OAS-- Israel Joint Program, Arequipa, Peru, 1971.

29. Other projects are: (1) replanning and settlement of the Lower Sisa; Central Huallaga Region (FAO/United Nations Development Programme and Ministry of Agriculture, Tarapoto, Peru, 1971), an area included in the reviewed case study; (2) resettlement project for the Cacatachi District, Lower Mayo Region (FAO/United Nations Development Programme and Ministry of Agriculture, Tarapoto, Peru, 1970); and, (3) Upper Mayo River Rural Settlement and Replanning Project (Ministry of Agriculture, Tarapoto, Peru, September, 1971).

30. Proyecto Integral de Reordenamiento y Asentamiento Rural del Huallaga Central, Ministry of Agriculture, Tarapoto, Peru, 1971; Nelson, The Development of Tropical Lands.

31. "Extraordinario Majoramiento Vial en el Perú," Urbanismo y Planificación, No. 43 (1981), pp. 30-42.

32. José A. Portugal Vizcarra, Crisis y Política Agraria en el Perú; Problema y Solución (Lima, 1981).

33. The main idea behind the nonresidential service center is to reinforce the communities of the agricultural settlement by adding nonfarming families engaged in related services. The service population itself would usually be too small to justify the establishment of a separate residential unit.

34. Proyecto Integral de Reordenamiento y Asentamiento Rural del Huallaga Central, Ministry of Agriculture, Tarapoto, Peru, 1971. A more efficient way to prevent "urbanization" would be to locate the centers in the vicinity of the towns, but beyond their jurisdiction. This would not detract from the mutual benefits resulting from the developmental activities, but would reduce the possibility of seizing economic opportunities from the rural sector.

35. In some settlements such as Badajoz (Spain) owners of excessively distant parcels were transferred to isolated farmsteads. A similar thing happened in a spontaneous way in Tingo Maria (Peru) where settlers moved to their remote parcels instead of building their dwelling in the designated "urban units."

36. O.A.S.--Israel Joint Program, Proyecto de Planificación--Colonización "La Joya," Arequipa, Peru, August 1967.

37. A Doak Barnett, "China's Road to Collectivization," Journal of Farm Economics, Vol. 35 (1953), pp. 188-202; and, C. K. Yang, Chinese Communist Society: The Family and the Village (Massachusetts, 1972). See also, Chung-Tong Wu and David F. Ip, "China: Rural Development--Alternating Combinations of Top-down and Bottom-up Strategies," in Walter B. Stöhr and D. R. Fraser Taylor (eds.), Development from Above or Below? The Dialectics of Regional Planning in Developing Countries (New York, 1981), pp. 155-182.

38. The need for organizing the family farm as the basic production unit is upheld by recent developments. A detailed account of agrarian reforms in Peru is rendered by Claude Collin Delavaud, "Agrarian Reform in Peru," in David A. Preston (ed.), Environment, Society, and Rural Change in Latin America (New York, 1980), pp. 37-52.

7
The Spatial Organization of Rural Services

HIERARCHICAL STRUCTURES

The crucial importance of the service structure at the village and intervillage level has been emphasized in the preceding case studies. Evidently, the coverage and efficiency of such services can be improved through systems of pooling or cooperation. Facilitating such cooperation is one of the chief objectives of spatial organization in land settlement. The physical plan does not merely prescribe the contents and locations of service facilities, but determines to a considerable extent their proper functioning. The correct timing of implementation, proper attitude, and community participation are also determinant factors in the actual development of services.

Services are generally structured in a simple hierarchy with three distinct levels: (1) the basic rural community or village composed of 60 to 120 families who receive their daily services from a communal center within the village, denominated center "A"; (2) several such villages grouped around a center "B"--a common or intervillage center which complements the preceding services; and, (3) a subregional service center "C," catering to a number of such village groups in the region, thus completing the basic structure.

Center "A" provides basic needs such as a primary school, grocery store, communal meeting place, and a small park. The area to be served depends mainly on the distances which the inhabitants have to transverse and the available means of transportation. Since small-sized communities cannot support such services economically, several villages may be grouped around a larger center (center "B"), which offers other economic, social, and cultural services in addition to these basic facilities. Center "B" may thus cater to a combined rural population of 300 to 600 families. Besides economizing the cost of services, another objective of center "B" is to attract the necessary professional and technical personnel, and to serve as a collection point for the produce delivered by the surrounding villages. Center "C" provides more specialized services such as secondary and vocational schools, processing plants, and marketing agencies, which warrant a greater number of users. Sometimes the "B" or "C" center will be located in an existing village or rural town because of its convenient geographical location or the opportunity to revitalize the locality by providing new facilities and functions.

Basically, the demands for services in rural settlements are similar to those for human settlements in general, although standards and design norms may vary from place to place. These demands usually fall into the following service categories:

1. Community or public--covering communications, transportation infrastructure, government agencies, public administration, utilities, etc.
2. Production--comprising all those services affecting agricultural production, processing, storage, and farm machinery and equipment.
3. Social and educational--covering cultural, religious, medical, and community development aspects.
4. Commercial--covering shops and stores of all frequency groups and other enterprises.

Planning standards for the design of services and siting requirements will vary according to local circumstances. Location must be based on criteria such as optimal efficiency, access, and frequency of usage. Not all services can be expressed in physical dimensions. Some facilities have institutional and organizational features such as agricultural extension services, the provision of production credits, programming and marketing functions, planning educational and cultural events, etc.

A further step in the service hierarchy includes the regional center "D" for specialized production facilities demanding higher volumes. Finally, the urban centers assume the more complex commercial, industrial, and governmental administrative functions. This sequence is described schematically in Figure 7.1. The lower stratum of services--especially the "A" and "B" centers--has been incorporated into many new settlement schemes. The building of such centers is sometimes slow, facilities are incomplete, and maintenance is lacking; nevertheless, they have a clear place in the planning model. In a few large-scale projects there are elements of center "C" in operation (Tingo Maria in Peru, Majaguas in Venezuela, Chontalpa in Mexico, and others). In some instances where projects assume bigger proportions the functions of the "C" center are delegated to existing rural towns along customary lines of regional planning. To date, the services infrastructure is expected primarily to provide basic amenities and only a few of the production services. The latter are generally the most difficult to implant. Tractor stations,

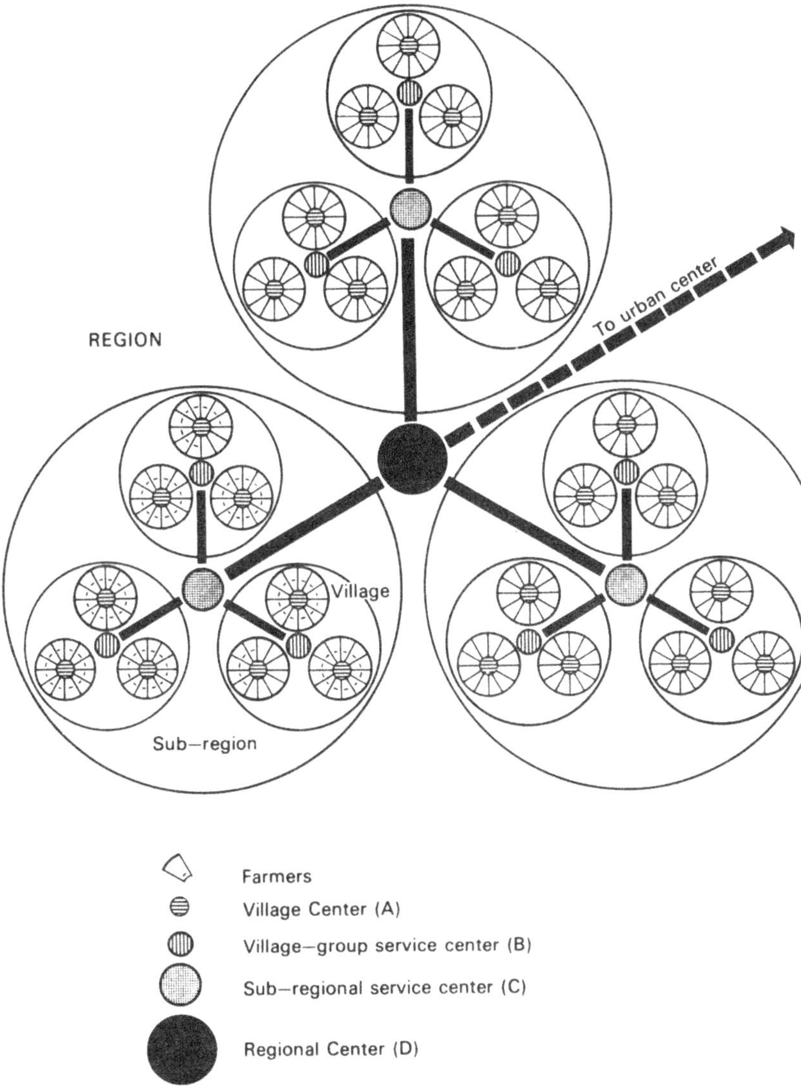

Figure 7.1 Dendritic structure of rural services. (Source: United Nations, Report of the Interregional Seminar, p. 114.)

cold storage, grain silos, cotton gins, rice mills, etc., exist under various combinations of private, cooperative, or state ownership arrangements, but are seldom integrated into a systematic spatial framework.

One of the difficulties in developing a perfect structure of services is the unavailability of contiguous areas suitable for settlement. The rural space destined for colonization may be intercalated by large private farms, as in Italy or Spain, or by empty areas of noncultivable land. Consequently, only in large-scale projects have some initial plans for a broader network of services been made. Another dubious situation is created by the existence of traditional villages or small rural towns interspersed among contemplated settlement schemes. A logical solution would be to integrate the new and existing settlements by attributing some service functions to the older rural centers which already possess some facilities. However, the special characteristics of many rural areas and the interrelationship between rural towns and their periphery may warrant additional inquiry into this subject.

Rural services need not, as a rule, evolve in a dendritic fashion as sometimes depicted in literature. The Israeli settlement model of the early fifties stands as a case in point. The physical master plan was originally conceived as a conventional hierarchical system of central places. Accordingly, the settlement system was to consist of the following levels: (1) the single village "A" center; (2) the rural or village group "B" center--itself with a population of about one hundred families--serving four to six villages; (3) a regional "C" center--usually a township of about 15,000 inhabitants with close economic ties with the rural areas for employment and services; and, (4) the "D" center--a medium-sized town of 20,000 to 60,000 inhabitants, designed as a service center for the planning region and for the location of industries not directly related to agriculture. At the top of this structure were the large urban district capitals functioning as centers for large-scale industry and a higher range of private, public, and government services (see Figure 7.2). The introduction of such a structure into a development area with existing population centers seemed relatively simple; the location of new services was linked to a physical master plan, while many other vital facilities were channeled through official settlement agencies.[1]

Since the build-up of rural services is a gradual process, however, the real development took a different turn. Growth and location were influenced to a great extent by the population itself, and by the underlying doctrine which aimed not merely at improving the efficiency of services but on narrowing the social and cultural gaps between town and country. A similar approach is frequently avowed by other agrarian reform and land settlement programs in Latin America. In the Israeli model, centers "A" and "B" retained their central-place functions with

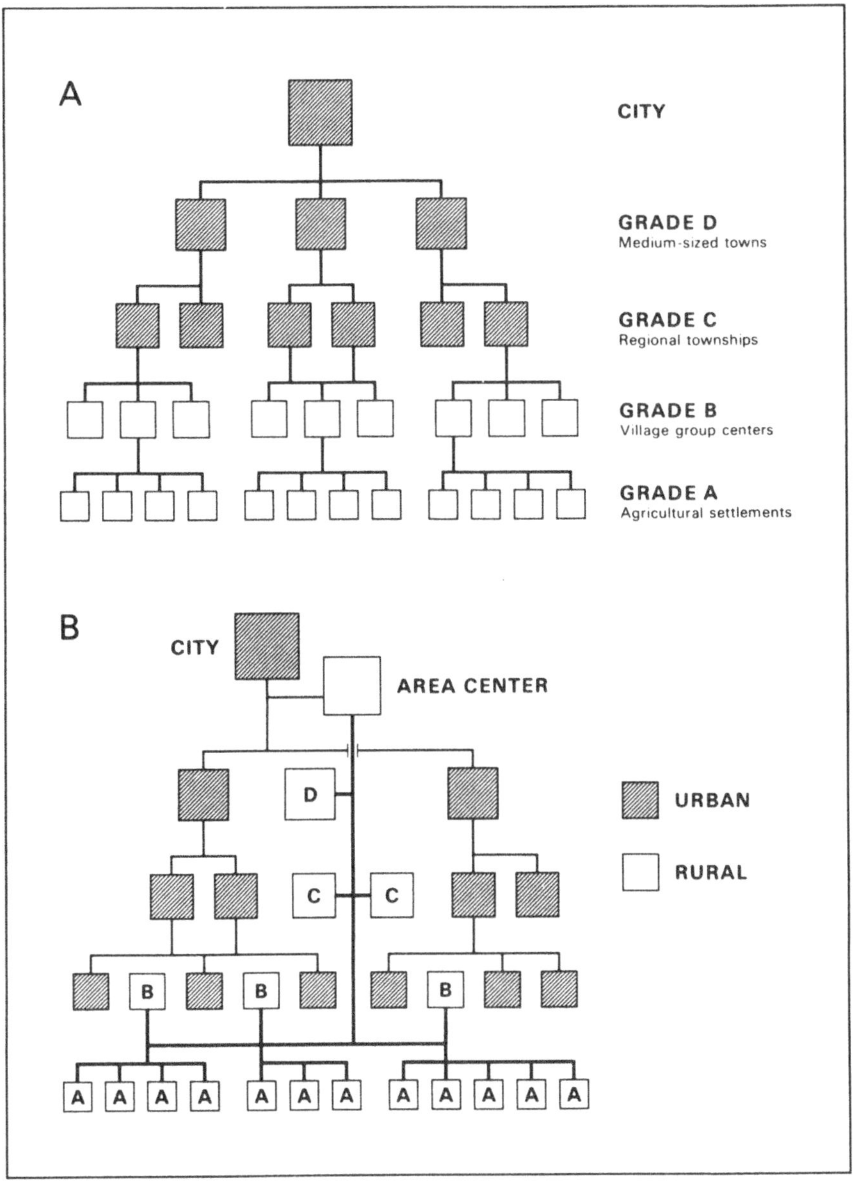

Figure 7.2 Planned and existing structure of central places in Israel.

A. Originally planned hierarchy according to rank order.

B. Evolved juxtaposition of separate urban and rural systems.

only slight variations. Center "A" developed as a community core for basic services, and center "B" became an intervillage center serving four to six agricultural settlements with individual public and economic services, mainly in the preliminary handling of produce such as sorting, packing, etc. Center "B" evolved into two different patterns: a residential center with housing for employees; and a nonresidential center consisting only of plants, stores, and other installations, with employees usually residing in nearby villages or towns.

At a higher level, the service structure became completely dissociated from the urban system, sharing with it merely such broader infrastructural aspects as communications and transportation networks. Today's subregional center "C" is mostly a nonresidential center providing more specialized public and economic services, such as the handling and processing of agricultural produce to about ten to twenty-five farm settlements. The regional center "D"--also a nonresidential service core--engages exclusively in the broadening of production for a group of about twenty-five to fifty settlements. Uppermost in this hierarchical service structure is the Area Center--a physical facility in which are located all the large enterprises owned by the regional bodies and their respective settlements. The Area Center usually belongs to a cooperative framework including up to two hundred farming settlements.

The unique juxtaposition of urban and rural structures is described schematically in Figure 7.2B. As can be seen from the diagram, the relationship differs from the urban hierarchy of central places such that the smaller rural settlements relate to higher-order centers in a selective or functional pattern. Contrary to the conventional theory of central places where each higher center contains the services of the lower center,[2] the rural structure in Israel--more rational by necessity--assigns specific functions to each center. The users from the rural settlements can by-pass any of the existing rural centers, depending on specific needs. Most of the rural services are owned and administered by the agricultural settlements they serve, but there is also a farming-related service sector owned by private and public companies. The physical location of rural facilities is most often outside urban jurisdiction, although some market-oriented installations such as cold storage warehouses are located in larger urban centers.[3]

The entire system reflects the farmer's desire to broaden the base of the production process and to retain the accrued added value thereof. It is interesting to observe that originally the plan was intended to provide only basic amenities and a socially durable structure that would survive the hardships of early settlement. This initial cooperation at the village and intervillage level was consequently instrumental in building bigger cooperative enterprises and in overcoming spatial constraints for including larger territories. The resulting returns from scale in economic and social areas bestowed the rural sector with an unexpected windfall benefit--the creation of new sources of employment. This, in turn, enabled the absorption of the younger generation, thereby counteracting the universal tendency of depopulation that usually follows the rationalization of agriculture.[4]

The development of two parallel spatial systems may have somewhat retarded the growth of the region's urban centers--a phenomenon viewed with concern by some planners who fear that the segregation of rural communities may deplete the region of its "urban" population.[5] However, there is no absolute separation between urban and rural, but rather a symbiotic relationship based on the use of common public infrastructure; and, the rural sector has free access to urban centers at all levels for any particular needs. Notable in these juxtaposed structures is the absence of the traditional center-periphery relationship and subordination to local intermediary channels. There exists, of course, the dependence on markets for agricultural outputs, but these are primarily related to national demand for which diverse rural sectors compete according to their comparative advantages.

Self-sufficiency, maintained through rural services for storage, handling, processing, and marketing, and the economies derived from the services' independent operation enables the rural sector to better absorb dynamic changes in production functions and to protect itself from extreme market fluctuations. The rural system finally "succumbs" to the advantages of urban concentration in highly specialized services, such as exports, industry, finances, government, and higher education. It does so, however, as an equal partner in other economic sectors and can thus resist the gravitational forces exerted by urban areas to emigrate. The vitality inherent in this rural structure is of special interest to other developing regions with a predominant rural-agricultural sector since the described system grew "from below," contrary at times to official planning policies and resource allocations.[6] Development in this pattern was possible because the basic elements of cooperation were built into the rural sector with the help of an adequate spatial organization at the village level.

Two situations occur in land settlement in Latin America. First, when there is no substantial supporting structure in the planning region, a decision must be made concerning the type of structure to be introduced into the area. Second, where an urban structure with supporting elements exists, a method must be found to integrate the old and new settlements. In the first situation--when land settlement occurs in a fringe region relatively devoid of urban infrastructure (e.g. Tingo Maria-Tocache in Peru, or the Amazon Highway settlement in Brazil)--the services for the new settlements will probably be developed along the lines enumerated above. While the physical planning and actual deployment will generally be based on access and land use, the guiding principle remains the prevention of redundant service facilities. Where sufficient resources are available, the settlement will contain village centers (center "A") and intervillage centers (center "B"), similar to the services included in the El Sisal settlement area (Table 6.1). Design norms, though, may vary according to local circumstances.[7] Larger schemes usually include an administration compound containing residential and service facilities for staff and employees and installations for offices, repair shops, storage, etc. This core will often be the forerunner of a subregional center (center "C"), which may later host the cooperative enterprises of the settlement as well as employee housing.

In the second case, where some urban services are available in the region, two possibilities exist depending on the scale of the settlement scheme: the new land settlement can be economically independent with its own basic services but related to the existing rural towns for additional facilities (e.g. Boconó, Venezuela); or it can be completely integrated with existing towns and settlements in terms of markets, production, and public services. However, in the present context of Latin American settlement areas, rural towns or villages with a nonfarming population must sometimes be regarded as antagonistic since these older central places may use their initial advantage to extract the vitality of the new settlements. Locating additional facilities in existing centers may increase even more the initial advantage of such centers over their peripheries.[8] In order to reduce the social and economic attraction of urban centers and to stimulate the initiative of new rural communities, it may be advisable to develop the settlement area as a self-sufficient enclave, independent as far as possible from the facilities existing in the region. Later, as the settlement consolidates socially and economically, the options for collaboration or competition with existing central places can be laid open on a more equitable basis. Admittedly, the sheltered development of new land settlements will tend to delay the growth of total output in the region, but such delay may well be worthwhile for the sake of achieving social and economic transformation, leading to a balanced and sustained development of the whole region.[9]

NOTES

1. Jacob Dash and Elisha Efrat, The Israel Physical Master Plan (Jerusalem, 1964).

2. Walter Christaller, Central Places in Southern Germany (Englewood, 1966).

3. As an example, 72 percent of the cold storage facilities in Israel are owned by nonrural bodies and about 82 percent of these facilities are located in urban areas.

4. I. Prion, Development Trends of Spatial Rural Cooperation in Israel, Publications on Problems of Regional Development, No. 3, Settlement Study Centre, Rehovot, Israel, 1968.

5. Alexander Berler, Urban-Rural Relations in Israel: Social and Economic Aspects, Publications on Problems of Regional Development, No. 8, Settlement Study Centre, Rehovot, Israel, 1970.

6. J. Maos, "The Spatial Organization of New Land Settlement: Experiences and Trends," GeoJournal, Vol. 1.4 (1977), pp. 29-35.

7. See United Nations, Report of the Interregional Seminar on Rural Housing and Community Facilities, ST/TAO/SER.C/103, New York, 1968; and United Nations Economic and Social Commission for Asia and the Pacific, Guidelines for rural centre planning (New York, 1979).

8. A. G. Frank, in discussing Brazilian agriculture, contends that it would be necessary to isolate agriculture, rather than integrate it (as is usually held) with the development-underdevelopment structure and to protect it from the exploitation and poverty the integration of such a structure generates. A. G. Frank, Capitalism and Underdevelopment in Latin America, Historical Studies of Chile and Brazil (London, 1971).

9. Resources for the Future, Design for a Worldwide Study of Regional Development (Baltimore, 1966).

8 Development of a Settlement Model

ASSUMPTIONS AND CRITERIA

The spatial problems at the microlevel, namely the village and intervillage complex, can be analyzed by means of graphical models in which various physical and conceptual features are simulated. These physical layouts can also be used as normative models that respond to preconceived criteria. While the building of these models demands a degree of abstraction in regard to details, sufficient verisimilitude must be preserved to enable its use as a planning tool.[1] The spatial variables involved in the model include: (1) the family farmstead; (2) the rural community; (3) the land allotment; and (4) distances to work and to central facilities. The illustrated graphical models (Figures 8.1-8.7) represent the basic physical components that ensure proper functioning of the settlement, apart from the prerequisites for agricultural production (soils, climate, markets, credits, etc.). At the macrolevel, adequate functioning of land settlement will depend primarily on the sum of input factors affecting production, as well as on the physical and institutional infrastructure. However, the quality of the microstructure--the planning and implementation of the basic units--is the factor that breathes life into the system by making it possible for individual initiative and community participation to unfold.

The spatial objectives of the model can be described as: (1) minimization of distances to work and services; (2) minimization of infrastructure costs; (3) maximization of land and crop concentration; (4) maximization of individual initiative and family participation; (5) maximization of farmyard efficiency; and (6) maximization of flexibility for future changes in land use. Some of these criteria are conflicting, e.g. distances to work versus distances to services or the concentration of holdings versus the concentration of crops. The model is expected to facilitate the optimization of the diverse requirements.

The methodological assumptions in respect to spatial

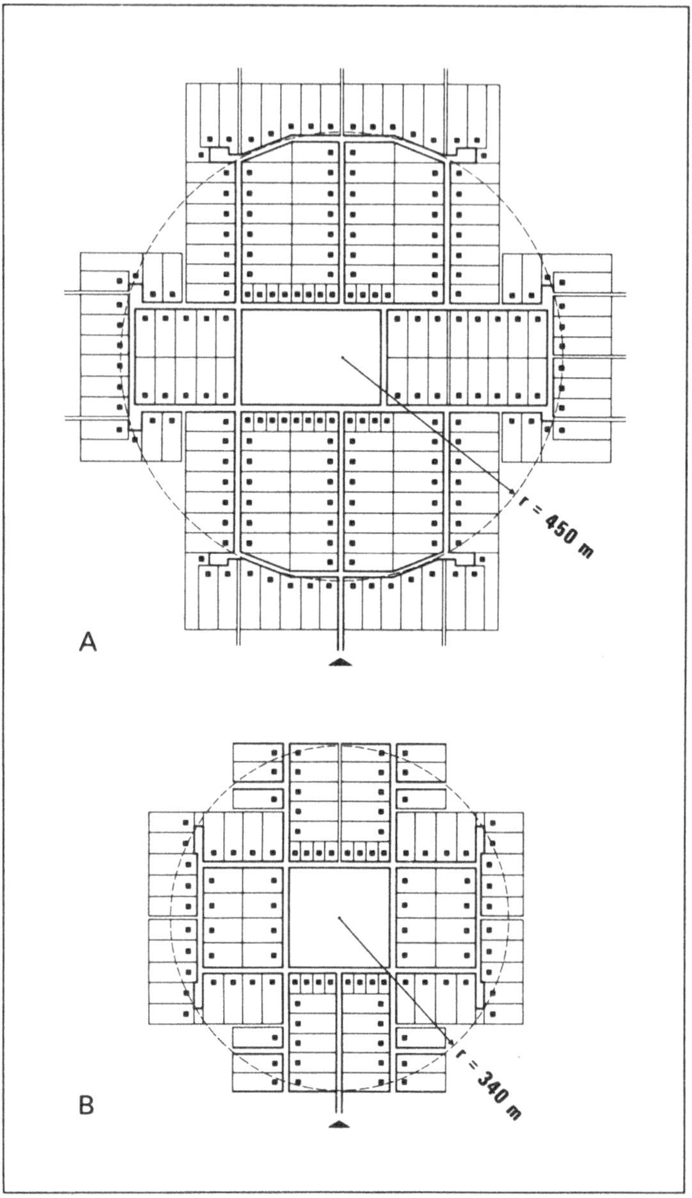

Figure 8.1 Model layout for agricultural village with 0.4 ha farmsteads.

A. "Big" village comprising 168 farms and 24 service families.

B. Medium-sized village comprising 84 farms and 16 service families.

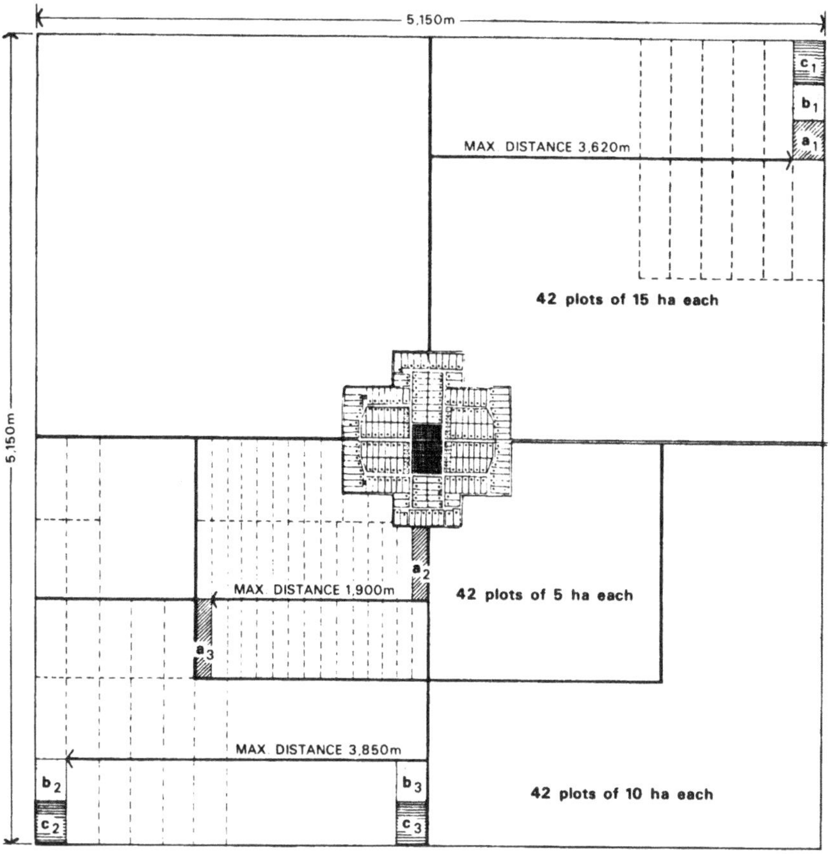

Figure 8.2 Model layout of a single-unit village for 168 farm families and 24 service families, with allotted holdings: 0.4 ha farmstead and 15 ha agricultural plot per family. Two variants are compared: (1) holdings (exclusive of farmstead) in one parcel of 200 x 750 meters, and (2) holdings divided into two parts, a near-lying parcel for intensive crops measuring 5 ha and a far-lying parcel for extensive crops of 10 ha.

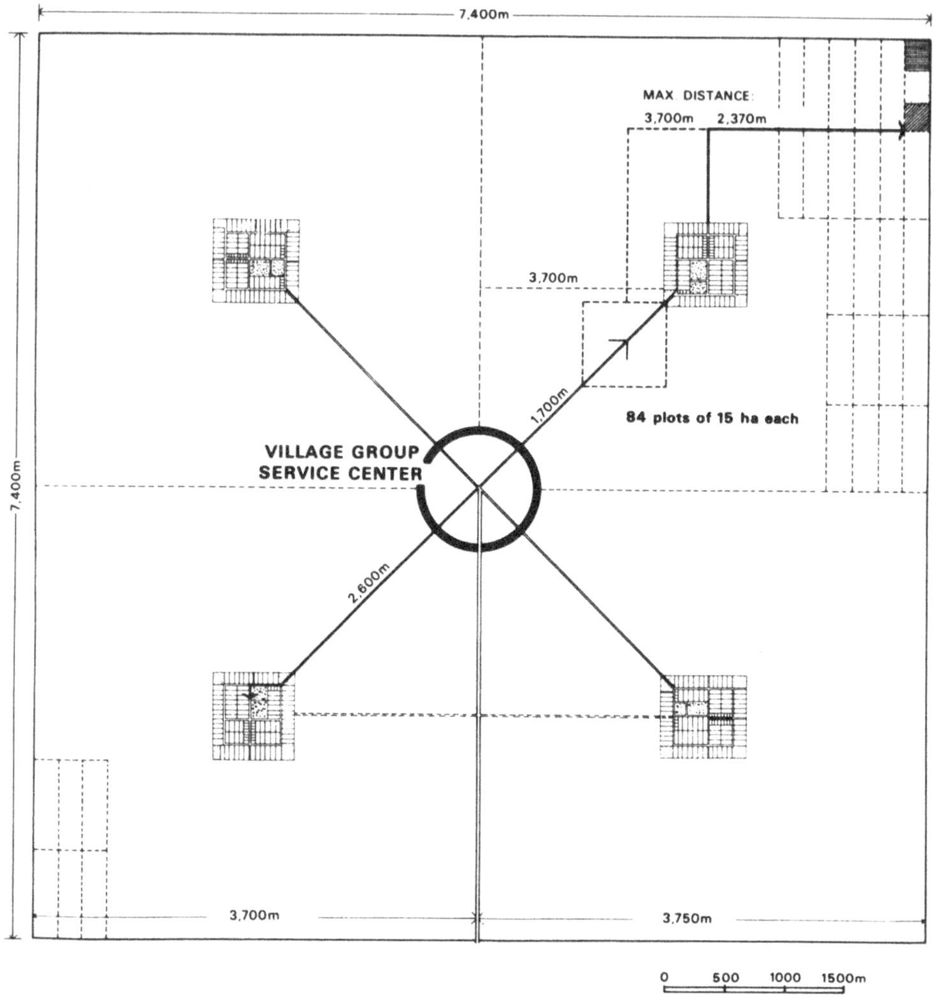

Figure 8.3 Model layout of four villages comprising 400 families grouped around a common service center. The holdings of each family are concentrated in one single plot of 15 ha. Maximum distances to fields increase according to the convergence of the villages toward the common center.

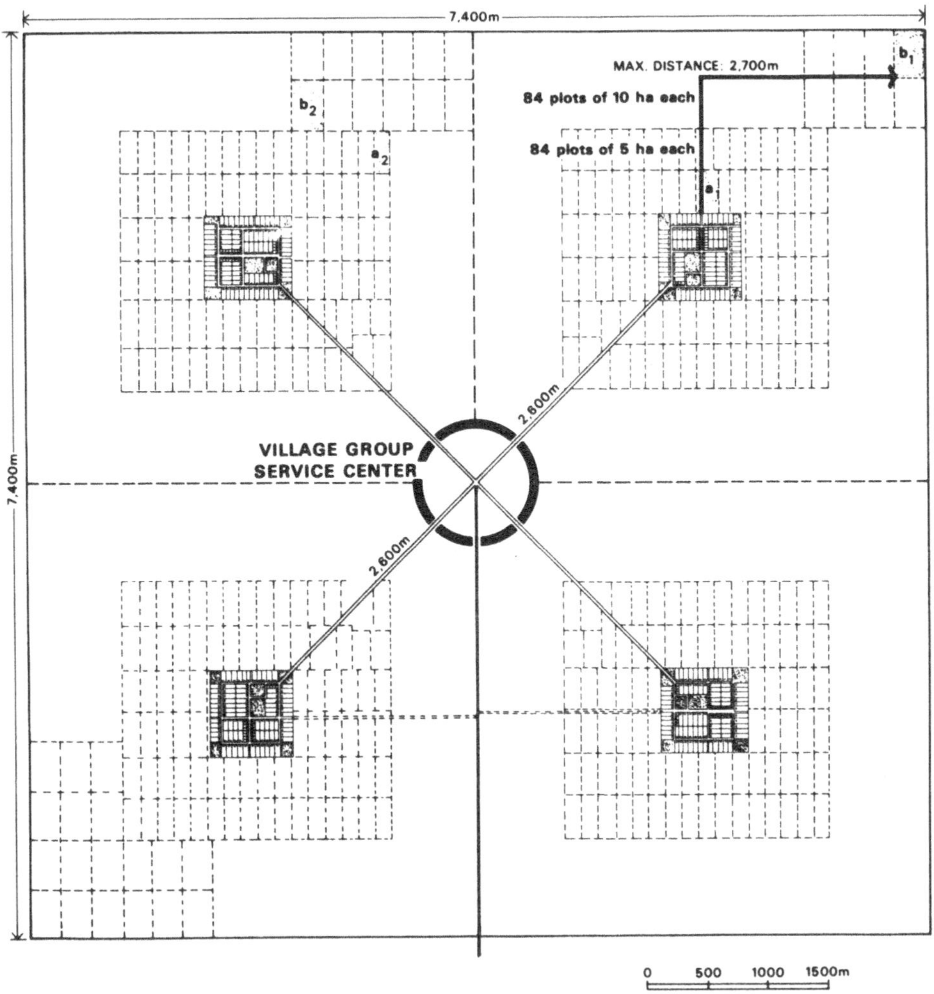

Figure 8.4 Variation of preceding model layout, with holdings divided into two blocks: a "near-intensive" parcel of five ha and a "far-extensive" parcel of ten ha.

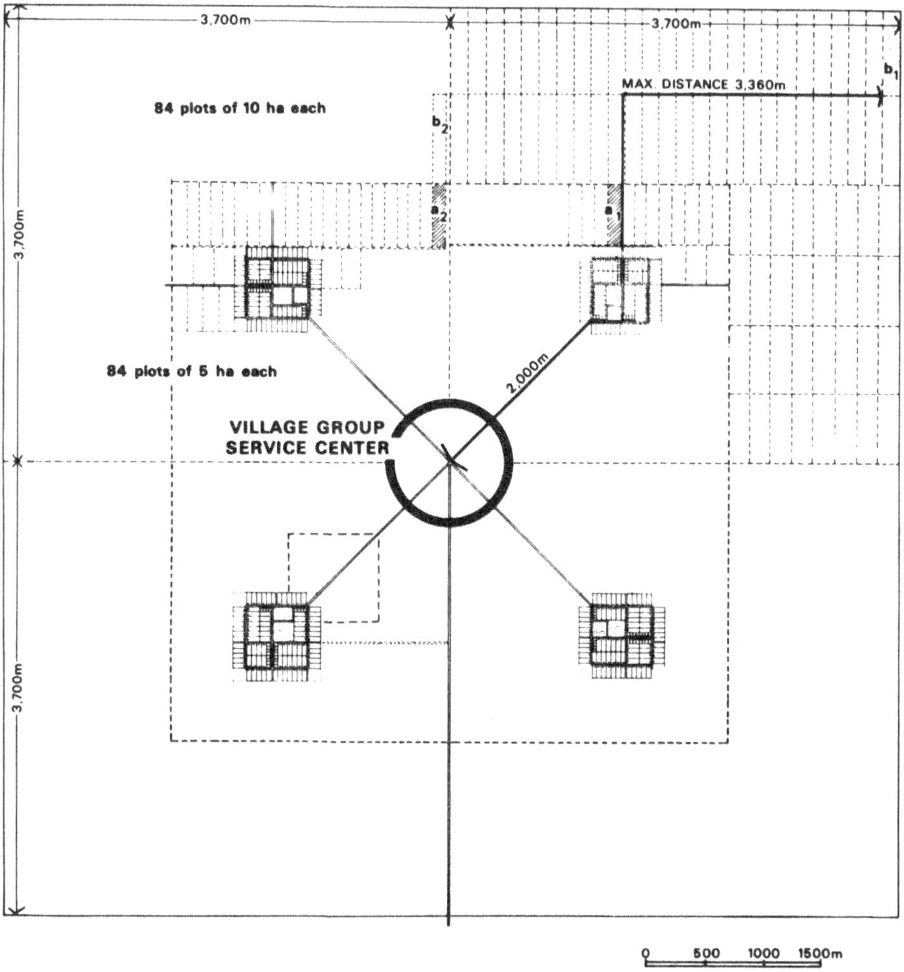

Figure 8.5 Variation of preceding model layout (Figure 8.4), with divided holdings gathered around the common service center. This layout enables concentration of blocks of homogeneous crops, as well as the converging of the village units toward the common center.

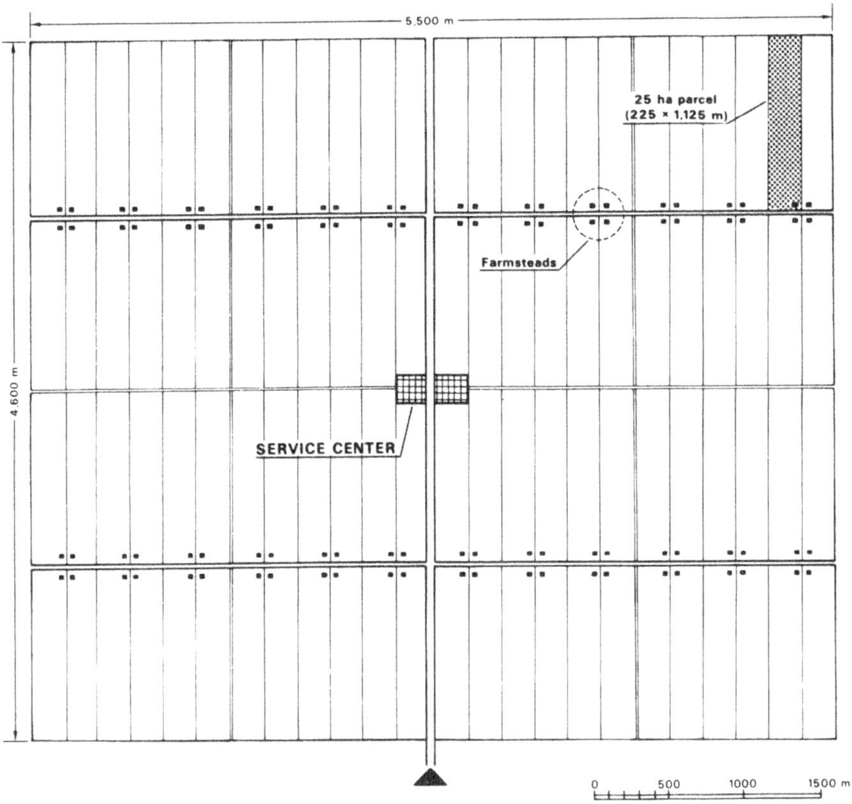

Figure 8.6 Schematic layout of dispersed settlement of pasture farms, comprising ninety-six farmsteads, each situated on its own twenty-five ha holding.

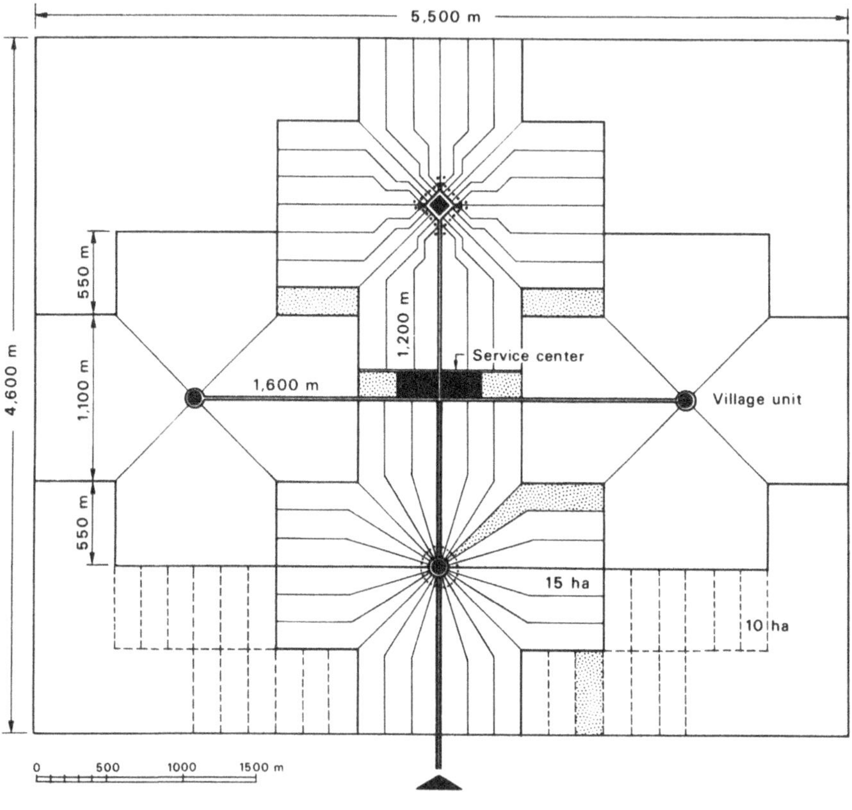

Figure 8.7 Concentrated version of layout for pasture farms (see Figure 8.6), each with fifteen ha of contiguous holdings and ten ha in separate parcels. The grouping in twenty-four farms facilitates provision of basic amenities and social interaction. Two alternative layouts are shown, but other variants along the same principle are possible. (See J. Maos and L. Kam, Criterios para el Planeamiento de Aldeas Agrícolas.)

and social organization conform to the conceptual framework described in the preceding chapters, as well as to the predominant trend of land settlement in Latin America. Accordingly, the model represents a concentrated settlement of family farms allowing for varying degrees of cooperation. The constraints to the model are principally: (1) equitable allocation of resources (in soil quality, distances, farm size, etc.); (2) production based exclusively, or foremostly, on family labor; (3) conditional land tenancy, to prevent fragmentation or competitive land uses; (4) continuity of the farmstead for new generations; (5) the possibility of developing the settlement in stages; and (6) a stipulated social cohesion.

The model is developed for family farms engaged in arable or a combination of arable and livestock farming. The time horizon and pace of implementation include the consolidation of the transitional phase from subsistence to mixed farming. Pasture farms, involving particularly low population densities, are also covered by the model although the social processes endemic in the bigger, compact villages are not as prominent in this pattern. Combinations of the two forms, where arable farming is accompanied by the use of marginal lands for pasture, lend themselves to modeling by the same method. The main variables comprising the model, the family farmyard, size of holdings, distances, and community size are described in the following sections.

THE FAMILY FARM AS BASIC SPATIAL UNIT

The family farm is the basic socioeconomic unit of land settlement. In the settlement model it also becomes the basic spatial element, aspects of which are determined by the size and quality of the land resources. These land resources are usually allotted on the basis of target incomes and the working capacity of an average farming family. The farmstead, as an integral part of this complex, merits special consideration.

The farmstead is usually defined as the farmer's dwelling and an enclosed farmyard containing farm buildings for the stabling, storage, and processing of agricultural products and materials, and buildings for the maintenance of farm machinery and tools.[2] In a nucleated settlement, the farmstead becomes a spatial element that influences village layout, distances to work and services, infrastructure costs, as well as social interaction and the efficiency of the farm itself. Considerable resources representing most of the farmer's savings are invested in the farmstead area in structures, equipment, and livestock, and an important portion of the farmer's working time is spent within the limits of the farmstead. Numerous engineering and agrotechnical disciplines deal with the planning and rationalization of farming operations carried out in this "built-up" area. Yet, the farmstead's significance as a vital component in the economy of the family farm is frequently overlooked. Even its historical role in shaping settlement patterns and generating breakthroughs in agricultural development has gone almost unnoticed. The emergence of new agricultural technologies which provide solutions to specific problems has dissolved the traditional aggregate structure of the farmyard into functional elements. As a result, the farmyard is no longer a compact harmonic unit but a complex of different functions. Structures and installations are put together and relocated, sometimes in a provisional manner, in order to accommodate specific production needs.[3] Many of the improvisations, experiments, and shifting of farming activities cannot be done without adequate and ample space.

The neglect of the farmyard in the physical planning of new villages could be explained by the fact that on isolated farms--where many notable achievements in agricultural productivity were produced--the farmyard area is almost inconspicuous. Actually, the farmstead built on its agricultural plot has unlimited space for its farmyard with all the needed flexibility for eventual changes. Apparently, the farmer is unaware of this asset--until it is lacking. In the U.S.A., for example, a farming manual notes factually: ". . . it is quite immaterial where the farmstead is located on the farm if it has the three requirements for a good site, sanitation, convenience, and beauty."[4] Consequently, in the planning of many small landholders' settlements, the farmstead has been "mutilated" by planners who wished to save infrastructure costs by increasing the compactness of the village. A case in point is the Badajoz project in Spain. The importance of providing adequate space for the farmyard can be summed up as follows:

1. The farmyard represents the principal workshop space and the main area for farm buildings, storage, etc., enabling better utilization of family manpower, being conducive to a working routine, and facilitating the acquisition of farming skills.
2. The farmyard area enables the accommodation of one of the farmer's sons on the farm and the continued participation of the parents, thus ensuring uninterrupted work on the holding and preventing the disintegration of the village community.
3. In the process of transition from subsistence to mixed farming, the farmyard area can be used for raising cash crops or food for self-consumption. The stabling of livestock, use of cut pasture, and utilization of farm waste can add considerably to the family's diet and budget.

The dimensions of the farmyard remain arbitrary because of the need to preserve maximum flexibility for developments on the farm. But there are certain limits to observe. Too small an area may stifle initiative for further development when congestion sets in. This has been the cause for outsettlement in past history as well as in new land settlement schemes. The consequent disruption of the village pattern may lead to increased disparities within the community and impair social stability. Since future usage of the farmyard cannot be predicted accurately, it is safest to plan for the critical stage of development, namely, the mixed farming stage in which there is an increased emphasis on livestock rearing or vegetable gardening. The area close to the farmer's house grows in importance as farming becomes more intensive and specialized. Experience indicates that an area of 0.4 to 0.6 hectare may be adequate for most requirements.[5] In some projects, planners have attached to the farmyard an additional tract of land--a so-called "homeplot." On this land, subsistence crops can be grown for some time until the family assumes modern production and consumption patterns, thereby countering the tendency to settle out on the main plot. Increasing the size of the farmyard and homeplot, however, makes it more difficult to group large numbers of farms in the village without negatively affecting distances to work and services.

THE SIZE OF FAMILY HOLDINGS

The allocation of land resources to the family farm deserves special examination because of the interrelationship between the size of holdings and physical distances. The amount of land allotted is usually determined by family income targets to be reached when the project is fully developed and consolidated. Income targets, however, are liable to different interpretations according to given conceptual frameworks. Examples of conceptual constraints in building income targets include the exclusion of hired labor, the determination of man-to-land ratios by purposely maximizing the spread of benefits in a given region, and intentionally dictating a moderate pace of growth to fit the capacity of the ecosystem to accommodate change. Any one of these constraints may present themselves in socially motivated settlement programs, and frequently they constitute a departure from conventional operational techniques used in planning the spatial equilibrium of agricultural production.

Quantifying land, labor, capital, and management is theoretically feasible when specific data are available or can be reasonably assessed. The size of holdings can then be computed according to the production function, based on estimated parameters of utility and on the optimum intensity of land use.[6] Many preinvestment studies for new land settlement schemes actually define the size of holdings according to approximate input variables based on both collated and hypothetical data. Similarly, the quantitative techniques used in determining the size of holdings per family reflect local or regional concepts of what size income is operative or acceptable. For example, an allotment of ten hectares is considered adequate in many Latin American countries for an arable family farm; ten to twenty hectares in mixed arable and livestock farming; and anywhere from twenty-five to eighty hectares is deemed adequate for extensive livestock farming. In irrigation systems, four to six hectares are believed to produce comparable family incomes. These dimensions are often biased upward to compensate for the marginal quality of tropical lands, remoteness from markets, and the lack of amenities and infrastructure--all of which are among the customary handicaps of land settlement. Brazil offers one hundred hectares per family in the Agrotowns planned along the Trans-Amazon Highway.[7] Ecuador grants twelve hectares to settlers in the tropical Northeast.[8] Peru uses a norm of sixty-five hectares in planning extensive pasture-type settlements in the Huallaga river basin,[9] and Nicaragua is developing a project with thirty hectares per family in a mixed arable and pasture farm.[10] Land is still used as one of the principal incentives to attract quality settlers. Only in areas where strong land pressures persist do land allotments reflect more realistic income targets, as, for example, in the Dominican Republic.

Aside from the question as to whether or not the size of holdings conforms to ultimate family incomes, it may take years before the family is able to prepare and cultivate its full land allotment. Most development programs assume eight to twelve years from settlement to full development, depending upon the successful coordination and timely input of the involved human and technical factors.[11] In several recent settlement schemes, the entire allotted area was brought under cultivation in a record time of two or three years, but these capital-intensive agrotechnical feats may be too costly to be used as standards. Moreover, the resulting increase in income has sometimes proven to be beyond the expectations of the settlers and has killed propensities to increase productivity through intensification or diversification. So-called shortcuts to specialized farming or the premature introduction of mechanization and labor-saving devices for cultivating larger tracts of land have often caused disguised and real underemployment and excessive investments in infrastructure.

One objective implicit in the immediate distribution of the entire land quota is to increase agricultural productivity through expanded acreage as opposed to higher productivity per unit area. But the notion that land has to be carved out in advance creates waste in infrastructure. If, for example, only half of the final land allotment were to be allotted to the settler with the rest held in abeyance until the first portion is fully developed, the savings in present value of infrastructure and administrative costs could be used to incorporate additional settlers into the scheme. The concept of higher productivity per unit area draws primarily on the human potential of the farming family, and is consistent with endeavors to form larger communities and to provide more evenly distributed employment.

DISTANCE CRITERIA

Theories of spatial organization are usually based on the principle of minimizing distances and maximizing the utility of points and areas within a given structure. Spatial interactions, however, are considered in economic terms, regardless of whether distances are measured physically, by time, by effort, or by perception. The distinction between physical as opposed to perceived distance is blurred by constantly changing environmental, social, and technological factors. The importance of distance as a socioeconomic factor is exemplified by the extensive efforts invested to date by European governments in consolidating historically fragmented holdings.[12] The relationships between distances from markets and optimal land uses, or distances between home and fields, have been treated in breadth mainly from the standpoint of economic rent.[13] Fewer studies exist on the patterns of rural settlements from the standpoint of social interactions,[14] even though such social underpinnings have been mentioned in economic and settlement geography.[15] In the following model, criteria of distances were chosen both from an economic and social point of view in an attempt to reconcile these conflicting requirements.

In the agricultural village, it is possible to distinguish two types of distances: (1) internal distances, from the farmer's house to the village center where services are located, involving social and economic activities; and (2) external distances, involving working activities. Both distances depend in varying degrees on the number, size, and shape of farmsteads in the village area and on the compactness of the site plan. External distances to the fields depend mainly on the size of holdings, topography, field system, and number of farmers in the village. Internal distances can be minimized by reducing the size of the family farmyard and homeplot included in the village area, and narrowing street frontage.[16] However, minimization of farmyard and homeplot, as noted earlier, can strip the farmstead of its usefulness. On the other hand, the rationalization of internal distances by differentiating between frequent and less frequent services, allows these services to encompass a larger clientele. The resulting improvement in range and quality may make it worthwhile to overcome longer distances to such services.

External distances can be minimized not only by

reducing farm size (e.g. through intensification), but also by concentrating plots of equal soil quality and crop suitability into large blocks of land. In this way, for example, a near block could be designated for more intensive cultivation while a far block would be used for extensive purposes. A citrus grove, to use another example, would need less frequent visits than vegetable farming. The system can be based on several blocks of land (e.g. three, in addition to the farmyard and attached homeplot). Although this system would break up the individual farmer's holdings, this disadvantage may be more than offset by savings in commuting time and the possibility of undertaking large-scale cooperative farming operations. It would also be possible to compensate the holder of a "far" extensive plot with a "near" intensive plot (and vice versa), resulting in a more balanced and equitable allocation of holdings. A similar differentiation has been applied in several projects, such as the Lakhish region in Israel or Cojedes in Venezuela, where part of the land allotment was planned for irrigation. Sometimes a "far" plot will be part of a communal tract for plantations or pasture, as in the Taanakh settlements in Israel, Chontalpa project in Mexico, or Tingo Maria-Tocache in Peru. The purpose of a two- or three-field system is to rationalize farming and to enable the introduction of cooperative working methods. The fact that improved equity in field allocation enables greater tolerance for long distances adds a secondary benefit to this system. This benefit is particularly true for the second or communal plot where work occurs less frequently. Calculations based on a settlement model for 168 family farms (Figure 8.2) showed that the average commuting time to holdings in a two-field system was about 50 percent less than the maximum commuting time in a one-field system.[17]

Both external and internal distances are important during the initial period of settlement. However, external distances to the fields have a higher "elasticity" than internal distances. In the beginning, the settler and his family may spend much time commuting to the agricultural plot with the simplest means of transportation or none at all. But the importance of this distance decreases as the settlement develops. The marginal labor of the family becomes concentrated on the farmyard area while field work is gradually improved by modern farming methods, mechanization, and cooperative management. Internal distances, in contrast, have a lower "elasticity" since they apparently do not change over time. All family household members continue to commute to central service points, mostly on foot, for a variety of daily needs and for social, cultural, or work-related purposes. Lengthy internal distances will often cause the appearance of redundant facilities which, later on, are apt to hinder the development of a cooperative spirit and the building of joint enterprises.

Various attempts have been made to establish distance criteria based on commuting time to the fields.[18] However, improved transportation or cooperative cultivation methods tend to render such criteria obsolete. Distance values, therefore, are still controversial. Generally, three or four kilometers are considered a substantial improvement over the subsistence farming stage. In more intensive agriculture, as in the Badajoz irrigation system, a norm of 3.5 kilometers has been used. Distances from the remotest house to services are acceptable within 600 meters for personal activities and within 1,300-1,600 meters for community facilities (equivalent to a 600-800 meter radius for a circle enclosing centers "A" and "B"). Some existing empirical evidence suggests that when this distance increases, the attraction of the center fades. In rural settlements in Israel, which were planned consecutively with increasing convergence on a common service center, there was little use of the center until a 600-800 meter radius was reached (see Chapter 4).

The successful social integration achieved in selected cases cannot be unequivocally and solely attributed to the distance factor. However, a trend can be observed in various schemes described in this study. Since the concept of distance in human settlement is a changing value,[19] questions arise regarding which of the distance criteria--social or work-related--will take precedence. A safe answer could be determined by evaluating priorities in light of future trends. Although current data regarding distances are still inconclusive, there is ample evidence that the tolerance threshold for internal distances is lower than that for external distances. As time goes by, distances to the fields are perceived as being shorter because of improved communications, while social distances, which affect the entire age group, tend to increase as activities spill to beyond the village perimeter.

COMMUNITY SIZE AND PATTERN

The number of farm families in a land settlement depends upon the following:

1. cultivable land available within a given perimeter and land allotment per family;
2. internal (farm to services) and external (farm to fields) distances;
3. community size conducive to the rational development and upkeep of services and amenities;
4. community size amenable to efficient organization and extension services.

The first two factors have been generally defined and can be optimized in conformity with the criteria described previously. Optimal community size, as compatible with other functional requirements of efficiency, begs some further clarification.

Many planners consider 80-120 families an optimal number for initiating intensive cultivation, as this size group keeps maximum distances to fields within three to four kilometers with holdings of ten to twelve hectares per family. A community of this size will be able to support basic facilities, such as two elementary school grades, grocery store, church, sanitary services, and basic utilities. Obviously, a bigger community, e.g. 300 families, could afford more efficient services, but would increase the distances to fields. Experience also shows that a larger community implies both longer external and internal distances, and is less amenable to agricultural extension services and community participation. It has been noted that villages of more than 100 families tend to become socially amorphous and difficult to organize as cooperative units.[20] The multinuclear pattern overcomes this latter difficulty by creating large villages composed of several community units, or neighborhoods. The problem of external distances, on the other hand, can be mitigated by dividing holdings into differentiated cultivation blocks and by improving roads or transportation.

ANALYSIS OF GRAPHICAL LAYOUT MODELS

Two model village layouts are used to analyze the relationship between distances to services and work under varying conditions of land use and spatial patterns. One village (Figure 8.1A) comprises 168 farming families and 24 nonfarming families employed in services. The number of "service" families will ordinarily increase in time but need not have noticeable effect on the initial village layout. A smaller village (Figure 8.1B) contains 84 farming families and 16 nonfarmers. Farmsteads within the village occupy an area of 0.4 hectare each. Houses of nonfarming families are situated on 0.1 hectare plots. The gross land allotment outside the village in this specific model equals fifteen hectares per family.

In the described rural agricultural setting, the degree of agglomeration is of primary interest rather than the population density per unit area. Agglomeration can be expressed by measuring the distance from the center to the remotest houses in the village area. This distance totals 450 meters in the big village and 340 meters in the smaller one. Any alternative assemblage of equally sized farmsteads (attempting to keep aggregate distances to a minimum) will presumably produce a similar cluster in size and form. The parcellation of the larger village's land and the resulting distances are also examined (Figure 8.2). Maximum distances to the fields vary between 3,400 and 3,800 meters. These distances can be "balanced" in a multiple-field system where separate parts of the family farm holdings are concentrated into blocks according to cultivation type. In a variant of the model, described also in Figure 8.2, holdings are divided into near-lying parcels of five hectares (for intensive crops) and into more distant parcels of ten hectares (for extensive cultivation). The remotest parcel in the near-intensive block lies 1,900 meters from the nearest house in the village.

Examples of two- or three-field systems are well known from history, though the reasons for their development vary. In current land settlement, the system is used primarily to concentrate specialized or irrigated crops, though it offers other important advantages in flexibility. For example, the system provides an opportunity to develop the project in stages and to achieve higher densities of rural settlements for the purpose of improving amenities and support services. Thus, a settlement may begin with only part of the programmed land allotment. Later, additional land can be provided in an area situated farther away, since distances become less critical due to improved communications and cooperative methods. In a case where land preparation is involved or where irrigation infrastructure is being built, it would also be possible to temporarily allocate larger holdings for extensive cultivation, reducing the initial land allotment when irrigation is introduced. The reduction in allotments would then enable the addition of a new group of family farms. Such a measure would also preclude uncontrolled squatting in the project area.

A subsequent model (Figure 8.3) shows the interrelationship between location and distances of a group of four smaller villages, each with eighty-four farm families deployed around a common service center. The total area involved is larger due to the increase in the farming population, but distances to fields remain within reasonable limits. As in the preceding model, distances can be further reduced by means of a two-field system (Figure 8.4) in which intensive parcels surround the village in a concentric ring, while the "extensive" parcels form the outer ring of the village's land allotment. In an attempt to even further reduce distances from the villages to the center, this system can be modified by moving the "intensive" blocks as closely as possible to the center, forming one contiguous area (Figure 8.5). Since the importance of distance to the extensive parcels is less crucial in a two-field system, even the village units can be drawn closer to the common center. Striking a balance between conflicting criteria of distances can thus be simplified; however, the trends and forces at play must be carefully observed. Past experience in land settlement indicates that distances to work become less problematic with improvement of economic and technological levels. The effects of "social" or "personal" distances on the other hand tend to remain stable over time. Moreover, converging villages upon a common center will typically prevent the growth of redundant competing services, and lead to closer cooperation.

The principle of differentiated cultivation blocks and the concentration of village units around common services can also be applied in pasture farm villages. Such villages are more problematic because of the larger holdings involved and the need to attach lands to the farmstead for circulating livestock between grazing areas and farm buildings. In a schematic layout for a settlement of ninety-six farms with twenty-five hectare holdings in a dispersed pattern (Figure 8.6), maximum distances to centrally located services would be around 3,600 meters--a distance which would increase further with larger holdings. A model concentrating these same pasture farms is illustrated in Figure 8.7 in which ninety-six farmsteads are grouped into four village units. Each farm has fifteen hectares of adjoining land and ten hectares in a separate parcel. In pasture farms the grouping of even twenty-four family farms facilitates social interaction and the provision of basic utilities, e.g. water supply and electricity, or certain production services such as a milk cooling tank. The four village units are located within 1,200-1,600 meters of a joint service center. Apart from savings in infrastructure, the concentrated model draws the community within acceptable distances from the village center.

Real-world conditions, such as available land resources, topography, existing infrastructure, etc., will naturally require modification and adaptation of the model to the terrain. The illustrated layout allows a degree of flexibility in the siting of village areas in order to achieve optimal environmental conditions. Figure 8.8 shows the layout for a series of nuclear villages in Cojedes, Venezuela, for 231 farm families about to be resettled from various hamlets dispersed in the area. The plan is based on the same principles applied in the preceding models, but is adapted to a given terrain and number of farming units. Although each nucleus is in itself a small neighborhood, the group of four nuclei constitutes a community that is able to maintain adequate municipal services. The plan for the two southern village units, A and B, has been finalized and is based on detailed topographical maps. Figure 8.9 illustrates the meticulousness that must be exercised in the actual siting and layout of villages. As in many other irrigation districts, maps that are scaled 1:10,000 or 1:5,000 convey little information, showing this terrain to be a flat plain. However, a 1:1,000 map with contour intervals of 20 centimeters revealed a relief of gullies and depressions explaining the frequent flooding of the proposed site. The detailed layout of village units A and B as shown in Figure 8.10 was consequently based on the drainage study of this area.[21] The layout for village units C and D is tentative, pending further physical data.

An aggregate model of spatial organization on a

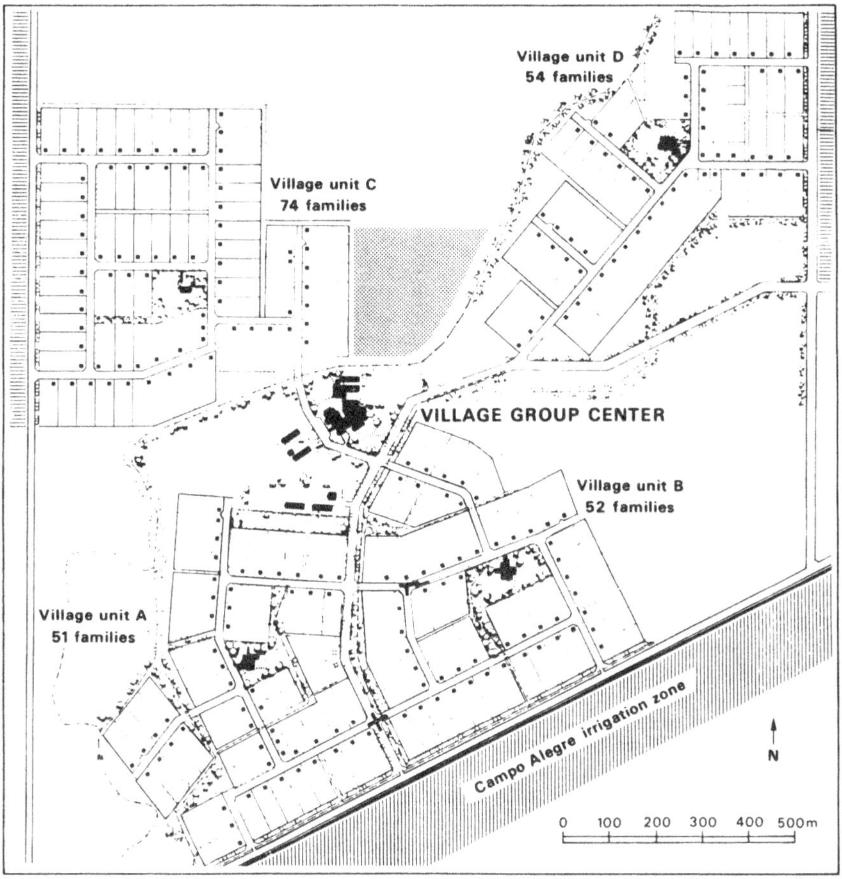

Figure 8.8 Proposed layout for Campo Alegre multiunit settlement in the Cojedes Project, Venezuela.

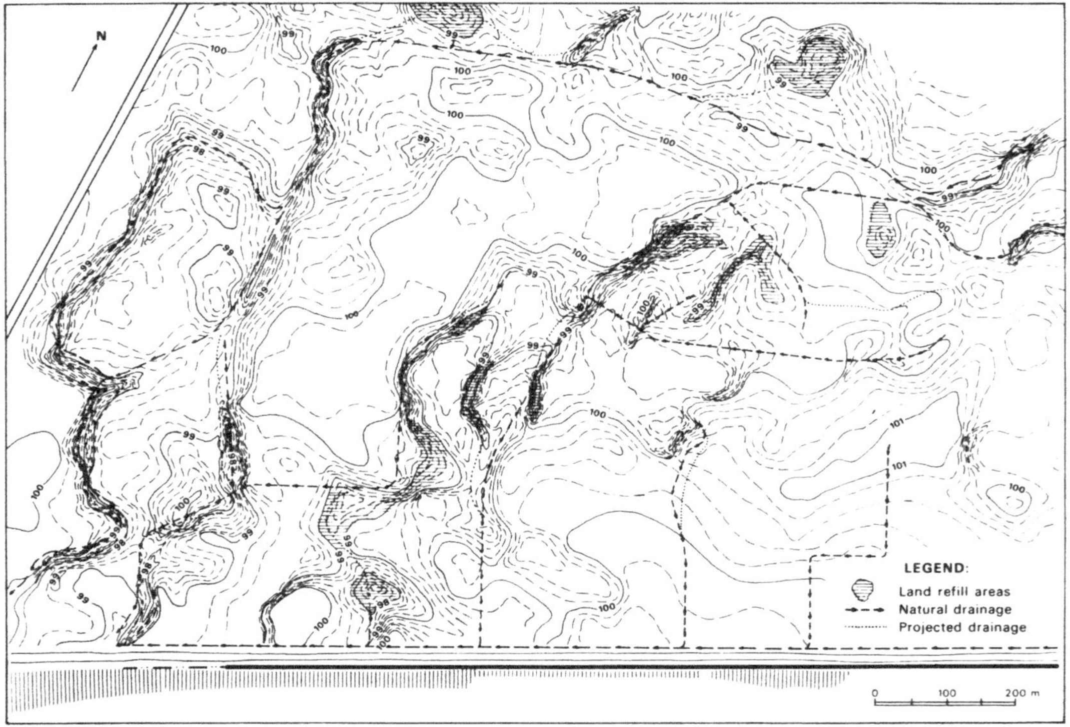

Figure 8.9 Drainage study of planned site for the Campo Alegre village in the Cojedes Project, Venezuela. The apparently flat terrain with a 0.5 percent slope was frequently flooded. A detailed topographical survey revealed considerable gullying and undrained ponds. Dotted lines show main natural drains which should be accounted for in the final layout.

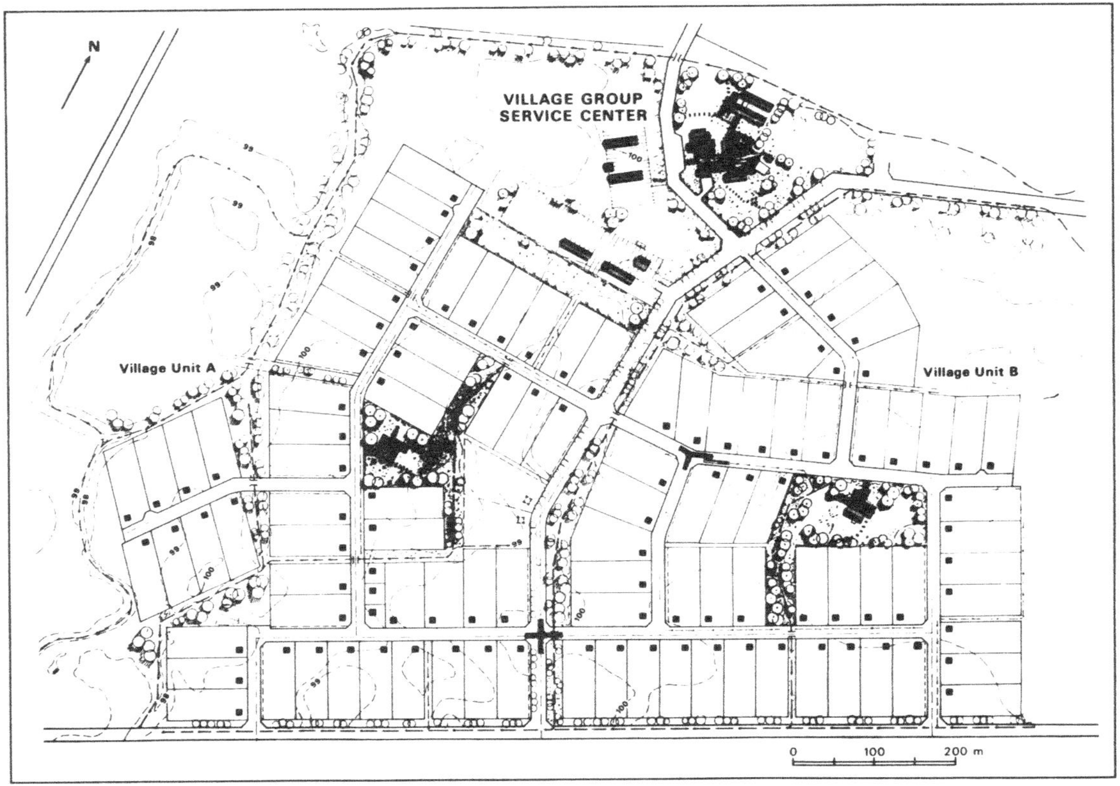

Figure 8.10 Detailed layout for the first two village units of the Campo Alegre settlement in the Cojedes Project, adapted to surface drainage conditions (see Figure 8.9).

regional scale is illustrated in Figure 8.11. This model is a further spatial extension of the basic units described previously. The principle of village units grouped around common service centers is applied in an ascending manner, with the village group center, subregional center, and regional or urban center integrated into one complete network. The urban center or rural town, a characteristic feature of the Latin American landscape, is interwoven into this structure by complementing rather than substituting the infrastructure developed in the rural settlements. This spatial model represents a composite rural-urban system which is bound by a reciprocal relationship in social and economic activities.

The application of this model to real-world conditions is exemplified by plans for the Central Huallaga Project in Peru (Figure 8.12), described in Chapter 6. In spite of the limitations imposed by a tropical river basin, which dictated linear development along the valleys of the Huallaga River and its tributaries, the planned structure accounts for existing localities and creates a new network of settlements directly involved in agricultural activities. The Central Huallaga Project uses many of the concepts elucidated in this study in order to produce a definite spatial structure of planned human settlements based on balanced distances between homes, fields, and services.

CONCLUSIONS

With the described objectives in mind, it is possible to define the spatial variables involved in the planning of land settlement, including the physical dimensions of farmstead and family holdings, distances to work and services, and size of the farming community. Although an exact quantification of each one of these variables is still problematic, it is possible to approximate a spatial model within acceptable latitudes. It is also possible to optimize several of the defined criteria of distances to fields and services based on a community of 80 to 120 families, a size considered more amenable to extension services and cooperation. More families would be needed, however, to improve the efficiency of services; therefore, the multiunit settlement comes closest to reconciling these conflicting needs by combining the advantages of the small community with the economies of scale derived from the association of a larger group of consumers and producers. The social aspects, represented by the constraints built into the described settlement model, have tangible spatial expressions, such as: equitable allocation of resources (i.e. soil quality, distances, farm size, etc.); production based exclusively, or primarily, on family labor; conditional land tenancy and controlled land use; continuity of the farmstead for coming generations; the possibility of developing the settlement in stages; and

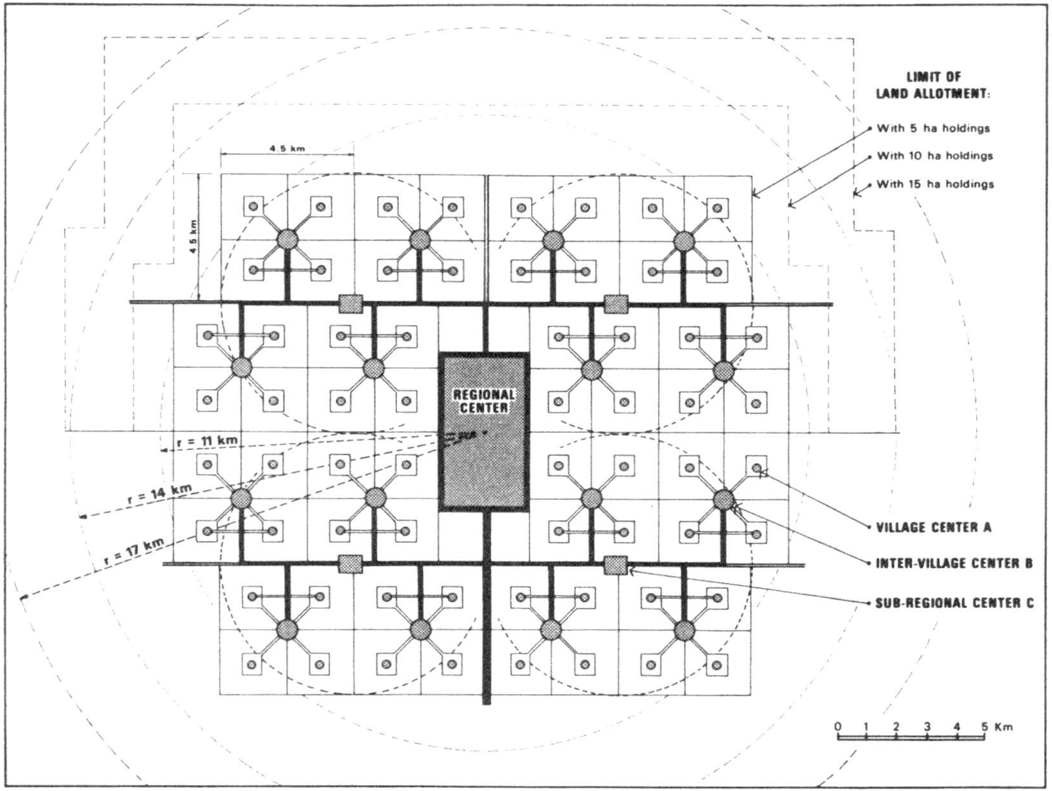

Figure 8.11 Regional scheme of agricultural settlements and their pertinent service centers, comprising 5,460 farming families besides the population engaged in rural and urban services.

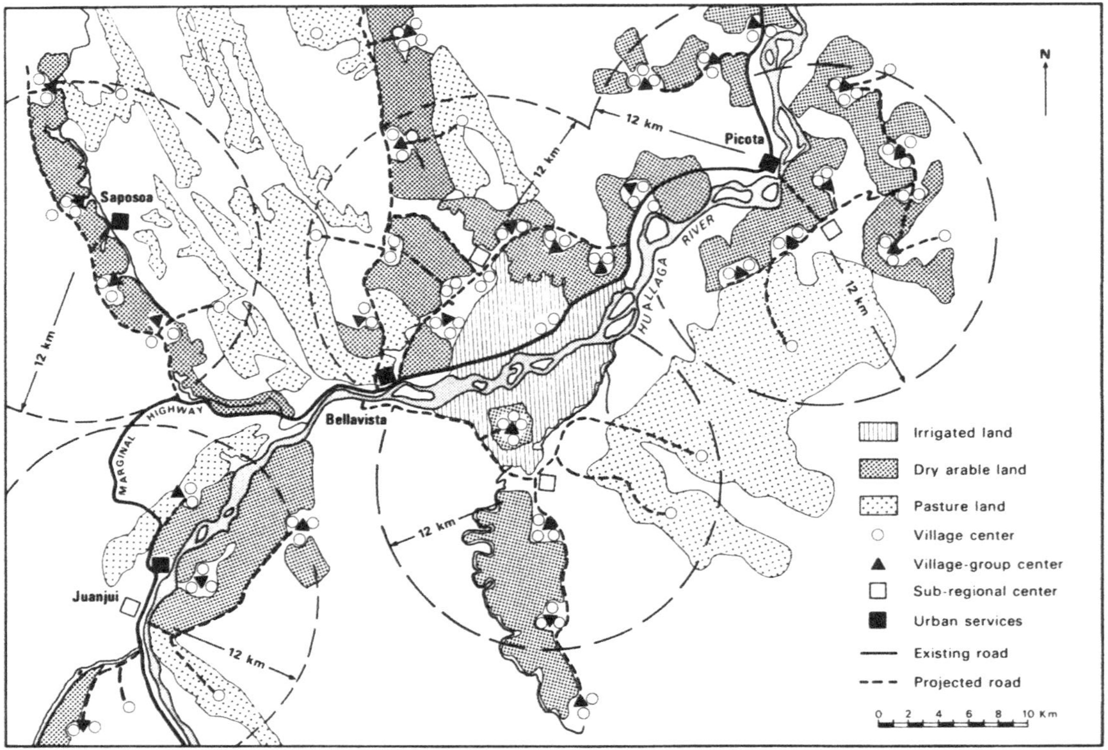

Figure 8.12 Spatial organization of land settlement in the Huallaga River Basin. (Source: Proyecto Integral de Reordenamiento y Asentamiento Rural del Huallaga Central.)

finally, social cohesion induced by the physical layout.

One of the primary functions of land settlement is the programmed transition from subsistence, to mixed, and finally to specialized farming. This transition entails constant changes in land use, the introduction of new cultivation and livestock branches, rationalization, and modernization. At the same time settlers undergo a sociocultural transformation during which they shift from a peasant economy to commercial farming incited by the market. This transformation entails changes in associative patterns and the creation of new institutional frameworks. It is difficult to predict the developmental trends of social patterns. These depend upon the human and social progress of the settlers, their prior behavioral traits, and the general sociopolitical environment. The spatial patterns, however, should be adaptable to any associative forms opted for in the future. Such adaptability dictates a high degree of flexibility in the physical planning in order for the settlement to move successively through various evolutionary stages, avoiding at the same time the pitfalls evidenced in the recent past.

The analysis of the described settlement models reveals that planned differentiation of holdings into several plots produces considerable savings in distances which, in turn, enable the formation of bigger villages. The multiunit village allows for efficient services while keeping within well-defined neighborhood units. Some patterns are limited, of course, to areas where adequate land resources are available within reasonable distances. However, the two-field system makes it possible to locate a portion of the allotment within a shorter distance, thus compensating for longer distances to the farther fields.

Both the external (village-to-field) and internal (village-to-services) distances are important, especially during the initial period of settlement. But the importance of distances to the fields decreases as the settlement develops. The marginal family labor concentrates on the farmyard area while work in the fields is gradually improved by modern farming methods, mechanization, and joint management. Internal distances, on the other hand, maintain their importance through time because all family household members continue to commute to central service points, mostly on foot, for a variety of daily needs and for social, cultural, as well as work-related purposes. Internal distances that are too long will often produce redundant and inefficient facilities which, later on, are liable to hinder the development of rational cooperative enterprises.

The main purpose of the two- or three-field system is to enable the progressive rationalization of farming and the eventual use of cooperative working methods. Greater distances to the fields, especially to the second or communal plot, can be tolerated--a secondary benefit of differentiation. This principle also implies that by reducing the initial land allotment per family, a given tract of land will hold a larger number of farming families. The remaining balance of land allotment can be allocated at a later point in time, either in the form of individual or communal plots, and at a greater-than-usual distance. By that time the average farm family may have fully cultivated the initial allotment, and may have started to exploit other possibilities for increasing income through intensification and farmyard activities (e.g. raising livestock or growing cash crops). In addition, after a number of years the farmer may be able to afford improved means of transportation to work, and the possible development of group farming will minimize the effect of distance to the second-stage land allotment area.

The phased allocation of land allows for a larger concentration of farming population and families engaged in related activities, resulting in more efficient and effective services. It is thus possible to spread the available resources and institutional efforts over a greater number of assignees or, alternatively, to offset initial costs by the present-value savings on deferred expenditures for the total land development. Implicit in the spatial organization as conceived herein is a slower paced, but pragmatic settlement process, through which the settler may adjust gradually to his new environment. At the same time, the settling entities may possess more leeway for mustering their resources and professional capacity in line with the planning needs generated by the project.

Despite the known problems of which the planner must be aware, there may be an untapped advantage in the fact that the people who are vying for settlement emanate from the most precarious living conditions. This situation implies that the land resources and related infrastructure required for attaining final income goals need not be meted out at once. As repeatedly shown, overproviding the settler can cause independence and incentive to fade and never develop. Similarly, an initially large land allotment rarely leads to higher productivity and is often above the working capacity of the individual farming family. Carving up limited land resources and spreading the settlements too thinly may impede the formation of a framework which eventually will provide the rural community with adequate services and allow the small landholder to operate within larger economic units.

NOTES

1. The use of spatial modeling to simulate typical layouts is discussed by George Chadwick, A Systems View of Planning (Oxford, 1971).

2. K. L. Bienheim (Coordinator), "Nomenclature of Technical Terms

in Rural Planning," Study Group on Problems of Individual and Group Settlement for Europe, OECD, 1965; and I. H. Adams, Agrarian Landscape Terms: A Glossary for Historical Geography (London, 1976).

3. Rudolf Schoch, "Bauliche Konsequenzen Neuzeitlicher Haltungs- und Arbeitsverfahren," Landtechnik, Vol. 19.9 (1964), pp. 295-302.

4. Farm Economy: A Cyclopedia of Agriculture for the Practical Farmer (Minneapolis, 1915), p. 468; see also, Farmstead Planning Handbook, Iowa State University, Ames, 1974.

5. E. Yalan, J. Maos, and L. Kam, Land Planning of the Agricultural Co-operative Village, The Rural Building Research Centre, Haifa, 1963; and, Raanan Weitz, From Peasant to Farmer (New York, 1971).

6. William C. Found, A Theoretical Approach to Rural Land-Use Patterns (London, 1971).

7. José Geraldo da Cunha Camargo, Urbanismo Rural; MA-INCRA, Ministry of Agriculture, Institute of Colonization and Agrarian Reform, Brasilia, 1973. See also, "Conquest of the Amazon: How High a Price?" Newsweek, 3 July 1972, pp. 24-27.

8. Instituto Ecuatoriano de Reforma Agraria y Colonización (IERAC), Proyecto Piloto de Colonización en el Nor-Oriente, Quito, Ecuador, 1971.

9. Colonización Tingo Maria-Tocache-Campanilla: Informe sobre la Reestructuración del Proyecto (Préstamo BID - 96/SF/PE), Unpublished report, Ministry of Agriculture, Lima, Peru, 1970.

10. Instituto Agrario de Nicaragua, Proyecto Rigoberto Cabezas: Primera Etapa (Managua, Nicaragua, 1972).

11. Plan de Operaciones para el Asentamiento de Familias de las Zonas de Acción Conjunta en las Areas de Colonización Tingo Maria-Tocache-Campanilla, Ministry of Agriculture and Interamerican Development Bank, Lima, Peru, 1971.

12. Erich H. Jacoby, Land Consolidation in Europe (Wageningen, 1959); and, "Group Farming: A New Experiment in Co-operation between Farmers," OECD Observer, No. 56, February 1972, pp. 31-33.

13. Michael Chisholm, Rural Settlement and Land Use (London, 1962); and, Found, A Theoretical Approach.

14. Among the few exceptions: Charles J. Galpin, "The Social Anatomy of an Agricultural Community," Research Bulletin No. 34, University of Wisconsin, Madison, 1915.

15. Walter Christaller, Central Places in Southern Germany (Englewood, 1966); and, E. A. J. Johnson, The Organization of Space in Developing Countries (Cambridge, Mass., 1970).

16. C. P. Barnes, "Economies of the long-lot farm," Geographical Review, Vol. 25 (1935), pp. 298-301.

17. J. Maos and L. Kam, Criterios para el Planeamiento de Aldeas Agrícolas en los Sistemas de Riego, Second Venezuelan Seminar on Irrigation, Working Paper No. II-7, Caracas, Venezuela, May 1966.

18. Chisholm, Rural Settlement; René Eyheralde, "Grouping of Rural Dispersed Population in Agricultural Villages," Paper submitted to the UN Seminar on Rural Housing and Community Facilities, Maracay, Venezuela, 1967.

19. David Harvey, Society, the City and the Space-Economy of Urbanism, Association of American Geographers, Resource Paper No. 18, Washington, D.C., 1972.

20. I. Prion, Líneas Generales de la Planificación Integrada Rural Regional en las Zonas de la Reforma Agraria, Ministry of

Agriculture, Israel, 1973.

21. Flooded houses is a common sight in new land settlement during rainy seasons as a result of insufficient topographical survey. The apparent ease of construction on flat lands often lures builders to develop housing on lands which are susceptible to inundation and engineering problems.

Bibliography

Abel, Wilhelm. Die Wüstungen des Ausgehenden Mittelalters. Stuttgart, 1955.

Abt, Yitzhak. "The Institutional Approach to Agrarian Reform and Related Tax Problems." Unpublished lecture, Lincoln Foundation, Hartford University, 1966.

__________. "Types of Agricultural Projects Used in Developing Countries." In R. Weitz (ed.), Rural Development in a Changing World. Cambridge, MA, 1971.

Adams, I. H. Agrarian Landscape Terms: A Glossary for Historical Geography. London, 1976.

Apthorpe, Raymond. "A Survey of Land Settlement Schemes and Rural Development in East Africa." East African Institute of Social Research Conference Papers, No. 352, 1966.

Arbel, Y., D. Freeman, and J. Maos. Proyecto de Desarrollo Rural Regional de Chira-Piura (Perú). Settlement Study Centre, Rehovot, 1980.

Augelli, John P. "Agricultural Colonization in the Dominican Republic." Economic Geography, Vol. 38, No. 1 (1962).

Balabanian, Olivier, Les Exploitations et les Problèmes de l'Agriculture en Estrémadure Espagnole et dans le Haut-Alentejo, 2 vols. Published doctoral dissertation, University of Clermont-Ferrand, 1980.

Banco Interamericano de Desarrollo--Secretaría de Recursos Hidraúlicos. Sinopsis del Informe sobre el Proyecto Piloto El Limon. Mexico, 1963.

Barnes, C. P. "Economies of the long-lot farm." Geographical Review, Vol. 25 (1935), pp. 298-301.

Barnett, A. Doak. "China's Road to Collectivization." Journal of Farm Economics, Vol. 35 (1953), pp. 188-202.

Barkin, D. and T. King. Regional Economic Development; The River Basin Approach in Mexico. Cambridge, 1970.

Basols, Angel and Gloria Gonzales. "Acerca de la Colonización en México y del Plan Chontalpa." Instituto de Investigaciones Económicas, Universidad Nacional, Mexico, 1974.

Becerra de la Flor, J. C. and S. I. Abarbanel. Proyecto de asentamiento campesino "Alexander Dothan" (El Sisal) Prov. de Azua, República Dominicana. OAS, Lima, 1974.
Belshaw, G. R. "An Outline of Resettlement Policy in Uganda, 1945-63." East African Institute of Social Research Conference Papers, 1963.
Berler, Alexander. Urban-Rural Relations in Israel: Social and Economic Aspects. Publications on Problems of Regional Development, No. 8. Settlement Study Centre, Rehovot, Israel, 1970.
Bienheim, K. L. (Coordinator). "Nomenclature of Technical Terms in Rural Planning." Study Group on Problems of Individual and Group Settlement for Europe, OECD, 1965.
Boerma, Addeke H. "Global Approach to Agriculture Problems." Survey of International Development, Vol. 10 (1973).
Il Borgo Gromola nella Piana del Sele. O.N.C.--Sezione Speciale per la Riforma Fondiaria in Campania, Napoli, 1960.
Brewster, John M. "Traditional Social Structure as Barriers to Change." In Soutworth and Johnston (eds.), Agricultural Development and Economic Growth. New York, 1967, pp. 67-98.
Browne, Soublette E. "Planificación Física para Reforma Agraria." In Seminario Interamericano de Planificación Física Rural. Instituto Interamericano de Ciencias Agrícolas de la OEA, Bogotá, Colombia, 3-9 December 1972, pp. 42-58.
Buck, W. F. Agriculture and Trade of the Dominican Republic. Washington, D.C., 1972.
Case Coloniche. Sezione Speciale per la Riforma Fondiaria in Puglia Lucania e Molise, Bari, 1958.
Chadwick, George. A Systems View of Planning. Oxford, 1971.
"Charter of Punta del Este." Boletín de la Oficina Sanitaria Panamericana, Vol. 51 (1961), pp. 477-493.
Chenery, Hollis B. "Development Policies for Southern Italy." In J. Friedmann and W. Alonso (eds.), Regional Development and Planning: A Reader. Cambridge, 1964, pp. 668-700.
Chisholm, Michael. Rural Settlement and Land Use. London, 1962.
Christaller, Walter. Central Places in Southern Germany. Englewood, 1966. (Translated by C. W. Baskin from Die Zentralen Orte in Süddeutschland. Jena, 1933.)
Clawson, Marion. America's Land and Its Uses. Baltimore, 1972.
Colonización Majes; Lineamientos para Determinar los Tipos de Asentamientos y Formas de Organización. OAS--Israel Joint Program, Arequipa, Peru, 1971.
Colonización Tingo María-Tocache-Campanilla: Informe sobre la Reestructuración del Proyecto (Préstamo BID--96/SF/PE). Ministry of Agriculture, Lima, Peru, 1970.
"Conquest of the Amazon: How High a Price?" Newsweek, 3 July 1972, pp. 24-27.

Cox, Paul. Venezuela's Agrarian Reform at Mid-1977. Land Tenure Center, Research Paper No. 71. Madison, Wisconsin, 1978.
Cunha Camargo, Jose Geraldo da. Urbanismo Rural--MA INCRA. Ministry of Agriculture, Institute of Colonization and Agrarian Reform, Brasilia, 1973.
Darwent, D. F. "Growth Poles and Growth Centers in Regional Planning--A Review." Environment and Planning, Vol. 1 (1969), pp. 5-32.
Dash, Jacob and Elisha Efrat. The Israel Physical Master Plan. Jerusalem, 1964.
De la Fuente García sj, Santiago. Geografía Dominicana. Santo Domingo, 1976.
Delavaud, Claude Collin. "Agrarian Reform in Peru." In David A. Preston (ed.), Environment, Society, and Rural Change in Latin America. New York, 1980, pp. 37-52.
Demangeon, A. "L'habitation rurale en France. Essai de classification des principaux types." Annales de géographie, Vol. 29 (1930), pp. 352-375.
__________. "Types de peuplement rural en France." Annales de géographie, Vol. 48 (1939), pp. 1-21.
Dorner, Peter, et al. Agrarian Reform in the Dominican Republic (The view your consultants). Madison, 1967.
Dorner, Peter (ed.). Land Reform in Latin America: Issues and Cases. Land Economics Monograph Series, No. 3. University of Wisconsin, Madison, 1971.
Dozier, Craig L. Land Development in Latin America; Case Studies of Peru, Bolivia and Mexico. New York, 1969.
Eckstein, Shlomo. "Collective Farming in Mexico." In R. Stavenhagen (ed.), Agrarian Problems and Peasant Movements in Latin America. New York, 1970, pp. 271-299.
Economic and Social Development Program for Spain: 1964-1967. Prepared by the Commissioner for Economic and Social Development Planning, Spain. Johns Hopkins University Press, Baltimore, 1965.
The Economic Development of Venezuela. Report of a Mission Organized by the International Bank for Reconstruction and Development. The Johns Hopkins Press, Baltimore, 1961.
Eidt, Robert C. "Agrarian Reform and the Growth of New Rural Settlements in Venezuela." Erdkunde, Vol. 29 (1975), pp. 118-133.
Enggass, Peter. "Spain." Focus, Vol. 20 (1970), pp. 1-8.
__________. "Land Reform in Spain." Focus, Vol. 20 (1970), pp. 9-12.
"Extraordinario Mejoramiento Vial en el Perú." Urbanismo y Planificación, No. 43 (1981), pp. 30-42.
Eyhéralde, René. "Grouping of Rural Dispersed Population in Agricultural Villages." Paper submitted to the United Nations Seminar on Rural Housing and Community Facilities, Maracay, Venezuela, 1967.
Farm Economy: A Cyclopedia of Agriculture for the Practical

Farmer. Minneapolis, 1915.
Farmstead Planning Handbook. Iowa State University, Ames, 1974.
Found, William C. A Theoretical Approach to Rural Land-Use Patterns. London, 1971.
Frank, Gunder A. Capitalism and Underdevelopment in Latin America, Historical Studies of Chile and Brazil. London, 1971.
Franklin, S. H. Rural Societies. London, 1971.
Friedmann, John and Mike Douglass. "Agropolitan Development: towards a new strategy for regional planning in Asia." In F. C. Lo and K. Salih (eds.), Growth Pole Strategy and Regional Development Policy. Oxford, 1978, pp. 163-192.
Friedmann, John and Clyde Weaver. Territory and Function: The Evolution of Regional Planning. London, 1979.
Galpin, Charles J. "The Social Anatomy of an Agricultural Community." Research Bulletin No. 34. University of Wisconsin, Madison, 1915.
Garofalo, S. "Investimenti netti e progresso tecnico nello sviluppo dell'agricoltura meridionale." Rivista di Economia Agraria, Anno 25 (1970), pp. 209-232.
Glikson, Artur. Planned Regional Settlement Projects: Comparative Study; Background, Experience, New Trends. Jerusalem, 1970.
Granott, Abraham. Agrarian Reform and the Record of Israel. London, 1956.
"Group Farming: A New Experiment in Co-operation between Farmers." OECD Observer, No. 56 (1972), pp. 31-33.
Hilhorst, J. G. M. Regional Planning: A System's Approach. Rotterdam, 1971.
Hirschman, Albert O. Development Projects Observed. Washington, D.C., 1967.
Horwitz, Abraham. On Health and Wealth. Pan American Sanitary Bureau, Regional Office of the WHO. Washington, D.C., 1967.
Houston, J. M. The Western Mediterranean World: An Introduction to its Regional Landscapes. London, 1964.
_________. A Social Geography of Europe. New York, 1968.
Iatridis, D. "Social Scientists in Physical Development Planning: a Practitioner's Viewpoint." International Social Science Journal, Vol. 18 (1966), pp. 473-493.
"Informe Técnico sobre el Desarrollo del Sistema de Riego Boconó--Edo, Barinas." Comisión Especial: MOP, MAC, IAN, BAP, SAS, CIARA, Caracas, Venezuela, October 1967.
Instituto Agrario Dominicano. Proyecto El Sisal. O.A.S.--Israel--B.I.D. Santo Domingo, 1969.
Instituto Agrario Dominicano. "Plan Regional del Valle de Azua No. 1." Santo Domingo, 1971 (five blueprints).
Instituto Ecuatoriano de Reforma Agraria y Colonización (IERAC). Proyecto Piloto de Colonización en el Nor-Oriente. Quito, Ecuador, 1971.
Instituto Agrario de Nicaragua. Proyecto Rigoberto Cabezas: Primera Etapa. Managua, Nicaragua, 1972.

Jacoby, Erich H. Land Consolidation in Europe. Wageningen, 1959.

Johnson, E. A. J. The Organization of Space in Developing Countries. Cambridge, Mass., 1970.

Kam, Lipa and Jacob Maos. "Report on Rural Housing and Village Planning in Venezuela." Pan American Sanitary Bureau, Regional Office of the WHO. Caracas, Venezuela, 1964.

Kindleberger, Charles P. Economic Development. New York, 1965.

King, Russell. Land Reform: The Italian Experience. London, 1973.

_________. "Italy." In Hugh D. Clout (ed.), Regional Development in Western Europe. New York, 1981, pp. 119-149.

Kuznetz, S. "The Present Underdeveloped Countries and Past Growth Patterns." In T. Morgan and C. W. Betz (eds.), Economic Development: Readings in Theory and Practice. Belmont, Calif., 1970, pp. 11-17.

Lahav, Avi. Proyecto El Sisal--Etapa C, República Dominicana: El Sistema de Riego y de Agua Potable, y la Planificación Física. Jerusalem, 1972.

Lakshmanan, T. R. "Integration of Physical and Economic Planning." Paper presented to the U.N. Group of Experts on Integration of Economic and Physical Planning, Ref. ESA/HBP/AC.10/4. August, 1973.

Land Reform in Apulia, Lucania and Molise. Arti Grafiche Laterza, Bari, Italy, 1964.

Maos, Jacob. "Standards and Patterns for Rural Community Facilities." Paper presented at the U.N. Interregional Seminar on Rural Housing and Community Facilities, Maracay, Venezuela, 1967.

_________. "The Spatial Organization of New Land Settlement: Experiences and Trends." GeoJournal, Vol. 1.4 (1977), pp. 29-35.

_________. "The Efficiency of Rural Services in Dispersed and Concentrated Land Settlement: A Comparison." Geographical Research Forum (Occasional Papers), No. 2 (1980), pp. 33-43.

_________ (ed.). Course on Rural Architecture: Work Prepared by the Participants. CIARA in collaboration with the Ministry of Health and the Pan American Sanitary Bureau. Caracas, Venezuela, 1967.

Maos, Jacob and Lipa Kam. Criterios para el Planeamiento de Aldeas Agrícolas en los Sistemas de Riego. Second Venezuelan Seminar on Irrigation, Working Paper No. II-7, Caracas, Venezuela, May 1966.

Maos, Jacob and David Pelley. "Agricultural Settlement Planning in the Specialization Era: New Approaches to the Physical Planning of the Moshav." GeoJournal, Vol. 5.3 (1981), pp. 269-276.

Matarrese, Nicola. "L'insediamento Rurale di Centri Satelliti." Annals of the Faculty of Agronomy. Bari, Italy, Vol. 18 (1963).

McNamara, Robert S. Address to the Board of Governors. International Bank for Reconstruction and Development. Nairobi, Kenya, 24 September 1973.

Medici, Giuseppe. "Pulverization and Fragmentation of Landed Property in Italy." In Roger N. Dixey (ed.), International Explorations of Agricultural Economics. Ames, 1964, pp. 153-163.

Meitzen, August. Siedelung und Agrarwesen der Westgermanen und Ostgermanen, der Kelten, Römer, Finnen und Slawen. Berlin, 1895.

Millikan, Max F. and David Hapgood. No Easy Harvest; The Dilemma of Agriculture in Underdeveloped Countries. Boston, 1967.

Mintz, Sidney W. "Peasant Market Places and Economic Development in Latin America." The Graduate Center for Latin American Studies, Occasional Paper No. 4. Vanderbilt University, Nashville, 1964.

Moscovitch, Edward H. Urban-Rural Investment Allocation in Venezuela. Unpublished Ph.D. thesis, Massachusetts Institute of Technology, 1966.

Mosher, Arthur Theodore. Creating a Progressive Rural Structure to Serve a Modern Agriculture. New York, 1969.

Myrdal, Gunnar. Economic Theory and Underdeveloped Regions. New York, 1971.

Naylon, John. "Irrigation and Internal Colonization in Spain." Geographical Journal, Vol. 133 (1967), pp. 178-191.

__________. "Iberia." In Hugh D. Clout (ed.), Regional Development in Western Europe. New York, 1981, pp. 359-387.

Nelson, Michael. The Development of Tropical Lands: Policy Issues in Latin America. Baltimore, 1973.

Organization of American States--Israel Joint Program. Proyecto de Planificación--Colonización "La Joya." Arequipa, Peru, August 1967.

Palerm, Angel. Observaciones sobre el desarrollo agrario en Israel. Estudios y Monografías, XIII, Panamerican Union, Organization of American States. Washington, D.C., 1964.

Pedregal, H. and H. M. De Pedregal. Principios Generales para la Planificación Física de Aldeas Agrícolas. Caracas, 1968.

__________. Aldeas Agrícolas en Venezuela. Ministry of Health and Social Welfare, Publication No. 73-03. Caracas, 1973.

Pihkala, K. U. "The Nature of Agricultural Economics as a Discipline and Science." In Roger N. Dixey (ed.), International Explorations of Agricultural Economics. Ames, Iowa, 1967, pp. 223-229.

Plan Badajoz: Presas y Zona Regable. Ministerio de Obras Públicas, Dirección General de Obras Hidráulicas, Confederación Hidrográfica del Guadiana. Madrid, 1965.

El Plan de Badajoz. Publicación de la Secretaría Gestora del Plan Badajoz, Instituto Nacional de Industria. Madrid, 1964.

Plan de Operaciones para el Asentamiento de Familias de las Zonas de Acción Conjunta en las Areas de Colonización Tingo María-Tocache-Campanilla. Ministry of Agriculture and Interamerican Development Bnak. Lima, 1971.

Portugal Vizcarra, Jose A. Crisis y Política Agraria en el Perú: Problema y Solución. Lima, 1981.

Prion, I. Development Trends of Spatial Rural Cooperation in Israel. Publications on Problems of Regional Development, No. 3, Settlement Study Centre. Rehovot, Israel, 1968.

________. Líneas Generales de la Planificación Integrada Rural Regional en las Zonas de la Reforma Agraria. Ministry of Agriculture. Israel, 1973.

Proyecto Específico de Recolonización del Distrito de Cacatachi. Ministry of Agriculture and F.A.O. Tarapoto, Peru, 1970.

Proyecto Integral de Reordenamiento y Asentamiento Rural del Huallaga Central. Ministry of Agriculture. Tarapoto, Peru, 1971.

Proyecto de Planificación Región Sur República Dominicana. Fundación David, Publicaciones sobre Desarrollo Rural Integrado, No. 1. Rehovot, 1981.

Proyecto Piloto el Limón. Secretaría de Recursos Hidráulicos, Comisión del Grijalva, Distrito de Riego de la Chontalpa. Tabasco, Mexico, D. F., 1963.

Ramadoro, A. "Insediamenti Rurali nelle Terre di Nuova Bonifica." In Commission Internationale du Genie Rural (ed.), Journees d'Etudes en Italie. Bari, 1961, pp. 5-30.

"Relaciones entre la Reforma Agraria, la Planificación Nacional y la Planificación Regional." Seminario de Planificación Agrícola Regional, Bogotá, Colombia, 5-10 June 1972.

Resources for the Future, Design for a Worldwide Study of Regional Development. Baltimore, 1966.

Rostow, W. W. The Stages of Economic Growth. Cambridge, 1971.

Rother, Klaus. "Das Mezzogiorno-Problem: Versuche des italienischen Staates zu seiner Lösung." Geographische Rundschau, No. 4 (1982), pp. 154-162.

Ruttan, W. Vernon. "Induced Technical and Institutional Change and the Future of Agriculture." In The Future of Agriculture: Theme Papers. University of Oxford, 1973, pp. 16-33 (presented at the 15th International Conference of Agricultural Economists, Sao Paulo, Brazil, August 1973).

Scardaccione, Decio. Land Reform: Experiences in Apulia, Lucania and Molise. Bari, 1965.

Schoch, Rudolf. "Bauliche Konsequenzen Neuzeitlicher

Haltungs- und Arbeitsverfahren." Landtechnik, Vol. 19.9 (1964), pp. 295-302.
Schwarz, Gabriele, Allgemeine Siedlungsgeographie. Berlin, 1961.
Settlement Study Centre. UDA Walawe Project; A Comparative Study of Two Regional Planning Alternatives. Rehovot, Israel, 1971.
Sharon, Arieh. "Collective Settlements in Israel." Town Planning Review, Vol. 25 (1955), pp. 225-270.
Singh, Tarlok. "Planning and Productivity in Agriculture." In Economic Development: Issues and Policies. Bombay, 1966, pp. 117-150.
Smith, C. T. An Historical Geography of Western Europe before 1800. London, 1967.
Smith, T. Lynn. Agrarian Reform in Latin America. New York, 1964.
________. Studies of Latin American Societies. New York, 1970.
"Some Regional Development Problems in Latin America Linked to Metropolitanization." Economic Bulletin for Latin America, Vol. 16 (1971), pp. 57-90.
"Special Meeting of the Ministers of Health of the Americas." PAHO Official Document, Vol. 90 (1969).
Statistical Abstract of Israel--1981, No. 32. Jerusalem, 1981.
Strauss, Estevam. Reestructuración del espacio económico latinoamericano. Santiago, Chile, 1969.
Symanski, R. and N. Burley. "The Jewish Colony of Sosua." Annals of the Association of American Geographers, Vol. 63 (1973), pp. 366-378.
Tassinari, Giuseppe. Ten Years of Integral Land Reclamation Under the Mussolini Act. Talura, Italy, 1939.
Thiesenhusen, William C. "Technological Change and Income Distribution in Latin American Agriculture." Paper submitted to the VI Interamerican Conference on Agriculture, OAS, Lima, 27 May-2 June 1971.
________. "A Venezuelan Agrarian Reform Settlement: Problems and Prospects." In R. D. Stevens (ed.), Tradition and Dynamics in Small-Farm Agriculture. Ames, Iowa, 1977.
Trewartha, Glenn T. "Types of Rural Settlement in Colonial America." The Geographical Review, Vol. 36 (1946), pp. 568-596.
United Nations, Centre for Housing, Building and Planning, Global Review of Human Settlements. Oxford, 1976.
United Nations, Statistical Office of the Department of Economic and Social Affairs. Global Review of Human Settlements: Statistical Annex. Oxford, 1976.
United Nations Economic and Social Commission for Asia and the Pacific. Guidelines for rural centre planning. New York, 1979.
United Nations, International Labor Organization. Toward Full Employment: A Programme for Colombia. Geneva, 1970.

United Nations. Report of the Committee for Development Planning, Document E/5126. United Nations, New York, 1972.

United Nations. Report of the Interregional Seminar on Rural Housing and Community Facilities, ST/TAO/SER.C/103. New York, 1968.

Vidal de la Blache, Paul. Principes de Géographie humaine. Paris, 1922.

Wagley, Charles. The Latin American Tradition: Essays on the Unity and the Diversity of Latin American Culture. New York, 1968.

Warriner, Doreen. Land Reform in Principle and Practice. Oxford, 1969.

Weintraub, D., M. Lissak, and Y. Azmon. Moshava, Kibbutz and Moshav: Patterns of Jewish Rural Settlement and Development in Palestine. Ithaca, 1969.

Weitz, Raanan. Spatial Organization of Rural Development. Publications on Problems of Regional Development, No. 3. Settlement Study Centre, Rehovot, 1968.

__________. From Peasant to Farmer: A Revolutionary Strategy for Development. New York, 1971.

__________. Integrated Rural Development; The Rehovot Approach. Publications on Problems of Regional Development, No. 28. Settlement Study Centre, Rehovot, 1979.

__________ (ed.). Rural Development in a Changing World. Cambridge, 1971.

Wilkie, Raymond. San Miguel: A Mexican Collective Ejido. Stanford, 1971.

Wood, Harold A. "Spontaneous Agricultural Colonization in Ecuador." Annals of the Association of American Geographers, Vol. 62 (1972), pp. 599-617.

World Population Estimates. Published by The Environmental Fund. Washington, D.C., 1981.

Wu Chung-Tong and David F. Ip. "China: Rural Development--Alternating Combinations of Top-Down and Bottom-Up Strategies." In Walter B. Stöhr and D. R. Fraser Taylor (eds.), Development from Above or Below? The Dialectics of Regional Planning in Developing Countries. New York, 1981, pp. 155-182.

Yalan, Emmanuel. The Design of Agricultural Settlements; Technological Aspects of Rural Community Development. Jerusalem, 1975.

Yalan, E., H. Finkel, L. Guttman, and Ch. Jacobsen. The Modernization of the Traditional Agricultural Village. Publications on Problems of Regional Development, No. 11. Settlement Study Centre, Rehovot, 1972.

Yalan, E., J. Maos, and L. Kam. Land Planning of the Agricultural Co-operative Village. The Rural Building Research Centre, Haifa, 1963.

Yalan, E., J. Maos, and L. Kam. The Influence of Farming Rationalization on the Planning of Scattered and Gathered Settlements. The Rural Building Research Centre, Haifa, 1964.

Yang, C. K. Chinese Communist Society: The Family and the

Village. Cambridge, 1972.
Yoshioka, Gary and Robert Athanasiou. "The Effect of Site Plan and Social Status Variables on Distance to Friends' Homes." Proceedings of the 79th Annual Convention, American Psychological Association, 1971.
Zalmanov, S. El-Sisal Development Project. Rehovot, Israel, 1973.
Zonas Regables de Badajoz. Ministerio de Agricultura, Instituto Nacional de Colonización. Madrid, 1972.
Zuvekas, Clarence. "Agrarian Reform in Ecuador's Guayas River Basin." Land Economics, Vol. 52 (1976), pp. 314-329.

Index

Dellplain Latin American Studies
Published by Westview Press

No. 8 *Studies in Spanish American Population History*, edited by David J. Robinson

No. 9 *The People of the Colca Valley: A Population Study*, Noble David Cook

No. 10 *Tierra Adentro: Settlement and Society in Colonial Durango*, Michael M. Swann

No. 11 *Andean Relfections: Letters from Carl O. Sauer While on a South American Trip Under a Grant from the Rockefeller Foundation, 1942*, edited by Robert C. West

No. 12 *Credit and Socioeconomic Change in Colonial Mexico: Loans and Mortgages in Guadalajara, 1720-1820*, Linda Greenow

No. 13 *Once Beneath the Forest: Prehistoric Terracing in the Río Bec Region of the Maya Lowlands*, B. L. Turner, II

No. 14 *Marriage and Fertility in Chile: Demographic Turning Points in the Petorca Valley, 1840-1976*, Robert McCaa

No. 15 *The Spatial Organization of New Land Settlement in Latin America*, Jacob O. Maos

Previous Dellplain Studies
Available from University Microfilms International

No. 1 *Social Fabric and Spatial Structure in Colonial Latin America*, edited by David J. Robinson

No. 2 *New Towns for Colonial Brazil: Spatial and Social Planning of the Eighteenth Century*, Roberta Marx Delson

No. 3 *Carl Sauer's Fieldwork in Latin America*, Robert C. West

No. 4 *Studying Latin America: Essays in Honor of Preston E. James*, edited by David J. Robinson

No. 5 *First Among Equals: Great Britain and Venequela, 1810-1910*, George E. Carl

No. 6 *Amazon Economics: The Simplicity of Shipobo Indian Wealth*, Roland W. Bergman

No. 7 *The Mining Society of Potosí, 1776-1810*, Rose Marie Buechler

For Product Safety Concerns and Information please contact our EU representative GPSR@taylorandfrancis.com Taylor & Francis Verlag GmbH, Kaufingerstraße 24, 80331 München, Germany

Batch number: 10732529

Printed by Printforce, the Netherlands